BEBE DANIELS

# Bebe Daniels
*Hollywood's Good Little Bad Girl*

## Charles L. Epting

*Foreword by*
Annette D'Agostino Lloyd

McFarland & Company, Inc., Publishers
*Jefferson, North Carolina*

LIBRARY OF CONGRESS CATALOGUING-IN-PUBLICATION DATA

Names: LeBlanc, Diane, 1964 May 15– author. | Swanson, Allys M., author.
Title: Playing for equality : oral histories of women leaders in the early
    years of Title IX / Diane LeBlanc and Allys Swanson.
Description: Jefferson, North Carolina : McFarland & Company, Inc., 2016. |
    Includes bibliographical references and index.
Identifiers: LCCN 2016039255 | ISBN 9781476663005
    (softcover : acid free paper) ∞
Subjects: LCSH: Sex discrimination in sports—United States—History. |
Discrimination in education—Law and legislation—United States—History. |
Sex discrimination against women—Law and legislation—United States—History.
Classification: LCC KF4166 .L43 2016 | DDC 344.73/099—dc23
LC record available at https://lccn.loc.gov/2016039255

BRITISH LIBRARY CATALOGUING DATA ARE AVAILABLE

**ISBN (print) 978-1-4766-6374-6**
**ISBN (ebook) 978-1-4766-2532-4**

© 2016 Charles Epting. All rights reserved

*No part of this book may be reproduced or transmitted in any form
or by any means, electronic or mechanical, including photocopying
or recording, or by any information storage and retrieval system,
without permission in writing from the publisher.*

Front cover: a publicity photograph from Paramount Studios
of Bebe Daniels in early 1922 (author's collection)

Printed in the United States of America

*McFarland & Company, Inc., Publishers
Box 611, Jefferson, North Carolina 28640
www.mcfarlandpub.com*

To Hadley Ann McGregor

# Acknowledgments

The two people who have helped me most in preparing this book are David McAleer and Annette D'Agostino Lloyd. David, my cousin, was instrumental early on as I was first discovering silent films, and has remained unbelievably supportive over the years. When I first conceived the idea for a biography on Bebe Daniels, he immediately understood why she was a deserving candidate for such a project. Trips to the TCM Classic Film Festival and William S. Hart Ranch and Museum provided ample opportunity to discuss this project, and he is now an expert on Daniels in his own right.

Annette D'Agostino Lloyd is not someone I knew before beginning the project, but I now consider her one of my closest friends in the hobby. As the leading expert on Harold Lloyd, she was already more familiar with Bebe's life and career than perhaps anyone else. Her assistance with every step of this project has been greatly appreciated, and it is my hope that the sections of this book dealing with Harold Lloyd do justice to the man she has spent so much time writing about.

For their assistance with archival research, I'd like to thank Rosemary Hanes at the Library of Congress, Ned Comstock and Sandra Garcia-Myers at the University of Southern California Cinematic Arts Library, and Faye Thompson and Jenny Romero at the Academy of Motion Picture Arts and Sciences Margaret Herrick Library. Helpful in acquiring original images for inclusion in the book were Bob Chatt, Ralph Bowman, Danny Schwartz, Larry Edmunds Bookshop and Jerry Ohlinger's Movie Material Store.

Social media has put me in touch with many people I may not have otherwise met, and for various reasons I have to thank Mike Baris, John Carpenter, Paul Gierucki, Lara Gabrielle Fowler, Bob Harned, Chuck Harter, Karie Bible and Ron Hutchinson for helping in their own ways.

# Table of Contents

| | |
|---|---:|
| *Acknowledgments* | vi |
| *Foreword by Annette D'Agostino Lloyd* | 1 |
| *Preface* | 3 |
| *Introduction* | 6 |
| 1. In a Snow-Flecked Dallas | 9 |
| 2. The Stage | 18 |
| 3. The Screen | 22 |
| 4. Meeting Harold Lloyd | 30 |
| 5. Leaving Rolin | 39 |
| 6. Mr. DeMille | 46 |
| 7. Realart Pictures | 53 |
| 8. Ten Days in Jail | 58 |
| 9. The End of Realart | 67 |
| 10. New York | 75 |
| 11. Valentino | 84 |
| 12. Romping Back into Comedies | 89 |
| 13. Engagement Rumors | 95 |
| 14. Dashing Screen Star | 105 |
| 15. The End of an Era | 116 |
| 16. Mrs. Bebe Daniels Lyon | 120 |
| 17. Leaving RKO | 128 |
| 18. Barbara Bebe Daniels | 134 |
| 19. To England | 143 |
| 20. Hollywood Holiday | 152 |

| | |
|---|---:|
| 21. Loyal to England | 160 |
| 22. War and Peace | 165 |
| 23. After the War | 174 |
| 24. The Lyons Take Television | 182 |
| 25. Still Only the Honeymoon | 187 |
| 26. "She Was My Life" | 191 |
| *Epilogue* | 193 |
| *Filmography* | 195 |
| *Chapter Notes* | 209 |
| *Bibliography* | 218 |
| *Index* | 219 |

# Foreword
## by Annette D'Agostino Lloyd

*I've been away so long ... they won't remember me.*—Bebe Daniels, *This Is Your Life*, September 29, 1954

As you hold this book, you are probably amazed that, upon learning that she was being honored with an episode of the long-running television roast *This Is Your Life*, Bebe Daniels was concerned that she was a forgotten entity. Those of us fortunate enough to have been touched by her immense contributions to both entertainment and civil industries, on both sides of the pond, know that her worries were unfounded.

In my years of chronicling the legendary life of Harold Lloyd—the man Bebe first supported on film, and the first man Bebe loved—I have come to appreciate the actress and the person Bebe Daniels was. She appeared in 144 comedies opposite Lloyd, between 1915 and 1919; in those formative years, both Harold and Bebe grew up, literally and figuratively, together, in front of appreciative audiences. Their pictures speak for themselves ... she brought out the greatness in her leading man, and definitely contributed to his rise to stardom. Their chemistry together was instant and lasting—and the young love that brewed behind the scenes was only conquered by ambition. On both their parts: Harold, though not ready for marriage, insisted on a stay-at-home wife; Bebe, after years of co-star status, received an offer of stardom from Cecil B. DeMille and took it. Though this sealed a professional severance, it did not break their lifelong affection and deep friendship. Harold and Bebe died within eight days of each other in 1971—this I view as the ultimate chapter in their tender story.

My admiration for Bebe Daniels transcends her Lloyd connection—her beautiful singing voice, her powerful dramatic films, her legendary patriotic work in the wake of D–Day, her final resting place at Hollywood Forever Cemetery, where I spent six years as celebrity biographer. Hearing of a new book on her life and times intrigued me greatly, and concerned me slightly. Knowing that such a challenge was in the most capable hands of rising star chronicler Charles Epting, well ... that relieved me.

I am 31 years older than Charles. And I was 31 when I began work on my first book, on Harold Lloyd. I remember, at that juncture, thinking back to when I first "discovered" Harold Lloyd, at the age of 17, and hoping that, someday, far in the future, new generations would do as I was doing, and keep the momentum of history appreciation rolling. I see my wish coming to fruition, through the fresh interpretation of, and reverence for, the classics, from young minds like that of Charles Epting.

I have always been historically minded and detail-oriented; Minutia would have been an appropriate name for me. I see those same qualities in Charles: his insistence on first-hand sources and quotes, his nitpicky adherence to detail, his resistance to blindly follow the research that preceded him, and his strong love for the times. Be it silent film, or philately, or American history, I have been continually impressed, and frankly stoked, by his work ethic and the quality of his writing. I am thrilled for Bebe that he chose her, and I am impressed with Charles, that she so captured his curiosity. This resulting book is a win-win, all the way around.

Charles Epting is a name that you might not have heard before—but I have not a smidgen of doubt that it is one you will remember. Just like that of Bebe Daniels.

*Annette D'Agostino Lloyd is the foremost biographer of Harold Lloyd and one of the leading authorities on silent cinema. Her numerous works include* The Harold Lloyd Encyclopedia, Harold Lloyd: Magic in a Pair of Horn-Rimmed Glasses *and two indices of* Moving Picture World *magazine.*

# Preface

As this manuscript was nearing completion, I boarded a plane from Los Angeles to Washington, D.C. My trip would last a mere 36 hours, affording me little time for the sightseeing that brings the majority of people to the nation's capital. But I had an important mission ahead of me.

My trip was designed solely to visit the Library of Congress, who have in their collections five Bebe Daniels movies that are either impossible or exceedingly difficult to view elsewhere. Within an hour of my plane landing, I was navigating the corridors of the James Madison Memorial Building searching for the Motion Picture and Television Reading Room.

When I arrived, I was seated at a 35mm film viewing station, and without any fanfare the title card for *You Never Can Tell* flickered on the screen. The film is 95 years old, and I was viewing the only print known to survive. I could hardly contain my excitement as, over the next five reels, Bebe Daniels played a checkroom girl attempting to seduce an older, moneyed gentleman.

The rest of the day was spent in that dark room, watching reel after reel of Bebe Daniels at work. There was *Sick Abed*, a farcical comedy she made with Wallace Reid, *Ducks and Drakes*, *Lovers in Quarantine* and an incomplete print of 1926's *Volcano!*. The quality varied from film to film (and even from reel to reel), but dealing with such rare material, quality hardly mattered to me.

I had already read newspaper and magazine reviews of each of the five films I watched that day. I had researched and written about countless aspects of Daniels' life, both public and private, for several years. But reading about films is one thing; watching them is something else entirely.

Remarkably few of Bebe Daniels' films from the 1920s survive. Of the 50 films she starred in over the course of the decade, only four are widely available to the public. The fact that I was able to view five on the same day was nothing short of remarkable. Over the course of that day my understanding of her career as an actress grew immeasurably, and likewise this book benefitted greatly.

I have always felt that Bebe was a victim of circumstance, and that her relative obscurity today is the result of factors outside of her control. It has troubled me for years that the only two books ever written about her are obscure and long out of print—not to mention biased and factually flawed. At a time when actresses such as Clara Bow and Louise Brooks are more beloved than ever amongst silent film fans, it is my hope

Early Bebe Daniels films on 35mm film at the Library of Congress.

that this book will help to restore Bebe Daniels to her rightful place in the pantheon of classic actresses.

Never before has a book solely focused on the life of Bebe Daniels; both her autobiography *Life with the Lyons* and the biography written shortly after her death, *Bebe & Ben*, are divided between her life and her husband's. Daniels' incredibly storied life is unquestionably deserving of its own book, which is what this work sets out to accomplish. Free from having to tell the dual stories of both Bebe and Ben, it instead traces the development of Bebe's career from her infancy on the stage in the American Southwest to her quiet and peaceful death in London.

Both prior works on Daniels are enjoyable, filled with firsthand accounts and personal anecdotes. As is inherent with personal stories, though, there is often no way to prove their validity and therefore this book has attempted to avoid relying on them. Instead, this work traces Bebe's life through newspaper and magazine articles, interviews, the words of her peers and other contemporary sources. There are many wonderful stories told by both Bebe and Ben in *Life with the Lyons* that have not been included here. It has been my mission, wherever possible, to tell Bebe's story through primary sources.

As strange as it sounds, I discovered Bebe Daniels twice—simultaneously. I watched my first Harold Lloyd short film, *Ask Father*, around the same time I first saw the classic

1933 musical *42nd Street*. I enjoyed both thoroughly, but it never crossed my mind that the gawky secretary who develops a crush on Harold could possibly be the same actress as the elegant Dorothy Brock. When I connected the dots, I was stunned.

My trip to the Library of Congress was the culmination of several years of research on her life. I visited some of the most prestigious archives in the country and scoured countless online auctions for photographs and lobby cards. I pored over century-old newspapers and magazines and tracked down rare, out-of-print films. And the more I learned about Bebe, the more I felt she deserved to have a modern biography written about her.

Bebe Daniels is forgotten by all but the most devout classic film fans today. For someone who acted alongside Valentino, Swanson and Fairbanks; who was hand-picked for stardom by Cecil B. DeMille; and who had a career that transcended all forms of mass media for six decades, it seems an unfair fate. But such is the fickle nature of stardom.

# Introduction

Defining the career of Bebe Daniels is not easy. She was a Shakespearean actress and she was a comedienne. She was a vamp and she was a flapper. She was a radio star and she was a war hero. She was a television personality and she was a singer. She was a mother and she was a criminal. In the entire history of Hollywood, there has been only one Bebe Daniels.

Few actors and actresses have conquered more media than Bebe did during her marathon career. She began her life as a child actress on the stage, then acted in silent films for a decade and a half. She was amongst the minority who successfully made the transition to talkies before retiring to England for much of her life. She was one of the most successful radio stars in the United Kingdom during World War II, before finally adapting her trademark radio show *Life with the Lyons* to television. Her career—from the stage to silents to talkies to radio to television—touched upon every form of mass-media in existence during her lifetime.

As popular as she was during her lifetime, though—she was a household name for decades on both sides of the Atlantic—time has not been kind to her legacy. Names like Mary Pickford and Clara Bow have maintained relevance, while Bebe's legacy has all but faded from public view. The reason is complex and involves film preservation, geography, her intensely private personal life and more than a little bit of misfortune.

Bebe Daniels departed from Harold Lloyd before he produced his widely celebrated feature films in the 1920s. Many modern-day fans of Lloyd are familiar with his leading ladies Mildred Davis and Jobyna Ralston, but the lack of availability of his early shorts ensures that all but the most devout film historians are unaware of how significant his partnership with Bebe was.

Furthermore, the vast majority of her silent films produced for Paramount during the 1920s are now lost, while most of her sound pictures from the 1930s are exceedingly difficult to get ahold of. There are, of course, exceptions. Her collaborations with Cecil B. DeMille and Rudolph Valentino were preserved, although none of these films can be considered classics. Several of her RKO musicals, including *Rio Rita* and *Dixiana*, are still commonly available, although these too are far from her finest work.

Undeniably Bebe's best-known movie to modern audiences is 1933's *42nd Street*, still considered to be one of the greatest musicals of all time. From hit songs ("You're Getting to Be a Habit with Me," "Shuffle Off to Buffalo," "42nd Street") to Busby Berkeley's masterful choreography to an all-star cast including a young Ginger Rogers and the debut of Ruby Keeler, *42nd Street* is still hailed by many as a masterpiece of pre-Code cinema.

It is somewhat ironic, therefore, that Bebe's role in the movie, Dorothy Brock, is an over-the-hill performer making her return to Broadway. Musical-director Julian Marsh (played by Warner Baxter) remarks, "These days, stars like Dorothy Brock are a dime a dozen." His statement rings true for the real-life Bebe. Silent stars trying to make the crossover into talkies were everywhere; while she was lucky to be given such prominent roles, there were dozens of once-famous actresses who simply faded into obscurity.

When *42nd Street* came out, Daniels was only 32, but the inimitable star had already lived an incredibly full life. Her career began during the earliest days of Hollywood, developing alongside the fledgling city. She had been traded between studios, been paired with different leading men, been pigeonholed into uncharacteristic roles. Time and time again, when it seemed like she was finally about to catch a break, she'd hit another setback—an injury, a part she didn't like, the differing views of studio executives.

Eventually she was able to survive the most strenuous crucible in Hollywood history when RKO entrusted her (and her previously unheard voice) to star in *Rio Rita*. Most silent actors simply faded into obscurity; Bebe was elevated to a new pinnacle of celebrity. Amidst a new wave of starlets—Ginger Rogers, Jean Harlow, Katharine Hepburn—Bebe Daniels stood out as a seasoned veteran, a relic of the silent era who managed to stay as relevant as ever before.

Her time in talkies would be short-lived, however. After a few years Bebe opted to settle in England with her husband, actor Ben Lyon, and her two children. Her decision for retiring from Hollywood was multi-faceted: her contract was expiring, she had a young daughter, and she and Ben hoped to return to the stage instead of making motion pictures. England seemed like the perfect place for the couple to settle and raise a family.

This is where the story would end for most actresses. Most would simply live out their lives as a footnote in the history of Hollywood; even some of the biggest stars of the '20s died in relative obscurity, all but forgotten by contemporary moviegoers. But Bebe's career was, in a way, still just beginning.

In 1940 Bebe and Ben premiered the immensely successful radio show *Hi Gang!*, which featured the couple as themselves. The program was so popular that broadcasts continued during the wartime blackout, helping to boost the public's morale. Her interviews with wounded American soldiers earned Bebe a Medal of Freedom from President Harry Truman.

After a decade-long run, *Hi Gang!* led to the spinoff radio sitcom *Life with the Lyons* (which also featured their children Barbara and Richard). *Life with the Lyons*, in turn, led to a television series, movies, books and a play, making the Lyons one of the most popular families in England.

However, her fame in England meant a serious decline in popularity in the United States. She did not appear in an American motion picture after 1935, and her radio shows and TV series were exclusively British. Although not a stranger to America (she returned, for example, to produce films for a short time in the 1940s), she was no longer a part of the Hollywood machine that continued to operate in her absence.

Her legacy in the U.K., however, will never be forgotten. She was a war correspondent during the darkest days of World War II, and her family continued their semi-autobiographical radio program in an effort to boost public morale. She helped millions of British cope with the harsh reality of war; her impact was so significant that John Lennon even released an album titled *Unfinished Music No. 2: Life with the Lions.*

Bebe suffered a near-fatal stroke in 1963 that largely ended her public appearances. She passed away eight years later with her faithful husband Ben by her side. Fans around the would mourned the loss of one of the greatest actresses ever to grace the stage, the silver screen and the airwaves.

Perhaps not much has been written about Bebe Daniels because her life lacks a defining characteristic. She did not sleep her way to the top of Hollywood, like Clara Bow. She didn't die of at the peak of her stardom, like Barbara La Marr and Rudolph Valentino. She didn't marry into a "power couple" like Douglas Fairbanks and Mary Pickford. She was never closely associated with one director, like Lillian Gish and D.W. Griffith.

One must dig deeper to find the trials and triumphs that crafted Bebe Daniels. An inherently private person, she rarely appeared on the front pages except for carefully orchestrated studio publicity stunts. She stayed out of the limelight that made—and broke—so many of her Hollywood peers. Keeping her nose clean proved both a blessing and a curse for her career—and in the long run, it accounts for her anonymity today.

Bebe's story is simultaneously tragic and triumphant. She was trying to be an actor's actor at a time when Hollywood placed higher value on spectacle. Audiences—and studio executives—would rather see her as a flirtatious coquette than a dramatist, so this is how she was cast more often than not. Throughout her prolific career, Bebe was never able to fully realize the serious acting dreams she had when she was a little girl.

While she might not have achieved her artistic ambitions, her career was still far from a personal disappointment. The immense fame she attained cannot be attributed solely to her flirty eyes or seductive lips. Beneath the veneer of a stereotypical vamp or flapper was impeccable acting ability, culled from her time on the stage as a toddler. Bebe truly was more than a pretty face—something that cannot be said of many of her peers.

It is my hope that this book will renew interest in the films of Bebe Daniels and help to restore her to her rightful place amongst the pantheon of Hollywood's greatest stars.

# 1

# In a Snow-Flecked Dallas

*She had never been called anything but Bébée.*—Ouida in *Two Little Wooden Shoes*, 1874

Little has been documented about the early life of Bebe Daniels' father. According to her, Melville Daniel MacMeal was born around 1865 in Edinburgh, Scotland. His father was a noted surgeon and religious zealot, a traditional Victorian gentleman if there ever was one. In recounting Bebe's pedigree, Ben went as far as to state, "MacMeal must have ranked high among the most intolerant men in Scotland, even in that period of the nineteenth century when religious intolerance was considered a virtue."[1]

The young Melville MacMeal lived in fear of his father's wrath. Each Sunday was spent indoors with the blinds drawn, listening to the elder MacMeal read from the New Testament. Singing, dancing and even reading were forbidden for Melville and his siblings—an obvious exception to the latter being made for the Bible. Bebe's father once remarked, "It was a case of holy reading, holy singing—or holy nothing!"[2]

Melville did not have much of a say in his future. As the eldest son, he was expected to follow in his father's respectable footsteps and become a surgeon. He obligatorily enrolled at the Royal College of Surgeons of Edinburgh, where he excelled. After passing the necessary exams, he was offered a job as a general practitioner—a prospect that did not necessarily excite the restless young man. He quickly devised a different plan.

At that time, many students looking to further their studies in the medical field would travel to America following their basic training in Europe. For Melville MacMeal, this provided a perfect opportunity not only to become a surgeon, but to escape his father's oppressive rule. Under the guise of receiving a better education, the elder MacMeal signed off on the plan whole-heartedly. Melville's departure for New York would mark the last time father and son were on good terms.

Upon his arrival in America, Melville was greeted by an unpleasant reality. Distinguishing oneself in the medical field was a long and bitter struggle that required years of hard work with little pay. Melville was not committed to his work to begin with; his decision to pursue surgery was more of a societal expectation than a heartfelt desire. The young man was no longer under his father's watchful eye, and New York provided him with unprecedented distractions.

Melville was instantly attracted to the stage. Whereas becoming a surgeon would require years of training with little immediate reward, the theater could provide him with short-term recognition and—perhaps someday—fame. Once bitten by the bug,

Melville began neglecting his medical studies, until finally they were little more than a distant memory. There was only one thing he had to do: inform his family of his sudden change in careers.

With trepidation, the younger MacMeal began crafting his note to his father. He dropped two bombshells, the first that he had abandoned medicine for the theater. The second, adding insult to injury, was that he had decided to change his last name to "Daniels" by adding a letter to his middle name. To his traditionalist father, both actions were an affront to the family. The first note Melville received in return warned the young man, "Anyone connected with the theater is an instrument of the devil." The next, in even harsher language, ended with a threat: "If you persist in this foolish and evil design I shall cut you off without a penny. The theater is a sink of iniquity, and if you continue we shall think of you as dead."[3]

The newly renamed Melville Daniels quickly suppressed any pangs of guilt. He had committed himself to the theater, and his father's moralistic letters would not deter him. Cut off from his previous life in Scotland, he set out to blaze a new trail all his own.

This story of her father's journey to America was recounted in both *Life with the Lyons* and *Bebe & Ben*, and for decades Melville Daniels' Scottish heritage has gone unchallenged. When closely examined, however, the entire story falls apart. In fact, there is no evidence to suggest that Melville Daniels ever even set foot in Scotland, let alone studied surgery there. His underdog tale was entirely fictitious, a clever work of the imagination created to hide his true upbringing.

Melville Daniel McMeal was born not in Scotland but in Pennsylvania, to Daniel McMeal and Sallie Bigley. Daniel McMeal was a well-respected physician, although not a surgeon. Melville was the third of the couple's four children. Both parents died within a year of one another when Melville was still a child. Beyond this, details about his youth are scarce.

Evidence for Melville's American heritage came from his own pen. On the certificate for his second marriage, he lists his birthplace as Pennsylvania and the ethnicities of his parents as American; likewise, census records consistently record Melville as hailing from the Keystone State. When the fabricated story about Scotland began—and why he was so determined to cover up his past—is unknown, but hardly unexpected from a man who built a career around deceit and deception.

Whereas Melville Daniels' lineage is clouded in mystery, Bebe's maternal pedigree was a source of much pride for the family. Phyllis Daniels was born on May 29, 1874, in Bogota, Colombia. Her father, George Butler Griffin, was something of a Victorian Renaissance man. His fascinating history was best described in an 1893 obituary:

> Col. George Butler Griffin was born in New York city September 8, 1840, and died in Los Angeles January 6, 1893, being 52 years, 4 months and 27 days old. His disposition was so retiring and his character so modest that few, even among his most intimate friends, knew of the greatness of the man.... [His] intellectual and moral qualities he largely inherited from a long line of honorable ancestors on both sides of the house. He was eighth to descent from Jasper Griffin, a Welch royalist who emigrated to Massachusetts in 1643, and ninth from Jesse de Forest, who founded New York city in 1636. His paternal grandfather, George Griffin, was a celebrated lawyer in New York city, and laid the foundation of that fine library which descended to his grandson. His father's mother was a daughter of Col. Zebulon Butler, the hero of the [Revolutionary War] Wyoming massacre, hence his middle name, Butler.
>
> Colonel Griffin was educated at Columbia college. He studied engineering, and in 1858, embracing

an opportunity to see something of the world, he went with a surveying party to Panama, and helped survey a ship canal across the isthmus. He went on is similar expedition to the isthmus of Tehuantepec [Mexico]. He then returned home, studied law, and was admitted to the New York bar in 1860.

At home he was married, but loving his wife and two children by death, in 1863 he went to the United States of Colombia as a civil engineer. He was rapidly promoted in the government service and was commissioned a lieutenant colonel.

He there Miss Eva Guadalupe, of a distinguished Spanish family, and, charmed by the prospect of a planter's life, he secured a large grant of land in the Cauca valley, and for four years was very prosperous.

He was seduced by relatives of his wife into taking an active part in politics, but, unfortunately, his was the losing side. His grand estates were confiscated, and he was glad to be able to escape from a probable death by coming to California.[4]

Further description of the celebrated Griffin family can be found in a 1920 newspaper article, shortly after Bebe Daniels had been elevated to stardom by Paramount:

Who says picture people don't belong to our best families? An inspection of the family tree of Bebe Daniels, Realart star, elicits the information that pictures of Pastora de Forest Griffin and Charles Alexander Griffin, Miss Daniels' great grandmother and father respectively, hang today in the Halls of Yale College. The "de Forest Medal," awarded yearly at Yale, was founded by David C. de Forest, great great grandfather of Miss Daniels. Mr. de Forest won historical fame as the First American ambassador to the Argentina after the recognition of that republic.[5]

Once in California, Colonel George Butler Griffin and his wife first settled in San Francisco, then in Los Angeles. Once there, his involvement in local politics continued. As the state was still in its early decades, the role he played in shaping Southern California was considerable. In addition, his historical writings were considered amongst the most significant works undertaken on the fledgling state.

George Butler Griffin and his wife Eva (her full name was Eva Guadeloupe de Garcia de Hidda de Hadda Solga Palagas de la Plaza, according to Bebe) had eight children: Eva, Pastora, Helena, Georgina, Francisca, Jasper, Alma and Georgia. Growing up on a sprawling ranch house in the foothills outside of Los Angeles provided the Griffin children with an idyllic, pastoral upbringing. In later years, Phyllis (as Pastora came to be known) often reminisced about her early years.

Phyllis Griffin's storied, honorable background was in direct contrast to Melville's nebulous early life. In later years, Bebe would show an obvious bias towards her mother's heritage, often invoking (alleged) Spanish noble blood and her grandfather's veritable résumé. Her dark features invoked images of South American beauty, allowing Bebe to successfully tout her mother's pedigree while ignoring her father's past.

As a young woman in Los Angeles, Phyllis Griffin found work as a stenographer while still living with her mother (her father died in 1893). Phyllis soon developed an interest in amateur theater. After acting in numerous small productions, she received an offer from a professional theater company. Her mother, from another place and era, was understandably concerned. But the young girl was unrelenting; and finally Eva consented and allowed her to enter the professional theater.

Newspaper reviews mention Phyllis in a number of plays in 1896 and 1897, ranging from Los Angeles to Sacramento. Now in her early 20s, she was beginning to make a name for herself, but the theatrical world provided little security in terms of income or lifestyle. It was a nomadic and irregular career, further complicated by the pushback she had already received from her mother. Phyllis needed to catch a break soon.

After she entered the theater world, Phyllis met a man and fell in love. Few details are known of their whirlwind romance; the *San Francisco Call* ran a single sentence about their wedding, stating, "News has recently been received here that on January 4 last Miss Phyllis Griffin, formerly of this city, and Melville Daniels were married at San Fernando Mission, San Antonio, Texas."[6] Within a year, the unlikely couple welcomed their first and only child into the world.

January 14, 1901. A traveling stock company of actors was headed to Waco, Texas, for their next performances. One of the repertoire's leading actresses was expecting her first child, so the company stopped in Dallas for several days. A Texas Norther—a special name for a type of cold front that sometimes brings very low temperatures—was coming in from the north, leaving a fine blanket of snow.

The actress, during the stressful days leading up to the birth of her child, was reading a book that her mother, descended from Spanish nobility, was particularly fond of: Ouida's *Two Little Wooden Shoes*, also known as *Bébée*. Because of the book—and because "bébé" meant "baby" in her native tongue—the actress decided it was to be the name of her newborn.

The story of Bebe Daniels' birth has become an accepted part of Old Hollywood lore. Throughout her entire life she maintained that she was born in Dallas, Texas, on January 14, 1901. Countless interviews recounted the story in varying degrees of detail. Bebe's resoluteness on the facts has left little reason for researchers to doubt their validity.

But, as is so often the case in the annals of cinematic history, the truth may be very different.

Corroborating evidence on Bebe's birth is difficult to find. The state of Texas did not issue birth certificates until 1903, and as her parents were traveling actors, local papers did not make mention of Phyllis and Melville's new child. The only hard evidence of Daniels' birth comes, surprisingly, in the 1900 United States Federal Census. It lists Melville and Phyllis G. Daniels as lodgers at a home in Stephenville, Texas. What is interesting is the fact that the line below Phyllis' name lists a daughter, Eva P. Daniels. The child was born in January of 1900, making her five months old at the time the census was taken. No other information is given.

Bebe was by all accounts Melville and Phyllis' only child, and the thought that they had a prior child who died in infancy seems far-fetched. The only scenario this leaves, then, is that Bebe Daniels was actually born Eva Daniels a year before her commonly accepted date of birth. Although she claimed that her parents named her Bebe at birth (a sentiment which Phyllis echoed), it appears that her actual given name was that of her maternal grandmother. For her entire life, Bebe Daniels was a year older than she claimed.

This truth was tantalizingly hinted at as early as 1933, when the *Austin Statesman* ran a blurb in their "Town Talk" column. The distinctly folksy column could easily be dismissed as nothing more than tall tales, although in light of the uncertainty surrounding Daniels' birth it takes on a whole new light:

> Originating in Minnesota, the land of a thousand lakes and a thousand Swedes for every lake, is the way Henry C. Smith describes R.M. Stene, "expert map maker now working in the highway department." And the thing most interesting in a very interesting life that Mr. Stene must live, is his state-

## 1. In a Snow-Flecked Dallas

ment that Bebe Daniels, the movie star, was born in Mineral Wells, Tex. But let's let Mr. Smith quote it as he got it from Map Maker Stene:

"Once Stene found a funny looking jigger near a lake. By looking through a catalog he discovered it to be a flute. Later he discovered how to play it, as well as other instruments. Adventure called and he became a band director in a road show. A Mr. Daniels was the manager. In 1900, while the show was stranded in Mineral Wells, Tex., a baby was born to Mr. and Mrs. Daniels. In much adversity Bebe Daniels had her beginning, another chapter for the silver lining group. Mr. Stene says that Mrs. Daniels was pure Spanish and that both she and Mr. Daniels were fine and likable people."[7]

Mr. Stene's claim that Bebe was born in the small town of Mineral Wells is obviously far from definitive, although coupled with the Daniels' residence in Stephenville in 1900 it certainly calls into question her claim that Bebe was born in Dallas. Stephenville and Mineral Wells are within 50 miles of one another, while both are less than 100 miles from Dallas. There is no doubt that Melville and Phyllis were working in the area; the canonical story of Bebe's birth in Dallas may simply have been created by selecting the nearest major city. Of course there is also the chance that the mysterious Mr. Stene was simply mistaken in his recollection.

What little is known about Bebe's infancy paints a grim picture. The harsh reality of Bebe's childhood would make itself known within hours of her birth. "I am told that my father took one look at me and then wanted to rush out for a drink to steady himself,"[8] Bebe would recount. For a woman whose positivity, unfaltering through good times and bad, would come to define her, it was a terribly depressing beginning.

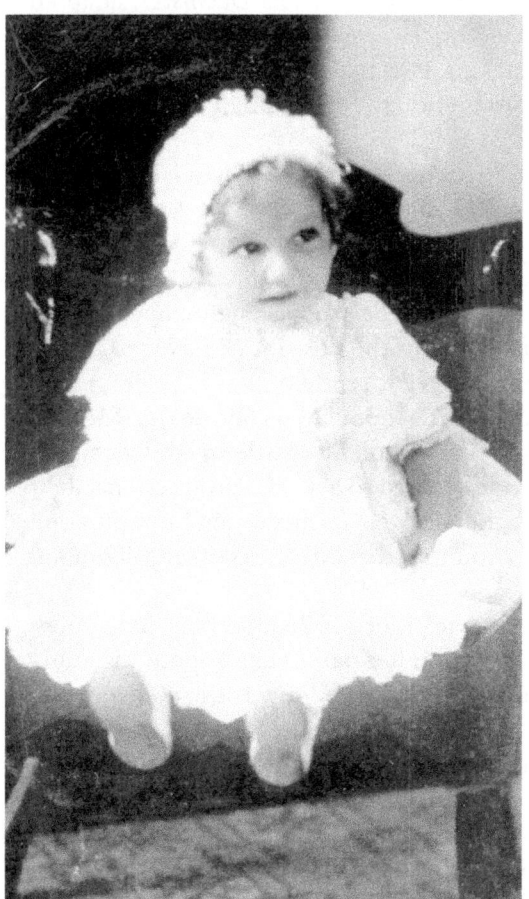

A portrait of Bebe Daniels at the age of 18 months.

Melville's brother Harry, traveling with the company at that time, attempted to cheer him up. "I tell you, she'll iron out and get pale-faced. All babies do."

"She'd better," Bebe's father replied. "Can you imagine anybody as beautiful as my wife, as my lovely Phyllis, having a ... a...." Unable to stand to look at his child, he buried his head in his hands.

For the first few weeks, Bebe's father was inconsolable. It wasn't until Bebe's Uncle Harry intervened again that Melville could bring himself to look at the infant. "Just look at her cute little face," Harry said. "It's got more dimples on it than a golf ball!"

But Melville would not truly come to love his daughter until he learned how he could exploit her in his theatrical productions. Bebe's introduction to the stage remains one of the most oft-recounted stories of her life. Whether there is any validity to it will perhaps never be known, but it is worth recounting if for no other reason than the importance Bebe later placed on the incident.

The company was still in Texas, and Melville was staging the play *Jane*. Even though there was no part for a baby in it, her father determined that he would carry her onstage during the performance. As he was delivering one of his lines, Bebe reached up and grabbed his nose. "Let go of my nose, you little rascal!"[9] he ad-libbed, and the crowd erupted in laughter. Bebe was a hit. From that point on, there was hardly a show where Melville wouldn't present his infant daughter for an easy laugh.

This is another point where Bebe's accepted history has overshadowed any original scholarship. In her interviews, Daniels would claim that both her mother and father carried her onstage during *Jane*, with her age varying from ten weeks to two years. While it is likely that Bebe's charming story had some basis in fact, exact details are impossible to ascertain.

Bebe's childhood was not as nomadic as she later claimed it was—but it was, in many ways, much more traumatic. In September of her first year, the infant Bebe found herself in central Pennsylvania for her father's production of *The Deemster*, adapted from the novel *Hall Caine*.[10] (Many of Melville Daniels' early productions were merely half-hearted adaptations of popular books, lacking in artistic merit but abounding in commercial appeal.) The company took the production to Maryland in November, followed by North Carolina the next month.

Bebe spent her first birthday somewhere on the road between North Carolina and Florida, where her father was staging an unremarkable show, *Where the Laugh Comes In*. After Florida, the company's next stop was Richmond, Virginia, a city that would serve as something of a surrogate hometown to 14-month-old Bebe. Although Richmond is never mentioned in either *Life with the Lyons* or *Bebe & Ben*, newspaper reports show that this is where Melville Daniels set up shop for the next four or five years, and where he achieved the closest thing to success in his entire life.

Bebe's father soon began promoting himself, ingenuously, as "Professor Melville Daniels." He never disclosed to his audiences that his "professor" title was better suited for surgery than theater—but then again, no one seemed to ask. His productions, light fare for a largely undiscerning audience, were generally well-received, and his reputation in town began to grow. At the very least, he encountered enough success in Richmond to put down roots for his wife and daughter.

Soon after his arrival in Richmond, back-to-back Melville productions lost money. One of Bebe's earliest memories was the conversation her parents had about his unexpected failures. "I think the reason show business is bad right now is the cold weather we're having," Phyllis said earnestly.

"Don't be silly, Phyllis," Melville replied. "In the show game we have hundreds of excuses for bad business. It's too warm, or it's too cold. Or there's the coming election, or Christmas, Lent or spring cleaning." He paused to think for a moment. "No, Phyllis, when business is bad there's only one answer: The customers don't like the show."[11]

He determined to remove himself from the front lines of show business; but his next scheme would be even more egregious than his acting company.

Melville established the "Daniels School of Acting & Physical Culture" in 1902 as a way to further spread his name. Theatrical productions in Richmond, which had a population of only 90,000, would never bring Daniels the fame he desperately sought. An academy, however, would provide some legitimacy to his operation (along with the self-serving side effect of better name recognition for himself). Almost-daily classified advertisements, obviously written by Daniels himself, frequently overstated the importance and influence of his school. (Daniels also served as the advertising manager of the city's two papers.) He assured readers that his pupils were practically guaranteed legitimate and lucrative acting gigs.

Daniels' operation was highly questionable from the start. In particular, the "physical culture" aspect of the school raises red flags, with Melville seeming more like a snake-oil salesman than an actual professor. Physical culture, a health movement based on exercise and athletics, was then sweeping the nation, and Daniels couldn't pass up the opportunity to capitalize on it. Using flowery language that exudes insincerity, he described his regimen as something of a cure-all for any imaginable medical problem. The following advertisement demonstrates just how cliched "Professor" Daniels' sales pitch was:

> LADIES, I HAVE CURED EVERY CASE of nervousness, indigestion, constipation, palpitation, weak heart, weak lungs, female complaints, eczema, weak, etc., that I have treated with my method of physical culture and deep breathing; physicians endorse it; established in Richmond two and a half years; hundreds of letters of testimonials from remarkable cures; a positive guarantee with each case; no cure, no charge; why not investigate at once; delays are dangerous. Call or address MELVILLE DANIELS, No. 627 East Broad Street.[12]

A much better salesman than father, Melville managed to build a small empire in Virginia. Perhaps it was because he realized that his future as a theater manager was bleak, but within a few years he was putting more focus on the "medical" aspect of his school than the dramatic. A syndicated article in 1906 called Melville Daniels a "physical culture expert" and described how he cured a man's case of hiccups that had "baffled two doctors."[13] In reality, this was probably not the "miracle cure" described, but rather the result of simple exercise. But, given the primitive state of medicine at the turn of the 20th century, Daniels was nevertheless hailed as a savior.

Other than Daniels' scant memories in her autobiography, little is known about the young girl's daily life in Richmond. One Richmond resident, Ethel Kelley Kern, is perhaps the only person to have later commented on Bebe's time in the city. Her quotes included here come from a 2008 article in *Style Weekly*,[14] a local magazine that, while not an academic source, nevertheless provides some interesting historical context.

Kern knew Daniels when she was a toddler playing in her father's studio in a building still standing at the corner of Broad and First Street. Amongst the local actors who frequented Melville's studio, "little Bebe was their pet," Kern said. A born performer, she would entertain the locals with nursery rhymes recited in a "loud, distinctive voice" (including her favorite, "Little Bo Peep"). Demonstrating from an early age the talent that would one day win her millions of fans, "[s]he would dance and pose, and when requested to show how she could faint, she would fall limp and gracefully to the floor."

It was also while living in Richmond that Bebe was first mentioned in print, although the article raises more questions than it answers. Published on September 19, 1902, the piece reads (in full):

> TURNED ON ITS MISTRESS.
> Greyhound Attacks Little Phyllis Daniels and Bites Her.
>
> Phyllis, the 3-year-old daughter of Mr. Melville Daniels, No. 213 north First street, was attacked by a greyhound belonging to her father and quite badly bitten about the head and face yesterday afternoon. The dog has been the playmate of the baby, and her family thought that he was to be trusted. Lately, however, the dog has been ailing, and when the little one started in for the customary romp yesterday, growled, and tried to avoid her. She persisted and followed the animal into the back part of the house, when it suddenly turned on her with a snarl and fastened its teeth in her upper lip. The lip was bitten completely through, and several other lacerations were inflicted. A visitor heard the child's cries, rushed to her assistance, and succeeded, after some difficulty, in beating the dog off, although it attempted to attack him also.
>
> There is no danger of hydrophobia, and the child was resting easily last night after she had been treated.[15]

The first points that must be addressed are Bebe's name and age, respectively. Adding fuel to the debate over Bebe's given name, this article provides evidence that the infant was known as Phyllis rather than Bebe. Given her father's prominence in town, this was presumably his doing. Regarding her age, Bebe was only two and a half when this article was published. It must be assumed that her age being stated as three years was either a mistake, or a tactic employed by Melville to make her appear older. The child was already performing in his plays by this time, so it does not seem impossible that Bebe's father inflated her age intentionally to fit his productions. While this is, of course, pure speculation, Melville's dishonest reputation makes it easy to believe that he would lie about his daughter's age.

In this article, a dismal portrait of Bebe's childhood is painted. Barely two and a half years old, she was left alone with no company but the family dog. Where her father was can only be speculated, but one gets the impression that this was not an isolated occurrence. As Bebe chose to whitewash much of her childhood, the true nature of her time in Richmond will never be known. However, the story of the dog attack (which she never mentioned later in life) is not indicative of an idyllic upbringing.

As an aside that demonstrates just how shameless Melville Daniels was: A classified advertisement placed only nine days after the attack reads: "For Sale—The Prettiest Greyhound in Richmond; a bargain. Call or address MELVILLE DANIELS."[16] Even in the wake of his daughter's near-disastrous encounter, he couldn't help trying to make a quick buck off the dog.

Conspicuously absent from Melville Daniels' public persona in Richmond was his wife. In fact, her name only appeared alongside his in the papers twice—and both times she was referred to as "Miss Phyllis Griffin." Daniels' desire to hide his marital status does not seem surprising, particularly given his penchant for providing "cures" to women. While the continued use of the surname "Griffin" could be explained as merely a stage name, the fact that she is specifically described as "Miss" on both occasions speaks to the quality of their marriage. Fortunately for Bebe and Phyllis, it would not last long.

At some point in 1904, Melville Daniels hired an actress by the name of Abon Hassan (real name Dell Lincoln). Born in England, Hassan travelled to America with her first husband, and both joined a circus troupe for a short time. As she had some theatrical training, she was one of the more qualified people in Daniels' operation. She quickly worked her way up the ranks with him; a city directory of Richmond lists Hassan as the directress of the Daniels School of Acting and Physical Culture.

Their relationship began innocently enough with Melville playfully teasing her by saying that she was "the clumsiest thing that ever walked in shoe leather."[17] But tensions grew between the married couple when Melville started refusing to talk about Hassan at home. Phyllis quickly began to worry that the association between director and directress had shifted from platonic to romantic. Even Bebe, at her young age, noticed that Hassan "wasn't young, nor even pretty. But she knew men."[18]

Already Phyllis and Melville's marriage was strained, undoubtedly exacerbated by the presence of so many young women in Melville's stock company. His affair with Abon was the final straw for Phyllis, and within six months of Hassan's arrival, the couple were separated. Bebe recalled the aftermath of the divorce vividly.

> "Mother was sitting in a high-backed chair window," she wrote, "sobbing her heart out and saying over: 'I don't want to live. I just don't want to live.'"
> 
> "I remember going up to her, putting my arms saying: 'What about me, Mother?'"
> 
> "And with that she threw her arms about me, clutched me to her breast and whispered: 'Forgive me, darling. Mother must have been crazy to say a thing like that. I promise I'll never say or even think it again. We're going to have a wonderful life together....'"[19]

Phyllis Daniels was true to her word. Sometime around 1905, mother and daughter moved to Los Angeles, where Phyllis' family still lived. While they did not have much, they were at least free from the harmful influence of Melville Daniels.

The rest of Melville's story will be recounted here briefly. In 1905, he and Hassan abandoned the acting ruse altogether and founded the Daniels Neuropathic Institute. In the same vein as his physical culture practice, the neuropathic institute was a pseudoscientific organization with no basis in actual medicine. In 1909, the couple moved the operation to Grand Rapids, Michigan, where Hassan's son from her first marriage came to live with them. Within three years, the Daniels Neuropathic Institute had branches in Cadillac, Ionia and Jackson.[20]

Daniels and Hassan were married in Essex, Ontario, on September 8, 1912. He continued to run his neuropathic institute out of Grand Rapids until his death on August 18, 1930.[21] He was reportedly 65 years old and had been ailing from pneumonia for some time. It is ironic that a man willing to lie and cheat his way to success, particularly in the theater, could not escape the shadow of his daughter, even in death. Obituaries make no reference to his traveling stock company or neuropathic practice; instead, he is merely cited as the father of the motion picture actress.

# 2

# The Stage

> *The miniature leading woman, Miss Bebe Daniels, is a delightful tot with distinct talent and shared the approval of the audience.*—review of *The Prince Chap San Francisco Call*, February 9, 1909[1]

Both *Life with the Lyons* and *Bebe & Ben* feature stories about Bebe's early life on the road, which is somewhat perplexing given her fairly constant residence in Richmond during the early years of the 20th century. One of the most pervasive stories is her battle with typhoid, when she was about four years old. "I was very ill, with a raging temperature," she recalled. "I can just remember the stage spinning round; the next thing, I was in bed in our hotel bedroom."[2] Treatment for typhoid often involved cutting the patient's hair off in the hopes it would give them strength. To Bebe, the idea was simply unbearable. In her delirium she begged her mother, "Don't let them cut off my hair!" When she awoke from a tumultuous night of sleep, she found her hair completely intact. Phyllis had not let the doctor touch it.

During the early years of the 20th century, typhoid was still a major killer in America. The top two deadliest disease outbreaks in American history were typhoid outbreaks in 1924 and 1903, respectively. Chlorination of water had not been developed, and vaccines were still in their infancy. It comes as no surprise that the episode was one of Bebe's most vivid childhood memories. Phyllis also recalled the incident vividly: "She had been playing on the stage in Shakespeare's *Richard III*," she stated in an interview, "and she kept saying the lines over and over again in her delirium. I found that [Bebe] had learned almost all of the play by heart, but in those days of dreadful anxiety, the fact didn't impress me much."[3] Ultimately, Bebe's mother was forced to relinquish her role in *Richard III* to nurse her daughter back to health. (Incidentally, Bebe often claimed to have been known as "the youngest Shakespearean actress in the world.")

There is no reason to doubt that Bebe played in a Shakespearean drama at such a young age, but there is no newspaper evidence to corroborate it. As with most of the stories of her folkloric childhood, it is only known directly from Bebe, undoubtedly tainted by personal biases and the selective memory of childhood. As such, many of the early anecdotes from Bebe's autobiography will be omitted from this work in favor of secondary sources that instead shed light on her quickly growing reputation in the theater world.

Bebe's earliest known newspaper review could not have been more positive. The July 2, 1906, *Los Angeles Herald* reviewed a performance of the 1890s naval drama *The*

*Ensign.* "INFANT ACTRESS MAKES BIG HIT," read the headline. Bebe was only five but was already a seasoned veteran of the stage, having just finished a production of *The Girl I Left Behind Me,* a Civil War story in which she played an African American boy. While the entire production of *The Ensign* was lauded, the writer was very careful to call attention to young Daniels:

> Bebe Daniels carried the day. She is such a little bit of tot that one cannot help holding one's breath when she first comes on, a fear perhaps that such a tiny baby could not even say lines. Bebe Daniels dispels all this the first time she opens her two pretty lips. She has a voice that penetrates to every corner of the house and she could give most of the stock actresses of the country pointers on acting.[4]

The performance was staged at the Burbank Theater in downtown Los Angeles. Noted theater producer Oliver Morosco had assumed the Burbank's operations six years prior and turned it into one of the city's most successful venues. Bebe's inclusion in his stock company marked a big step in her career, as Morosco often featured major players in his productions and was a respected figure in the legitimate theater world (as opposed to the lower-class vaudeville circuits).

The positive review of *The Ensign* was by no means an isolated incident. Over the next several years, Bebe would go on to make a minor name for herself with Morosco's Burbank stock company and later with the David Belasco stock company. A review of Henrik Ibsen's *A Doll's House* called her a "clever actress"[5] while an article about Belasco's production of *Zaza* mentioned that she was talented in "a degree far beyond the average child."[6]

The following year, 1907, saw Bebe perform in *A Royal Family* (after which she was erroneously referred to as "Master" Bebe Daniels because of her male role[7]) and *Her Own Way,* in which she was said to have a "naturalness all too rare among stage children."[8] Newspaper reviews provide the only record of Morosco and Belasco's stage productions, meaning that there is no way of compiling a complete list of the shows Bebe performed in. These few tantalizing glimpses suggest that, amongst Los Angeles theater circles at least, Bebe was beginning to turn heads.

These isolated newspaper reviews remain the only definitive evidence for Daniels' stage roles as a child. Her autobiography is understandably spotty when it comes to these early years, and as a majority of her roles were relatively minor it was common for her to not be mentioned in the press. While the reviews that do survive provide wonderful evidence of her early stage successes, they sometimes create more questions than they answer. They remain, at best, a tantalizing glimpse into the unconventional life of a young girl whose time was spent on the road or on the stage.

Another of Bebe's early successes came in 1909, with a San Francisco production of Edward Henry Peple's *The Prince Chap.* As originally written by Peple, the character of Claudia was to be played by a different actress in each of the play's three acts: "In Act First, a child of six; in Act Second, a child of eight years; and in Act Third, a slender, thoughtful girl of eighteen."[9] However, demonstrating her versatility, Bebe played both the first and second Claudia.

Although the play primarily served as a vehicle to introduce the Valencia stock company's new leading man Mace Greenleaf, the local papers cited young Bebe's performance as one of its highlights. She was called "one of the cleverest child actresses on the stage,"[10] and it was noted that her performance was "invariably rewarded with many curtain calls."[11]

The *San Francisco Chronicle*, in a moment of great irony, stated that "it is not always that precocity continues itself in later life, and Miss Daniels at 20 may not be a dramatic star, but at 9 she emphatically is."[12] Little did anyone in attendance at these early performances realize that, by the age of 20, Bebe would be starring in films.

Bebe's San Francisco debut also marked one of the only periods of financial security during her childhood, as it was reported that while with the Valencia stock company she was receiving $75 per week in addition to all accommodations for herself and her mother.[13]

The National Child Labor Committee formed in 1904 and over the course of the next few years ran a prominent publicity campaign against child exploitation. One of their targets was the theater, where young children were regularly employed full-time. Although not as detrimental as manual labor jobs that compromised the health of youths, theater jobs were nevertheless included in many of the state-level reforms advocated by the NCLC. It was such a law that threatened to put Bebe—and countless other children of the stage—out of business.

To circumvent California's new laws, Phyllis made Bebe a stockholder and partner in a theater company. Bebe was now self-employed and the child labor laws no longer applied to her. Such a scheme had been tried in other jurisdictions and upheld by the courts, so it seemed like the perfect solution. Almost instantly, newspapers picked up on the novelty of the arrangement:

### Nine-Year-Old Actress Is Now Youngest Theatrical Manager

The youngest theatrical manager in the United States lives in Los Angeles. She is Bebe Daniels, the 9-year-old daughter of Mrs. Phyllis Griffin Daniels. Today she was made a full partner in the Belasco Theater Company and she will receive 15 percent of the profits of the company. The contract shows that little Miss Daniels paid $100 for this business arrangement.

Bebe will now be able to play in any performance at the Belasco. This matter was brought into the courts in regard to the case of little Gertrude Hartman. Gertrude was a member of *Mary Jane's Pa*. Upon starting the company en-tour Gertrude was made a partner in all the Henry W. Savage enterprises. The Chicago courts decided that the authorities had no right to interfere with the child's property and as she owned an interest in the company the authorities could do nothing about it.

Bebe Daniels will play the child part in "*The Squaw Man*."

But local authorities saw through the charade and Bebe was not allowed to become a partner in the company at her young age. The incident was not a complete failure, as for the first time in her young life Bebe was a news story. Prior to this her references in print were limited to local reviews. The story of her promotion to theater manager was syndicated in papers across the country. It may not have been much, but it presented Bebe with her first sense of recognition. More people than ever were familiar with the name Bebe Daniels.

Notoriety cannot put food on the table, though, and the most pressing concern for Phyllis and Bebe was finding work. As Phyllis' time on stage diminished over the years, it became less and less feasible for her to support her daughter with the career she had once loved. Other options quickly needed to be explored.

William Selig was born in Chicago in 1864, and after a brief stint as a furniture upholsterer entered the vaudeville circuit as a young man. His entry into moving pictures is the stuff of Hollywood lore: After viewing one of Edison's films in 1894, he began trying to devise his own moving picture system at a photography studio he opened. With the help of a man who had once repaired one of the Lumière Brothers' cameras, he was able to create such a device. He formed the Selig Polyscope Company in 1896.

Initially all of Selig's productions were based in his hometown of Chicago. By 1909, he took his troupe of actors on the road and headed south to New Orleans, continuing to make films along the way.[14] They then headed west, arriving in Los Angeles on March 21. After leasing a plot of land behind a Chinese laundry on Olive Street for several months, Selig had an idea that would revolutionize Los Angeles and the movie industry. He bought a piece of land in the Edendale neighborhood, three miles from downtown, and established the city's first permanent motion picture studio.

Until a proper studio was constructed the following year, Selig's movies were filmed outdoors. A small barn on the lot was used to store props and scenery. During 1909 his company produced approximately 50 films in Los Angeles, most of which were 1000 feet—about 14 minutes—in length.[15]

Selig soon began assembling a new troupe of actors, combining those he brought from Chicago with new players based in Los Angeles. His two top directors, Francis Boggs and Otis Turner, were pioneers of the early motion picture industry. The studio's cheaply produced films were being sent to nickelodeons around the country. Their success helped to precipitate the mass movement of moviemakers to the Los Angeles area over the next several years.

It was against this backdrop that Phyllis Daniels took eight-year-old Bebe to meet with Selig in Edendale. Undoubtedly impressed by her extensive stage experience, Selig hired both mother and daughter on the spot. "He was wonderful, the way he helped us," recalled Bebe in her later years. "You see, acting in movies was so different from acting in the theater where you *feel* your audience, and each audience reacts differently. Mr. Selig taught us how to act to a camera—but forget it was there. We had to imagine our unseen audience's reactions—so timing movements and actions was very important."[16]

At the time, Phyllis had no idea of the momentous nature of their simple meeting with Selig. She was simply trying to put food on the table, and motion pictures were more lucrative than the stage. She certainly did not realize that by introducing Bebe to the world of cinema, she was planting the seeds for one of the most storied careers in Hollywood history. That fact would make itself known in due time; what was most important to the two ladies in Edendale was the fact that they would now be making a dollar a day between the two of them.

On the Selig Polyscope lot, Bebe and her mother were introduced to other actors who had made the transition from stage to film. Hobart Bosworth, a Broadway legend during the first years of the 20th century, had recently joined the company. Eugenie Besserer, too, had shared the stage with some of the dramatic world's biggest talent. The fact that other legitimate actors were working for Selig certainly helped to assuage the concerns of Phyllis about the movie industry.

# 3

# The Screen

*Those who have observed the child's work in the pictures concede for her a brilliant future when she leaves the school and again takes up dramatic work.—Moving Picture World, 1911*

In *Bebe and Ben*, Daniels recalls that the first Selig Polyscope film she and her mother worked on was *The Common Enemy*, released on April 4, 1910. A brief description of the plot for the long-lost film can be found in *Moving Picture World*:

> Let us imagine ourselves back to the period of turmoil and strife and fight of brother against brother, in 1860–1864. In the States, at that time, guerrillas, better known as "unlawful warfarers," were the pest and fear of both North and South. We see a Southern family gathering, interrupted by this fearful band. Their behavior in the home brings to the rescue of her mistress the old negro mammy, the family cook, who is daunted by nothing. A secret message is dispatched by the young daughter to Col. Morgan's camp—the anxious household awaiting with abated breath the result. The child, determined to reach her father, is wounded by a picket before her identity is known. Message received—Morgan commands, surrounds and annihilates the guerrillas.[1]

Bebe played the "young daughter of a proud Southerner" who delivers the message to Colonel Morgan. It was a significant role for her first, certainly the result of years of training on the stage. Unfortunately, examination of surviving stills from *The Common Enemy* do not appear to show Daniels.

During the early days of Hollywood, films were not made with longevity or posterity in mind. Studios produced shorts quickly, shipped them around the country and moved on to the next production. These were the days before movie stars; studios did not advertise the appearance of specific actors, and audiences were not conditioned to expect such information. Therefore, it is exceedingly difficult to determine exactly which Selig Polyscope pictures Bebe acted in.

There exists a great deal of controversy over whether Bebe starred in Selig's 1910 production *The Wonderful Wizard of Oz*. Selig had worked with L. Frank Baum two years earlier during the multimedia production *Fairylogue and Radio-Plays*, which combined film, theater and magic lantern slides to fully immerse the audience in the author's fictional world. Although *Fairylogue* was a financial disaster, the company attempted to tell the story again through a much more conventional medium. Like nearly all of Selig's films, *The Wonderful Wizard of Oz* was a 1000-foot one-reeler. It was released on Easter, March 24.

Its production records apparently do not exist. The earliest known reference to Bebe as Dorothy Gale comes in Einar Lauritzen and Gunnar Lundquist's seminal 1976

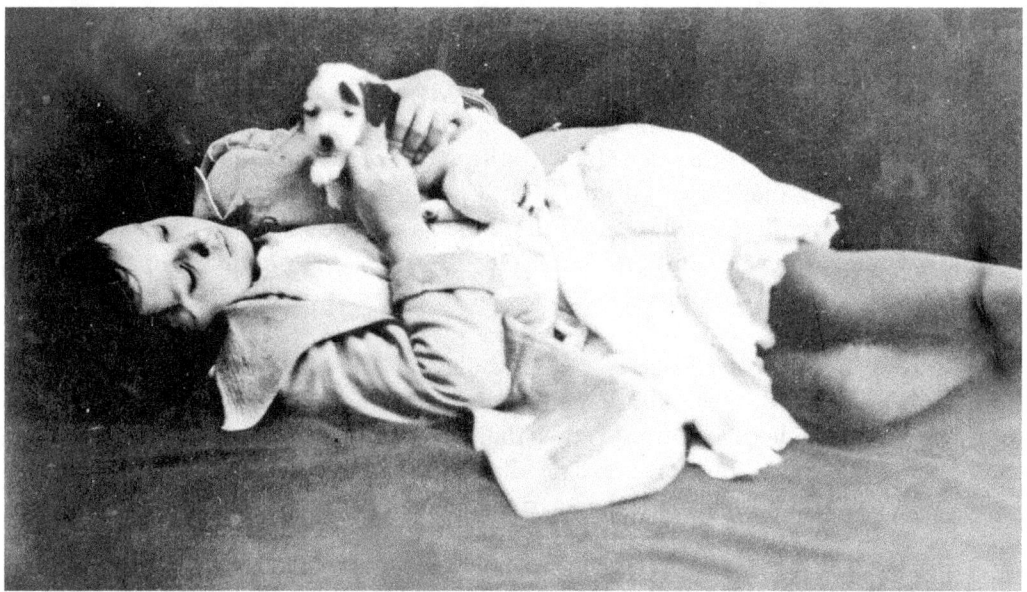

**Bebe Daniels at the age of 11 (ca. 1911), shortly after getting her start in motion pictures. Her pet dog she is seen holding was named "Spot."**

work *American Film-Index 1908–1915*. At the time of the book's writing, the film was considered lost, and the source for Lauritzen and Lundquist's claims is unknown. Otis Turner is listed as the director, and the film's alleged cast list includes Daniels, Hobart Bosworth, Eugenie Besserer, Robert Leonard, Lillian Leighton and others.

Even the filming location of the movie is a matter of dispute. If, as alleged, it was directed by Turner, then production most likely would have taken place in Chicago. Francis Boggs was Selig's leading West Coast director at the time, so it seems unlikely that Turner would have directed the film at Edendale.

Mark Evan Swartz makes a case in his book *Oz Before the Rainbow* that the film was indeed produced in Los Angeles, based on the presumed appearance of Bebe Daniels and Hobart Bosworth.[2] Daniels, being so young at the time, would not likely have made a trip to Chicago for the film. (Furthermore, such a trip would almost certainly have been mentioned by Bebe in her later writings.)

Bosworth, on the other hand, moved to California in 1908 as treatment for his tuberculosis. Swartz argues, therefore, that he almost certainly would not have travelled to Chicago for the filming of *Oz*, thereby placing the movie's filming location in Los Angeles in the opinion of Swartz.

Swartz's claims are entirely conditional on the accuracy of *American Film-Index*. The more one looks at the circumstances surrounding the film's production, the less likely this becomes. Although Bebe's appearance in *Oz* has become an accepted fact for many, it is imperative to reexamine all available evidence on the subject.

Visual examination of the film, which was discovered in 1983, does not bring the question of Dorothy's identity any closer to resolution. The film's quality is far from perfect, leaving the identity of all of the actors open to much debate. Enlargements of Dorothy bear some resemblance to known early photographs of Bebe, although the similarities are not enough to confirm her identity. Ultimately, there is simply not enough—no closeups, no unmistakable features—to say whether or not it is Bebe based solely on the film.

The January 8, 1910, *Moving Picture World* acknowledged that both Otis Turner and Frank Baum were "under contract with the Selig Polyscope Company in Chicago,"[3] strongly suggesting that *Oz* was produced in Chicago. Furthermore, Bebe very clearly stated that *The Common Enemy* was the first motion picture she acted in. *The Common Enemy* was released a week and a half after *Oz*. While it is very possible that production of *The Common Enemy* took place first, it seems strange that *Oz* would elicit no mention from Bebe.

Perhaps the strongest piece of evidence placing *The Wonderful Wizard of Oz* in Chicago can be found in the film itself. The lavish sets were obviously built indoors, and the lighting is clearly artificial rather than natural. Selig's Edendale studio simply did not have the capabilities for such a production. Prior to 1910, "the LA company had been staging its productions in the open on a concrete stage."[4] Because the company's films were often westerns, outdoor filming worked perfectly. Selig's Chicago studio, on the other hand, was well-suited for this type of interior filming.

It will probably never be known with certainty if Bebe portrayed Dorothy Gale in Selig's 1910 production. If it is indeed her, it represents her earliest surviving film. Arguments on either side are plentiful, but it is the opinion of this author that she did not appear in Selig's *Oz*.

Richard Braff's notorious *Silent Short Film Working Papers* lists Bebe in three short films between 1910 and 1914 but there is no corroboration. These films, mentioned here in brief, are not listed in this work's filmography as it is the opinion of the author that Braff's book alone is not sufficient evidence.

*The Courtship of Miles Standish*, based on a Longfellow poem, supposedly featured Bebe alongside Hobart Bosworth, Betty Harte and other Selig stock players. Released in January 1910, it predates *The Common Enemy* and is therefore unlikely to have featured Daniels. Another enigmatic title is 1911's *A Counterfeit Santa Claus* (which seems to have no connection to a picture with the same title released the following year). Again, there is no evidence outside of Braff's unsourced book to suggest that Bebe acted in the film (or that the film was ever released). Lastly, *Justinian and Theodora* (another Bosworth and Harte picture) was also released in 1911.

Without knowing Braff's sources, it can only be assumed that he inferred Bebe's presence in these films based on the fact that she was known to be with the Selig Company at the time. In lieu of further evidence, it seems irresponsible to accept these one-reelers as part of Daniels' filmography (despite many sources that accept Braff's flawed work at face value), so they are omitted from this book.

In her autobiography, Bebe tells stories of acting in Westerns and riding horseback with Hoot Gibson during her pre–Rolin film career, although she unfortunately does not mention any specific titles. A cast photograph places both Bebe and Phyllis Daniels at the Bison Film Company in 1911, which is backed up by the following quote in *Moving Picture World*:

> Little Bebe Daniels, the well known professional child actress, lately appearing in Bison Stock, has given up picture work for the present, and is now attending the Dominican Sacred Heart School.[5]

Those who have observed the child's work in the pictures concede for her a brilliant future when she leaves the school and again takes up dramatic work.[6]

It was presumably while with Bison that she made many of her early westerns, the majority of which are lost to time. Her stint at the Sacred Heart School is also notable as her only traditional education; for the rest of her adolescence, she was taught by tutors while pursuing her acting career.

Years later, a letter sent to *Screenland* magazine sheds some light on Daniels' early childhood:

> Dear Editor: I have something on Bebe Daniels. I think it's pretty funny, myself and I bet you'll laugh when I tell you.
>
> I once knew Bebe as a demure little convent girl, who "stepped softly, looked sweetly and said nothing." She wore a black veil to mass every morning except on Sundays. Then she wore a white one and looked more like a saint than ever.
>
> Picture her kneeling in a quiet little chapel with only the light from many candles and the soft red lamp that swings above the altar, while all about her the shadowy saints were peering skeptically from their corners.
>
> I never actually saw her saying a rosary, but as she would probably say in her latest picture, *You Never Can Tell*.

A 1911 group photograph of the Bison Film Company. Bebe Daniels can be seen seated in the front row, second from right. Her mother, Phyllis Daniels, is seated in the second row (fourth from left, in white shirt) (courtesy Academy of Motion Picture Arts and Sciences).

Anyway, as a last word from an old school mate, I will say, that in spite of her past, Bebe is the cutest little devil on the screen.

Sincerely,
Betty Burke,
Los Angeles, Cal.[7]

Burke's recollection provides a glimpse into the early life of an actress about whose childhood very little is known.

Further information about Daniels' early short films is remarkably scant. A photographic still is the only evidence that she acted in Kalem's one-reel comedy *Dr. Skinnem's Wonderful Invention*. Released on September 11, 1912, it was summarized in *Moving Picture World*:

> Dr. Skinnem is flat broke and greatly distressed. His maid-of-all-work notifies him of her intended departure, which completely crushes the doctor. Making himself comfortable in a lawn chair, the Doctor falls asleep and dreams of a wonderful invention that enriches him and causes the departure of all his troubles. What the invention accomplishes and its final results are laughably depicted by the Kalem players.[8]

Bebe's involvement in *Dr. Skinnem* is perhaps most notable in the fact that it places her at the Kalem Company in mid–1912. The vast number of films the studio

**Bebe Daniels (left) in *Dr. Skinnem's Wonderful Invention*, a 1912 Kalem Company production.**

was producing (over 200 in 1912 alone), combined with the fact that so few of their productions survive, means that it is probably impossible to glean which other Kalem films Bebe acted in.

Bebe's first actual screen credit didn't come until 1914, when she was a player with the Vitagraph Company. *Anne of the Golden Heart* starred Anne Schaefer, George A. Holt and George Kunkel alongside 13-year-old Daniels. Bebe played the protagonist's "pretty young daughter" Lucy, who is placed in a convent by her father.[9] After a change of heart that turns her away from her religious calling, Lucy returns to her father—who must bid farewell to his love interest for the protection of his daughter. A brief synopsis appeared in *Moving Picture World*:

> Upon the death of his wife, George Blake, an attorney, leaves the East. He first places his pretty young daughter, Lucy, in a convent. After traveling for a few years from place to place, in an endeavor to find some location which he might be happy in, he settles in Lariat Hollow, a mining town. He soon falls in love with a woman of the dance hall named Anne. This incites the jealousy of Larkin, the political boss of the town. To break George Blake, Larkin nominates him for mayor, purposing to have him defeated. Anne suspects the plot and tries to influence Blake to refuse the nomination. But Blake has given his word to enter the contest and goes in to win.
> Blake's daughter writes to her father that she wishes to remain in the convent and become a nun. The father gives his consent. Now with every Eastern tie severed, he asks Anne to marry him. She accepts, but says they will wait until after the election, fearing to ruin what political chances he might have by an alliance with a dance hall woman. The election occurs and Larkin's confederates defeat Blake. On the night of the election, Lucy arrives unexpectedly from the convent, having decided that she has not the religious vocation after all. Blake, in his hour of trouble, is glad to have her with him. Anne wanders out alone through the autumn forest, living through her "Gethsemane." She returns to the cabin in which Blake lives and says to him: "Lucy, your daughter, has the first claim on you. You must take her back East, away from me to the surroundings in which she belongs." Anne takes the girl in her arms and kisses her, then she turns to Blake, and bidding him a last farewell, goes out into the forest alone.[10]

The one-reel film was released on January 22 amidst a lineup that featured other screen icons. Anita Stewart and Norma Talmadge were two of Vitagraph's leading ladies. John Bunny had a little more than a year left in his fleeting career. Appearing in the production of such a distinguished film company was certainly a major credential for young Bebe.

A June 1915 article in *The Movie Magazine* mentions Bebe acting in a one-reel comedy titled *Aunt Matilda Outwitted*. The Albuquerque Film Manufacturing Company had recently moved to the Norbig Studios at 1745 Alesandro Street (just blocks from the Daniels' home in Edendale). Albuquerque, which released its shorts under the name Luna Films, was nearing bankruptcy by the time *Aunt Matilda Outwitted* was produced. The small production company was out of existence by the end of the year.

One of Albuquerque's main actresses, Dot Farley, managed to maintain a film career through the 1940s. Her films were typically comedic westerns which she starred in and wrote. *Aunt Matilda Outwitted*'s cast also included Winna Browne, Evelyn Thatcher, Major J.A. MaGuire, Pete Pairier and Raymond Zell.[11] Besides the cast, all that is known about the long-lost film is a brief review in *Moving Picture World*:

> A rather amusing western comedy.... Aunt Matilda, appointed guardian over her two pretty nieces, has her troubles keeping them away from their cowboy lovers, who to overcome the difficulty dress as girls and hire out with Aunt Matilda. They manage to get to the parson's with the girls, and the ceremony is performed before the desperate relative catches up with them.[12]

*Aunt Matilda Outwitted* is a notable addition to Bebe's filmography, as her employment by the Albuquerque Film Manufacturing Company was previously unknown. Practically nothing is known about another film allegedly produced by Albuquerque. A brief article in *Moving Picture World* in June 1915 read, "The Albuquerque Farce Comedy company is this week producing *Crazy with the Heat*, a rural subject, with Raymond Zell and Beebe Daniels [sic] playing the principal parts. The direction is in charge of Nick Cogley. The subject deals with the adventures of a decidedly romantic girl who has a number of suitors who are all willing to do or die to win her heart."[13] No additional information about the film is available, and Zell remains an elusive figure. Cogley was well-known for his work with Keystone during the 1910s.

A film around which there exists much misinformation is the 1915 film *The Savage*. It is commonly listed as having been produced and released in 1913, but two independent sources place it two years later. Directed by James Young Deer (an enigmatic figure of early Hollywood on whom much has been written), the five-reeler starred Bebe, George Gebhardt and Al Garcia. Like *Aunt Matilda Outwitted*, it was produced at the Norbig Studios in Edendale, this time by the Pathé Company.

Production began the second week of July 1915, when *Moving Picture World* ran a brief entry that read: "James Youngdeer is putting on a big Indian five-reeler at the Norbig studios this week with Bebe Daniels as the leading woman. Many Indians, cowboys and settlers will be used in the big cast."[14] The publication did not review the film when it was released later that year.

*The Movie Magazine* contains a bit more information: "*The Savage* was originally intended to be a one-reel story and was begun in the early part of 1914, at which time Mr. Gebhardt was working with Mr. Young Deer. The picture not being completed then, Mr. Young Deer recently decided to make a feature of it, and in order to complete the picture it was necessary that he secure the services of Mr. Gebhardt, who was one of the principal characters in the beginning of the story."[15] George Gebhardt, mentioned numerous times, was an actor who appeared in dozens of D.W. Griffith's early pictures, as well as some Paramount films.

Despite the interest in James Young Deer's life in recent years, no additional information has come forth regarding *The Savage*. Whether the film, apparently an ambitious project, was even released is unknown as no contemporary reviews have been located. At the present time it remains a mere footnote in the early life of Bebe Daniels.

A good deal of misinformation exists regarding Bebe's relationship with Mack Sennett, the silent era's "King of Comedy." Quite often it is stated as fact that Bebe was one of Sennett's famed Bathing Beauties, alongside future leading ladies Gloria Swanson and Marie Prevost. This claim can often be traced back to Daniels' 1971 obituaries, which included a stint with Sennett amongst her numerous other entertainment successes.

Around 1913, Phyllis Griffin Daniels took charge of Keystone's wardrobe department as it provided a more steady source of work than acting. Bebe would often accompany her mother to the studio, as acting jobs were sporadic. But while Bebe's presence at the studio is undeniable, her role as an actress in any of Keystone's productions is highly suspect.

Sennett himself addressed Bebe's involvement with his pictures in his 1954 autobiography, claiming, "Bebe Daniels was a Mack Sennett girl over my objections."[16] Confirming that Phyllis was working for him at the time, he continued, "When I heard that the child had charmed several of my directors into giving her Bathing Beauty parts, I threw up my hands like a pious Irishman and ordered them to cease and desist." Ironically, Bebe's first big break would be acting alongside another future star who had been fired from Keystone: Harold Lloyd.

Bebe recalls her relationship with Keystone much differently. "It has so often been rumored and published in movie magazines that I worked for Mack Sennett," she wrote, "that I had better tell what really happened. When Hal [Roach] made one of his first trips to New York we had no idea whether he would manage to sell the pictures satisfactorily through Pathé, so Mother suggested it might be a good idea if I went along to the Sennett Company." Melancholically, she added that "the insecurity of those days made this a wise suggestion on her part."[17]

Upon entering Mack Sennett's office, she informed him, "I'm not working for two weeks, and probably not the next week either."

He replied, "I'm sorry, I don't think…."

Brazenly, the 14-year-old continued, "So far as the money goes, Hal Roach is giving me thirty dollars a week, but I will work for you for fifty, Mr. Sennett."

"I'm sorry, I don't think I have anything for you right now," was all he could muster in response. Bebe's time with Keystone was, according to her, over before it began.

Bebe did, however, remain friendly with many of Keystone's top players. Charlie Chaplin, who she first met while he was working at Keystone in 1914, became a longtime friend. She also counted Mabel Normand and Buster Keaton amongst her acquaintances.

Bit parts at small studios was hardly a sustainable job for Bebe, and frequently she and Phyllis found themselves in desperate need of money. But Bebe's break was just around the corner.

# 4

# Meeting Harold Lloyd

*At the end of a year, I suddenly fell head over heels in love with Bebe and for four years we went together continually and expected to get married when we were old enough. Bebe was awfully young for her age, but she was the sweetest kid that ever lived. We both know now it was only what we call puppy love, but it was mighty important in those days.*
—Harold Lloyd, *Photoplay*, June 1924[1]

One afternoon towards the end of 1915, cowboy-turned-actor Jim Kidd stopped by the Daniels house. Born James Willoughby, he was a Wild West legend, renowned for his riding ability and strong moral character. During the last years of his life he became a well-known figure in Hollywood, even playing a bit part in *Birth of a Nation*. So beloved was he in the movie colony that when he died in 1916, his pallbearers included Harry Carey and Douglas Fairbanks.

Phyllis and Bebe were both friendly with Kidd, and the latter was ecstatic when he told her that a new film company had moved into the nearby Norbig Studio.[2] Located along the same stretch as Mack Sennett and Selig, Norbig was a rental studio where various companies could stage their productions. Recently a subsidiary of Pathé had begun filming one-reel comedies on the lot. "Their leading man is Harold Lloyd," Kidd said, "and they're looking for a girl to play opposite him."[3]

Bebe could hardly believe what he was saying because it almost seemed too good to be true. "They really want a blonde, and I don't think you are old enough," Kidd added, tempering her excitement. "But it won't do any harm to try. Dress as old as you can, and get over there as soon as possible."[4]

Even at her young age, Bebe was resolute. "I'll make myself *look* older," she replied, "and I'll tell them I'll wear a wig." Kidd wished her luck and went on his way.

Looking older would prove easy for Bebe: Phyllis' college-aged sister Alma was living with them at the time, and Alma's clothes were both fashionable and Bebe's size. "I almost literally tore the clothes off her back," Bebe later joked. She quickly put on her aunt's blue silk suit, high-heeled shoes and matching hat—an ensemble that added several years to her age—and was on her way.

The Norbig studio was only about a half block from the Daniels residence, and Bebe's heart and mind raced the entire way. A steady job with Pathé could give her and her mother some stability in life, something the two desperately desired. Bebe had had her fair share of business meetings already—certainly more than most 14-year-olds—

and she was prepared to use everything she had learned during her brief film career to get the job.

The Pathé subsidiary that Jim Kidd had mentioned, Rolin Films, was a small production company managed by Dwight Whiting and Hal Roach. Whiting was Rolin's general manager, handling the business side, while Roach was a struggling actor-turned-producer and director. The pair began making inexpensive comedic shorts to be distributed by Pathé.

Already their star Harold Lloyd was beginning to attract some attention in the motion picture world. After appearing as an uncredited extra in numerous productions for several years (not at all unlike the trajectory of Bebe's career), Lloyd developed his first unique character, Willie Work. Following the one-reeler *Just Nuts*, Pathé agreed to distribute all of Lloyd's subsequent work with Rolin. Roach and Whiting, with Lloyd in tow, were slowly working their way up the hierarchy of production companies.

It made sense that Lloyd was looking for an actress to play opposite him. Most comedic actors had steady leading ladies—Arbuckle had Minta Durfee, Chaplin had Edna Purviance—and while Roach and Lloyd obviously could not have predicted the duration of the actress they were to hire, it was not beyond the realm of possibility that their choice would have long-term effects on Harold's career.

Little did Hal Roach know who was about to knock on his door.

"I'm Bebe Daniels. I believe you're looking for someone like me to play opposite Harold Lloyd?" Her tenacity was unmistakable, especially for such a young girl. Roach did not know what to make of the young girl, poised and rigid, standing in his doorway.

The two must have made the oddest couple as they sat and talked for the next half-hour. Roach was nine years her senior (to the day), but their shared experiences in the movie industry helped to level the playing field. Exactly what Bebe said to impress him so quickly has been lost to history, but he almost immediately offered her a four-picture contract (with the potential for further collaboration). As the conversation came to a close, a look of concern came over his face.

"We *were* looking for a blonde."

"I'll wear a wig!" Bebe had come this close to landing the job; she wasn't going to let the color of her hair get in the way.

"For me you're fine as you are. We'll see what Harold says."

"She was only 14 then, and she had skinny little legs, but she was sure pretty," Lloyd told *Photoplay* in 1924. "We could get her cheap and she'd had stage experience, so we decided to take her."[5]

Bebe's recollection of the meeting was somewhat more romanticized. "[Hal] took me out to meet Harold and said something to him about me playing opposite him. Harold said 'Wonderful!' We shook hands, and from the very way Harold spoke, Hal knew that he'd okayed me." She added, "I liked him instantly, and I sensed that he liked me, too." Their affection was natural. In the moment, Bebe thought she was simply being hired for four movies. She did not realize the role that Lloyd would go on to play for the rest of her life.

So, with Harold's approval, Bebe became the leading lady for the Rolin Film Company. The final detail that needed to be discussed was her salary. Without hesitation,

Bebe asked Dwight Whiting for $35 a week. Whiting countered with $25. The barely teenaged Daniels proved an expert negotiator. She explained that if she was going to need two or three outfits per week, she would need more money than that. They settled on $30.

"Be here at eight o'clock in the morning," Roach said at the end of the day. "We're going on location."

"What shall I wear?"

"What you've got on will do fine."

"Do you want me to wear a hat?" Bebe asked.

"Never mind the hat," he smiled. "Just come bare-headed."

Bebe raced home with the good news. However, a sinking thought soon crept into her mind: What if Aunt Alma needed her suit tomorrow? She was worried that her limited wardrobe, which she had not told Roach about, might come back to haunt her. Fortunately, Alma assured her that she could borrow her clothes whenever she liked, even if it meant she had to stay in bed all day. Young Bebe anxiously paced around the house, waiting for her mother to return from work. Upon her arrival, Bebe informed her that she had secured work at a rate of $30 per week. It seemed as if the Daniels' luck had changed.

Lloyd and Daniels on their own were not a viable comedic team for Hal Roach. Harold was not yet the comic genius he would one day develop into, and Bebe was still untested in comedic roles. Lloyd needed a foil, someone with whom he could compete for Daniels' attention.

The third piece in the brilliant comedic trio crafted by Hal Roach was veteran vaudevillian Harry "Snub" Pollard. Most readily identified by his trademark mustache—variously described as a walrus mustache or a Kaiser Wilhelm mustache—he was a beloved Hollywood comedian for more than 50 years. Playing opposite the eccentric Lloyd, Snub often acted as a serious but lovable foil. Often down on his luck and never ending up with the girl (that was Lloyd's job), Pollard nevertheless contributed greatly to the comedic success of Roach's films.

Born as Harold Fraser in Melbourne on November 9, 1889, Pollard first toured the U.S. with his acting troupe in 1910. When the troupe broke up, Pollard was faced with a decision: return to Australia or try his hand at motion pictures in America. He ultimately decided on the latter and quickly found himself in minor uncredited roles. Notably, an un-mustached Pollard can be seen as the ice cream vendor in Charlie Chaplin's 1915 short *By the Sea*.

Pollard joined Roach's studio at almost the exact same time as Bebe, and very quickly all three actors came to be associated with one another. Pathé advertisements from the time refer to Lloyd, Daniels and Pollard as "the trio that causes the laughs heard 'round the world."[6] While Lloyd was obviously the leader of the pack, Daniels and Pollard's contributions to the Lonesome Luke comedies shouldn't be understated—a fact which Hal Roach understood very well. To be successful, Charlie Chaplin needed Edna Purviance, Roscoe Arbuckle needed Mabel Normand, and Harold Lloyd needed both Bebe Daniels and Snub Pollard.

The first film Bebe made with Lloyd was *A Foozle at the Tee Party*, although *Giving Them Fits*, filmed several weeks later, was the first Daniels-Lloyd collaboration to be released. Reviews of these films make no mention of Bebe as Lonesome Luke's new leading lady; the focus was put on the star himself, and Daniels was initially interchangeable with Lloyd's other main actress, Gene Marsh. No one could have predicted the longevity of their relationship, nor the comic heights that she herself would attain in the shadow of one of the screen's greats.

Before 1915 was over, Bebe had already filmed eight films with Lloyd and was quickly becoming an integral part of the Rolin operation. Internal communication at the company made frequent mention of their leading lady, and promotional material for Lonesome Luke comedies increasingly relied on the presence of Daniels and Pollard. After a short time, "Bebe Daniels" pennants were being created to distribute at movie houses. Lloyd's rise to stardom was meteoric, and Bebe was following very closely behind him.

Nineteen sixteen, her first full year with Rolin, saw the release of another 34 Lonesome Luke one-reelers. Seemingly without end Lloyd's popularity grew nationwide, with theater owners noticing a quickly growing rivalry between Chaplin's Little Tramp and Lloyd's Lonesome Luke as the screen's most popular comedian. It was not highbrow art that Lloyd and Daniels were producing, but it was immensely successful and allowed both of them to develop their craft. The frequency with which new films were being churned out was remarkable and ensured that the Rolin company's prized stars were always on the minds of the public.

A 1915 group photograph of the Rolin Film Company. Bebe Daniels is seated in the front row (center). Directly behind her is Harold Lloyd in his Lonesome Luke costume; to Lloyd's left is Harry "Snub" Pollard.

Beginning with *Lonesome Luke's Lively Life* on March 18, 1917, it was announced that Lloyd's pictures would now be two-reelers. While the addition of a second reel might not seem like a major development, the ramifications it had on the careers of both Harold and Bebe were long-lasting. Production schedules immediately slowed down; as opposed to a film every week or two, Roach was now producing one Lloyd film per month. Two reels also allowed for the development of slightly more significant plots—although in many regards these films were still highly derivative of the frenetic Keystone comedies.

The switch to two-reelers was warmly received by critics. *Moving Picture World* wrote, "To say that these [two-reel] comedies are a great improvement on the 'Lonesome Luke' one-reelers made by the Rolin Company is merely stating a fact."[7]

Through the first few months of 1917 Lonesome Luke proved an immensely popular character. "Lonesome Luke Comedies give better satisfaction than any we have played, and we play them all,"[8] reported one theater owner. "Lonesome Luke Comedies are the best we receive and certainly deserve praise,"[9] stated another. Although other players (most notably Bud Jamison) joined Roach's lineup at various times, the three core actors—Harold, Bebe and Snub—always remained the same.

During the Lonesome Luke days, Bebe did not have a public persona separate from Lloyd. Whenever she was mentioned in trade journals or fan magazines, it was invariably in passing (always some variant of "Lloyd is supported by Bebe Daniels and Snub Pollard"). Being so closely associated with a single actor had its blessings and its curses; it provided Bebe with steady work and a sufficient income, but it also prevented her from acquiring anything more than a supporting role. Her often nameless characters were certainly critical to the Lonesome Luke shorts, but their one-dimensionality often makes Bebe seem like more of a prop than an actress.

Things began to change as 1917 came to a close. Harold and Bebe's dancing prowess became a popular news item, and even such trivial things as a two-week illness in September were picked up by the press. She was still a long way from becoming a bona fide star, but people were beginning to take notice. Pretty damsels in distress were a dime a dozen in short comedies; nameless bathing beauties were too numerous to count. Slowly but surely, Bebe was distinguishing herself.

On September 9, 1917, a momentous film in the career of Harold Lloyd was released. Tucked between the release of *Lonesome Luke's Wild Women* and *Lonesome Luke Loses Patients*, a one-reeler called *Over the Fence* was released. The plot was fairly forgettable: Lloyd and Pollard, both working for a tailor, fight for Daniels' attention. Harold happens upon two tickets to a baseball game which Snub then steals, forcing Lloyd to get creative with his means of entry into the ball park.

But this one simple comedy would go on to change the course of cinematic history. For the first time since his "Willie Work" days, Harold did not appear as the immensely popular Lonesome Luke. Instead, he shed the novelty of his absurdly tight clothes in favor of something much more simple: a pair of horn-rimmed glasses. No longer an exaggerated comic stereotype, as Luke had always been, his *Over the Fence* character is realistic and relatable—the type of boy you might find working for a tailor in real life, not just in motion pictures.

This new character was not an overnight invention. In early 1916, Lloyd had begun toying with the idea of a new persona. The reason was simple: He was tired of being deemed funny simply because of his outlandish appearance, and instead wanted to "present the humor to be found in real life, reflecting his audience on the screen, and allowing them to see themselves in the hilarious process."[10] He began searching for a costume that would compliment, but not overshadow, his humanity.

The idea for his trademark look came while watching a dramatic picture that featured a main character who wore a pair of glasses. Despite the standard stereotypes associated with glasses, the minister in the film "turned out to be a regular virile he-man, which belied the whole thing."[11] Lloyd decided to emulate this juxtaposition with his new persona, producing a uniquely comic character whose humor laid not in a mustache or ill-fitting costume, but in his universality. Lloyd's "Glasses Character" would eventually go on to embody the All-American ideal of the 1920s, but the process would not be a quick one. Convincing Roach about his new character was challenging enough; convincing audiences would prove even tougher.

*Over the Fence* did not mark the end of Lonesome Luke; Lloyd went on to make six additional two-reelers. But as far as he was concerned, the character might as well have been abolished immediately. His head and his heart were in his new creation, "a fellow that you see walking down the street that you pass all the time. He wears ordinary clothes; he wears glasses as his only distinguishing mark."[12] Through early December 1917, Lloyd released (on alternating weeks) his final two-reel Luke comedies and his first several "Glasses" comedies.

Unlike Willie Work and Lonesome Luke, this new character did not have a given name. Today he is often referred to as the "Glasses Character," although many contemporary audiences simply called him "The Boy" (embodying Lloyd's everyman appeal). It seemed only fitting that his perpetual love interest, both on screen and off, quickly became known as "The Girl." Mary Pickford may have been known as "America's Sweetheart," but Bebe was right behind her in embodying youthful innocence and naiveté.

Bebe's roles in these early "Glasses" shorts remained trivial at best. In *By the Sad Sea Waves*, she's a beach-goer who elicits Harold's attention; in *Bliss*, she's the socialite Harold falls for. Often Bebe served as an archetypal damsel in distress. For example, in *Rainbow Island*, she's to be eaten by cannibals. These first one-reelers with the new character were not all that different from Lloyd's Lonesome Luke shorts—merely sequences of gags strung together for comedy, not poignancy. While the scenarios, costumes and settings may change from film to film, the essence is always the same: Harold must fend off other suitors to win the hand of Bebe. But audiences were enthralled.

Working for Hal Roach had its perks. On days when they weren't filming, the cast and crew would pile into buses to Venice or Ocean Park in Santa Monica. Bebe, still a teenager, and Harold, in his mid-twenties, enjoyed the amusements like any normal youngsters would have. Bebe fondly remembered playing boardwalk games and eating hot dogs and popcorn with her fellow Rolin employees.

During these outings, Harold first began to show affections toward Bebe. "Harold used to take every opportunity to sit next to me in the bus or on the rollercoaster," she later wrote, "but it took six months for him to pluck up enough courage to ask me to go out with him alone."[13] Bebe was overjoyed. Apart from a silly childhood crush, her relationship with Harold was her first experience with romance. Just one thing stood in the way: Phyllis Daniels.

"I was working all day with Harold, and we had so many interests in common that it seemed the most natural thing in the world I should go out with him, so the first time he invited me I rushed home and asked Mother. She agreed, as Harold is such a decent type, and so shy. His shyness had caused him to wait quite a while before asking me out." Fortunately for Bebe, Phyllis took a liking to Harold that caused her to relent on her strict "no dating" policy for her daughter. The two were spending so much time together at the studio, it does not seem like Phyllis had much of a choice.

Throughout their time together, Bebe and Harold took Hollywood by storm with their dancing. In February 1918, Mae Murray held a competition at Watts Tavern,[14] a popular dance club south of Los Angeles where men such as Valentino performed in his early days. The silver trophy Murray provided for the event was added to the ever-growing Lloyd-Daniels collection, and Murray's competition remains just one anecdote amongst a litany of competitions won by Hollywood's beloved couple.

The two Rolin stars began gracing the pages of the local papers more and more frequently. When wrestling champion Walter Miller visited Los Angeles for his next match, Lloyd and Bebe were called upon to appear in promotional photographs. One showed Miller and Daniels making eyes at one another while the middleweight champ held a noticeably worried Lloyd in an expert arm-lock.[15] Such photographs contributed to Harold and Bebe's onscreen personas, and worked to further their beloved status amongst the movie going public.

As her fictional character developed over the course of her work with Rolin, so too did Bebe's personality off-screen during the late 1910s. Her piquant, charming attitude, innocent and uncorrupted by the burgeoning movie industry, was a hit with audiences. Her roles with Harold were largely successful for that exact reason; the character she played with him was not actually a character, but rather the teenage Daniels being herself in front of a camera. This earnestness translated well both in her films and her personal life.

**A promotional photograph of Bebe Daniels in 1918 which was used in Rolin advertisements the following year.**

## 4. Meeting Harold Lloyd

One morning in late 1918 a reporter found Bebe alone on the beach near Venice, wearing a bathing suit and curiously running in place. The reporter inquired why she was acting so strangely. "The best warming-up exercise I know when one comes out of the water on a chilly day is the 'sand piper trot,' as I call it," Daniels replied. "Physical culture teachers may call it 'the stationary run,' but I like to name it for one of my beach bird friends. In one's wet bathing suit it is a bit shivery to run across the beach in the breeze. This is much warmer and more comfortable."[16]

On another occasion, Bebe threw a party for her closest friends, to raise money for the Red Cross. "Bebe Daniels ... is forever figuring out freak ideas for parties," a report read. "One evening lately she gave a kid dress up party at the Chestmere Apartments, where she gathered about seventy-five couples, the girls bringing basket lunches, which were raffled off to the highest bidder among the men present."[17]

In many ways Bebe was still a child; her unconventional upbringing had deprived her of traditional schooling, and her formative years were spent on a studio lot rather than a playground. Whereas contemporary actresses like Mary Pickford were playing "little girl" roles as grown women, Bebe actually *was* a little girl.

One evening in late 1917, Bebe and Harold visited the Sunset Inn in Santa Monica for a dancing contest. They were ringers, almost as well known for their prowess on the dance floor as on a movie screen. Bebe recalled wearing a white satin gown, making her appear much older than her 16 years. It started out as a night like countless others; it would quickly transform into a night Bebe would never forget. As she later recalled, at some point that evening a note arrived at Bebe and Harold's table. According to the note, Cecil B. DeMille was visiting the Sunset Inn that night and wanted to speak to Bebe. The couple were both shocked at the famed director's request. What could DeMille want to speak to Bebe Daniels about?

Bebe and Harold wandered over to DeMille's table, where he was seated with his writer and mistress Jeanie MacPherson. Quickly, the tone of the conversation turned serious. "How would you like to come and work for me?" he asked her directly.[18] Bebe was stunned and speechless; Harold, on the other hand, was alarmed that he might be losing his leading lady and girlfriend. A heavy and anxious silence hung over the table.

Even Harold, her confidant and closest friend, did not know how she would respond. Bebe was a key piece of the Rolin operation, and her sudden loss would be detrimental to the company. At the same time, he understood that an offer to work for DeMille was not something to be passed up lightly.

Finally, Bebe worked up the courage to reply. "Thank you, Mr. DeMille, but I afraid it is absolutely impossible for me to accept," she said earnestly. "I am under contract to Hal Roach, and"—she paused—"I'm very happy."[19]

Harold was relieved. The success of his pictures, and his love affair with Bebe, were both safe—for the time being. It would be another year and a half before Bebe's career aspirations would finally overcome their relationship.

While Harold may have been relieved that Bebe did not accept the offer that night, Hal Roach and his business partner Dwight Whiting certainly were not keen on DeMille and Lasky's advances. A series of letters preserved in the Hal Roach Collection at the University of Southern California displays the fallout from the meeting:

My dear Mr. [Frank A. Garbutt, of Famous Players–Lasky],

In has come to my attention that one evening at one of the local beach cafes Mr. Lasky and Mr. DeMille noticed our star, Miss Bebe Daniels, on the dance floor, and after calling her over to their table, offered her a position on the Lasky forces. Miss Daniels replied that she was satisfied to remain where she was as she was under contract and receiving her salary regularly, whereupon they told her that they would be glad to have her join their forces at any time she could arrange to do so, and that they would pay her a figure of around twice what she is now receiving.

Evidently Mr. Lasky and Mr. DeMille are not familiar with the resolution now in force with the Producers Association which covers this controversy. Would you be so kind as to call the matter to their attention and have them see to it that the slip is not repeated?

Kindly acknowledge receipt of this letter and oblige.

With very best personal wishes I am,
Yours very truly,
[Dwight Whiting]
May 4, 1917[20]

The following day, Garbutt responded:

Dear Mr. Whiting,

I have your kind letter of May fourth, regarding Miss Bebe Daniels, and immediately communicated with Mr. DeMille.

Mr. DeMille advises me that he and Mr. Lasky saw Miss Daniels dancing at the Cafe, as stated, and thinking she was an attractive girl, and not knowing who she was or that she was employed, asked her to call at the Studio. Later, when Mr. Lasky found that she was employed and under contract, he told her frankly that he could not pursue the matter further, and the question of salary, Mr. DeMille says, was never mentioned at all.

I think, therefore, that possibly there may have been a misunderstanding as to what was said for I am sure that neither Mr. Lasky nor Mr. DeMille would talk to anyone whom they knew was under contract or regularly employed by any member of our Association. I thank you for bringing the matter to my attention in such a frank way and feel sure that if we would all do this, it would save many misunderstandings.

With kind personal regards, I remain
Yours very truly,
Frank A. Garbutt

A schism had been created between Hal Roach and DeMille. It would come to a head two years later.

# 5

# Leaving Rolin

*Bebe Daniels, principal comedienne with the Harold Lloyd comedies, has signed with Famous Players–Lasky. Miss Daniels will be assigned to the Cecil DeMille Co., starting work at Los Angeles next week.*
—Variety, July 4, 1919[1]

When Bebe first began starring in comedies with Harold Lloyd, her physical attributes were not of the utmost importance. While Lloyd recalled noticing that "she was sure pretty" upon their first meeting, Roach and Lloyd were less interested in finding a beauty queen than they were in finding someone with on-screen experience, comedic timing and—most importantly—who would work on the studio's limited budget. As Bebe met all of these requirements, her childish good looks only enhanced her value to Rolin.

As she matured alongside Lloyd, however, audiences were quick to notice that her youthful cuteness was quickly developing into full-blown beauty. Newspaper advertisements once promoted Lonesome Luke films as co-starring Bebe Daniels; now these same movies co-starred "pretty Bebe Daniels." Under a photograph of the demure Daniels, many papers ran the following syndicated exaltation of her beauty:

> It is to be expected that as soon as eligible young men see this picture they will emigrate to California in large numbers, and not because of the shortage of coal in the east. The smiling beauty with the parasol and barber-pole clothes is Miss Bebe Daniels, who acts as a foil for Harold Lloyd in Pathé-Rolin comedies. Personally we fail to see why anybody should live in the east when Los Angeles trees grow such fruit as this.[2]

As Bebe's 18th[3] birthday approached, Lloyd took it upon himself to plan the festivities at the Rolin studios. He told a reporter that he would serve as the master of ceremonies, and promised to present Bebe with a cake sporting 300 candles.

"But why 300?" demanded the reporter. "Bebe is only 18, isn't she?"

"Sure," replied Harold with a smile. "Each candle stands for some fellow that is crazy over Bebe."[4]

Harold certainly counted himself amongst those 300, as it was also in the months leading up to Bebe's 18th birthday that marriage rumors first began circulating.

A facet of Bebe's life at Rolin Studios that has been wholly forgotten in the ensuing years is her homefront work for World War I. Apparently an incredibly spirited and patriotic girl, Daniels did everything she could (on and off the set) to contribute to the war effort. Although Rolin—like many Hollywood studios—was making American propaganda films such as *Kicking the Germ Out of Germany*, Bebe's interest in assisting the troops went above and beyond what was expected of her.

Bebe's work began humbly; in mid–1918, she had organized a knitting club in the Rolin Studio, putting everyone (including her male peers) to work. The result was "several boxes of warm knit-goods for the boys in the trenches."[5] The fact that she found time to knit while also producing a one-reeler a week demonstrates her remarkable dedication.

The knitting club was just the beginning of her war work, and before the year was over she had established a salvage branch of the Red Cross at the Rolin Studio (an organization for which she was an "ardent worker"[6]). She also enrolled the studio in the Motion Picture War Service Association, going as far as to nail a sign to the studio's facade promoting their role in the program. It was noted that Bebe had "taken an active part in Liberty Bond campaigns, Red Cross, Red Star and many other branches of war work."[7]

Perhaps her most dedicated involvement came in the form of public appearances; she made several for the Red Cross and other organizations. She even traveled to San Diego's Camp Kearney to perform to Army units scheduled to ship off to France. It was reported that the rising movie star "sang jazz songs that brought the laughs from the boys."[8] Although she was only 18 and not yet a household name, Daniels sought any way that she could to serve her country. In 25 years she would once again be providing entertainment to American troops.

A ca. 1919 glamour shot of Bebe Daniels taken by famed Hollywood photographer Albert Witzel.

Unfortunately, Bebe's war work was cut short by the Spanish Influenza. Late in 1918, she, Snub Pollard and several other Rolin employees were stricken by the pandemic that would end up claiming 50 to 100 million lives worldwide. Without two-thirds of the studio's leading comic trio, Roach was forced to cease productions for several weeks.[9] By the time she recovered the war was over, with Rolin Studio having led the way in terms of patriotic duty.

During the summer of 1918, Bebe took a trip to nearby Seal Beach to compete in the second annual Seal Beach Bathing and Fashion Parade. With 50 participants, including many aspiring starlets from a number of studios, the event was witnessed by more than 35,000 spectators—a remarkable turnout for the diminutive Seal Beach. The pageant host was Roscoe "Fatty" Arbuckle, one of Hollywood's most famous comedians.

Bebe finished in the top three, no doubt helping to spread her popularity throughout Southern California. The spectacle was filmed and released to local theaters the following month. A panoramic photograph of the event shows Bebe front and center; even in a still image, Daniels' magnetism in front of the camera separates her from the dozens of other young girls in attendance.

Even at this early stage of her career—still years before the infamous speeding arrest that would come to define her for a time—automobiles played a major role in Bebe's life. In 1917, her car of choice was a Chandler. The next year she opted for something a little faster, a Mercer Raceabout. At only 16 years old Bebe was a very early adaptor to the fledgling car culture, and very quickly her love of cars—particularly fast ones—became an important part of her public persona.

An exemplary demonstration of Bebe's automotive interests (and unwavering patriotism, which would become more pronounced in adulthood) came in an interview she gave in May 1918. Because of the desperate need for young men overseas, Daniels decided to learn how to maintain her own automobile in order for her mechanic to enlist. After a week of intensive training, Bebe concluded that "every woman in the country ought to take care

This insert from a panorama photograph of the 1918 Seal Beach Bathing and Fashion Parade shows Bebe Daniels (center), who finished in the top three of the contest (Library of Congress).

of her own automobile. In the first place it will release the men for war work. But, aside from that advantage, it is the most interesting diversion in the world."[10]

The young girl's love of mechanics—which would later manifest itself as a love of aviation—was clearly not contrived. "There was a time when I thought dancing was more fun than anything else ... but it can't compare to the pleasure I get out of jumping into my overalls and spending the morning keeping my automobiles in shape." At the time, Bebe was not only becoming one of the most celebrated youngsters in Hollywood, she was quickly developing into something of a sex symbol. Yet rather than try to attain the glamorous image of many other starlets, Bebe maintained her inner tomboy. The rough-and-tumble girl who once rode around on horses was now riding around in automobiles.

Bebe Daniels and Harold Lloyd in the 1919 film *Ask Father*.

According to Harold Lloyd biographer Annette D'Agostino Lloyd (no relation), the one-reeler *Ask Father*, released on February 9, 1919, marked a turning point in Lloyd and Daniels' on-screen relationship. She calls it "the first example of romance in which the audience can fully believe."[11] The plot deviates from the duo's typical shorts. Instead of Harold pursuing Bebe from the start, he is instead taken by the daughter (Marie Mosquini) of a prominent businessman. Throughout his unsuccessful attempts to ask her father's permission to marry, Bebe—a lowly secretary—slowly wins Harold over with her selfless compassion.

As Annette Lloyd points out, "We, the audience, notice her *way* before Harold does; thus, in the course of the reel, we are rooting for Harold and *Bebe* to get together. And, by the end, they do: this is perhaps the first case of Lloyd film romance made believable—Lloyd's and Daniels' characters are not just thrown together for the sake of plot."[12]

The culmination of Bebe's character development came in the only two "Glasses Character" two-reelers she produced. *Bumping Into Broadway* (and to a lesser extent *Captain Kidd's Kids*) show a full-fledged relationship between Rolin's leading man and leading lady. The addition of a second reel allowed Lloyd to develop his "Glasses Character" more fully, just as he had done for Lonesome Luke two years earlier. Today, these films hold up as the best example of Harold and Bebe's on-screen rapport. Unfortunately, there was already turmoil behind the scenes when they were being made.

On May 19, 1919, a desperate telegram was sent from Hal Roach to Pathé's offices in New York. Although Daniels had forgone DeMille's offer of a higher salary almost two years earlier, the expiration of her Rolin contract in early 1919 forced her to reconsider. Although the story was told (in a somewhat fictionalized manner) by Bebe later in life, the telegrams between Roach and Pathé's Paul Brunet provide the only contemporary account of her departure:

MAY 19, 1919
    BEBE DANIELS HAS SIGNED CONTRACT WITH THE LASKY COMPANY TO BE FEATURED BY CECIL DEMILLE IN BIG PRODUCTIONS STOP
    IMPOSSIBLE TO KEEP HER WITH US STOP
    HAVE YOU ANY SUGGESTIONS TO ADVICE [sic] FOR LEADING LADY WITH LLOYD STOP
—HAL E. ROACH

MAY 20, 1919
    REGARDING BEBE DANIELS WE HAVE NO SUGGESTIONS TO MAKE AS TO HER SUCCESSOR STOP
    AS YOU ARE MORE FAMILIAR WITH COMEDY SITUATION SUGGEST YOU ATTEMPT TO FIND SOMEONE IN LOS ANGELES STOP
    IF YOU LEARN OF A PROSPECT WORKING IN NEW YORK WE WILL BE PLEASED TO INTERVIEW HER IN YOUR BEHALF STOP
—PAUL BRUNET

MAY 22, 1919
    I AM TRYING TO GET MILDRED DAVIS WHO PLAYED LEAD IN BRYANT WASHBURN PICTURE ALL WRONG TO PLAY LEADS WITH LLOYD STOP
    KINDLY ASK THE OPINION OF THE PEOPLE THERE REGARDING THIS GIRL STOP
—H.E. ROACH

MAY 22, 1919
    MILDRED DAVIS VERY SATISFACTORY WE SUGGEST THAT YOU GET HER STOP
—PAUL BRUNET[13]

Both Tom Dardis and Richard Schickel's biographies of Harold Lloyd seem to insinuate that Bebe's departure from Rolin was more personal than professional. Specifically, Dardis states that "there is some indication that she was anxious to marry him, but he felt he was far too young to shoulder the responsibilities that went with marriage."[14] He provided no source for his claims that Bebe's move to Lasky and DeMille was intended to spite Lloyd (or force Harold to "call her bluff"[15]), even going as far as to selectively edit telegrams to suggest a growing bitterness between Daniels and Roach. Dardis' thesis echoes the writing of Schickel, who bolstered his argument for Bebe's spitefulness with unverified quotes from Hal Roach.

Bebe was certainly in love with Harold, and marriage was certainly on the minds of both of them at one time or another. But when the evidence is examined, there is little reason to believe that Daniels' move to Famous Players–Lasky was anything but practical. As early as 1917, Bebe was quoted as saying "I like my present work, but some day I want to do really big things. When I was a little girl, I played in a great many Shakespearean plays.... I wouldn't care particularly about playing the Shakespearean roles [now], but I do want to play fine modern parts that require hard work. I'll never be satisfied until I do."[16]

Although an aspiration for dramatic roles was Bebe's explanation for leaving Lloyd later in life, this early interview demonstrates that this was far from a fictitious cover story. While there may have been a personal component to the split, an offer from DeMille—particularly one for $1000 per week (versus Roach's $150)—would have perfectly satisfied Daniels' interest in acting in dramatic parts. DeMille was, after all, renowned for the dramatism of his films, and an offer from him could hardly have been turned down in good conscience (no matter how much she loved Lloyd).

The details of Bebe and Harold's breakup have become a part of Hollywood lore, with various stories alluding to their unrequited love for one another. It has been variously reported that Bebe kept all of the dancing trophies the couple had won until the time of her death, or that she wore a ring or necklace that Harold had given to her for years after her departure from Rolin. Perhaps the most poetic story revolves around a ring that was given to Daniels by Lloyd; when she announced her new contract with Lloyd, she allegedly had the ring's stone recut into a pair of cufflinks that Harold wore for the rest of his life.

Although all of these stories may be more myth than fact, they do demonstrate

**Harold Lloyd and Bebe Daniels perched above downtown Los Angeles in *Look Out Below*.**

the lingering feelings that undoubtedly lasted between Harold and Bebe. It was the first serious relationship that either of them experienced, and the fact that it ended so abruptly has contributed to its fabled reputation amongst film historians. Their love was no more (officially, at least), but as the years went on, the two developed a friendship that spanned their entire lives.

# 6

# Mr. DeMille

*Her mother is Spanish; her father Scotch; why is she the perfect Oriental type? What must a girl be to earn this distinction? Why did Cecil DeMille select Bebe Daniels, who first appeared on the stage at the age of ten weeks, as a true Oriental? She lives in the splendor of vivid Babylonian color and the weird mysticism of the Far East. Even her dressing room is draped in gold lace and black velvet, richly splashed with red.*
—Motion Picture Magazine *advertisement, October 1919*

*Male and Female*, Bebe Daniels' first picture under the direction of Cecil B. DeMille, was released on November 23, 1919. Based on J.M. Barrie's *The Admirable Crichton*, the film is perhaps most notable today as an early collaboration between fledgling Hollywood's greatest director (DeMille) and most famous leading lady (Gloria Swanson). Film historians also often note that *Male and Female* marks Bebe's first dramatic role that, albeit brief, presumably worked to fulfill many of the ambitions she had when leaving Rolin.

Incidentally, the scene that featured Daniels would prove to be not only the most famous in the movie, but also one of the most enduring scenes of the silent era. The movie is considered a "rather free adaptation of Barrie's story"[1]; the most glaring addition by DeMille is a Babylonian fantasy sequence that exudes the flamboyance of early Hollywood.

The scene features Thomas Meighan (otherwise the titular Crichton) as a Babylonian king atop his throne with Bebe, known as "the king's favorite," at his right hand. The king condemns Swanson, the "Christian slave," to a fearful death in a den of lions. The scene was so dangerous that DeMille considered cutting it from the movie; at Gloria's insistence he eventually decided to include it.

In her autobiography, Swanson recalled that "the only people who could be inside the wire mesh with the lions were Tommy [Meighan], Bebe, Mr. DeMille, the cameraman, the trainers and I."[2] Although Bebe did not directly interact with the lions—she simply watches with glee as her rival is sent to her death—it certainly was a unique introduction to dramatic acting for the former Hal Roach comedienne.

In stark contrast to her comic roles opposite Harold Lloyd, *Male and Female* marked the beginning of Daniels' onscreen persona as a "vamp"—a characterization that would follow her closely for the next several years. Continuing in the footsteps of Theda Bara and Louise Glaum, Bebe's dark features and Hispanic heritage make it seem inevitable that this trope would eventually be applied to her.

A rare photograph by Karl Struss of Bebe Daniels on the set of *Male and Female* (courtesy Academy of Motion Picture Arts and Sciences).

Her sheer dress and cape in *Male and Female*, remarkably revealing by contemporary standards, call to mind Bara's Cleopatra and Nazimova's Salome and provide a sharp contrast to Swanson's leopard-print tunic. However, the elegant outfit (and outrageous headpiece) also serve to detract from Daniels' performance and render her little more than a visual foil to Swanson. Very few contemporary reviews even mention Bebe's presence in the film.

The production of *Male and Female* was emotionally taxing on the young Daniels, who had been used to the relaxed, enjoyable atmosphere of making movies with Hal Roach. Overwhelmed by the celebrity of both Swanson and Meighan, the typically exuberant Bebe "became shy and self-conscious"[3] for the first time in her life.

Bebe later reflected on this period of her life: "I often cried and wished I had never left Hal Roach, or at least had listened to him and Harold when they said, 'You won't be happy at Lasky's.' Then I snapped out of it. This was ridiculous. I had wanted to go into drama. And here I was wallowing in self-pity."[4]

The month after *Male and Female* came Bebe's second dramatic picture, *Everywoman*. An allegorical story based on Walter Browne's 1911 play of the same title, *Everywoman* starred Violet Heming in one of her only motion picture roles. Featuring an incredibly diverse cast, *Everywoman* served as a morality tale about the struggles of a young woman seeking fame. Along the way, Heming (the "Everywoman") encounters "Beauty," "Passion," "Truth" and other tropes. Bebe, now beginning to be known as a vamp, fittingly played "Vice."

Largely as a product of the large ensemble cast, Bebe's role as Vice was only briefly mentioned in contemporary reviews. Her part was invariably compared to her similar performance in *Male and Female*; indeed, Daniels' depiction in the media at this time was resoundingly one-note. While she may have been attempting to carve out a dramatic career for herself, Bebe was having a hard time overcoming the public opinion that she was the exotic, mysterious vampire-type.

Interestingly, as late as 1922 Bebe was voted the top movie "Vampire" by the readers of *Motion Picture* magazine, showing the lasting effect of the stereotype on her career. In fact, she received more votes than Theda Bara, Pola Negri and Louise Glaum combined. Daniels also came in fifth amongst comediennes—her Harold Lloyd shorts were still fresh in the minds of many moviegoers, in large part due to their frequent theatrical re-releases—and tenth amongst leading women, evidence of her ongoing transition from bit parts to more prominent roles.

Being paired with "The Screen's Most Perfect Lover" in the film *The Dancin' Fool* was a major step forward for Bebe's career. Wallace Reid was much closer to Daniels' age than Thomas Meighan was, and therefore made for a more believable love interest. Anna Q. Nilsson, Lila Lee, Wanda Hawley and Ann Little had all benefitted from high-profile pairings with Reid, and so did Bebe. The two sequential films she made with him provided the perfect transition from her early work with Paramount to her first starring roles.

*The Dancin' Fool* came less than a year after Reid's tragic accident during the filming of *The Valley of the Giants*, which sparked his long-running battle with opiate addiction. Already, the strain of Hollywood was beginning to take its toll on his body; in 1919, he made eight feature films, followed by seven the next year. The harder he worked, the more he spiraled into substance abuse. The vicious cycle claimed his life in early 1923.

Based on a *Saturday Evening Post* story by Henry Payson Dowst, *The Dancin' Fool* featured Reid in the uncharacteristic role of Sylvester Tibble, a country boy who travels to the city to work for his uncle's jug business. His restlessness soon finds him in dance clubs, where his talent on his feet earns him extra money. Junie Budd (Daniels) becomes his dancing partner and love interest. At the end of the film's admittedly thin plot, he saves his uncle's jug business and marries Junie.

A majority of reviews focused on the fact that Reid was terribly miscast in the film. He was known for his daredevil stunts in automobile racing films, so the role of a dancing country boy seemed incongruous (even the name "Sylvester Tibble" seemed to contradict Reid's personality). This in turn confused Reid's countless female adherents, expecting to see him depicted a certain way. *Variety* mused that "he isn't the hick rube type, doesn't look the part, acts it but passably and the majority of Reid admirers won't care particularly for it."[5]

Bebes, however, was prepared for the part after countless real-life dancing contests with Harold Lloyd. She was by all accounts an incredibly gifted dancer, and played the part of Junie quite naturally. While Reid's performance was critiqued by all, Bebe's was complimented. "She's as pretty as a picture," read one review, "and she doesn't let any grass grow under her slippered feet."[6] Another stated that Bebe is "the type of girl who makes the average man anxious to play the sturdy oak."[7] Playing opposite someone so beloved (and objectified) as Reid helped call attention to Bebe's physical allure. This would prove greatly beneficial as she continued her rise to stardom.

Only the month after *The Dancin' Fool* was released came Bebe's next film with Wallace Reid: *Sick Abed*, based on a play by Ethel Watts Mumford. Reid played Reginald Jay, a young society man who finds himself in the midst of a divorce scandal. To avoid appearing in court, he feigns a serious illness and must be attended to by pretty Nurse Durant (Daniels). His deception succeeds perfectly, and in the process he wins the affections of his nurse.

Reginald Jay was a role much better suited to Reid than Sylvester Tibble had been, and accordingly *Sick Abed* was massively successful. Reid's admirers were pleased to once again see him play a suitable part, and the film's mile-a-minute comedy left audiences roaring. With a much more sound plot than his previous film, *Sick Abed* was viewed as something of a return to form for the actor and was considered by many critics to be one of his better films.

As Bebe's fame continued to grow, she transformed from merely an actress into a popular culture icon. Postcards, metal tins, felt pennants and other paraphernalia began to appear bearing her likeness. Daniels even served as the subject of a 1921 song, "Bebe-D (Sing Love's Alphabet With Me)." With lyrics by Billy James and A.V. Hendrick and music by Max Kortlander and A.S. Brooks, the sheet music featured a large photograph of a doe-eyed Daniels. The lyrics, while not explicitly about the actress, could nevertheless easily conjure up an image of her:

> Just the other evening I was handed quite a treat,
> I got tired strolling thru the park and took a seat;
> Spied upon a girl and fellow cooing like to doves,
> Here's the way these two were making love:
>
> First he'd call her Bebe "A" for "Angel,"
> Then he'd call her Bebe "C" for "Cute,"
> Then he'd call her Bebe "D" for "Darling,"
> Each loving thing he said to her just seemed to suit.
>
> Like busy bees a-buzzing after honey,
> They would kiss while she sat on his knee;
> Then they'd start that honeysuckle alphabet of Loveland.
> Bebe A, Bebe C, Bebe D.

**The 1921 sheet music for "Bebe-D (Sing Love's Alphabet With Me) depicts the actress on the cover.**

"Bebe," a novelty fox trot, was published two years later. While neither of these songs were sanctioned by Daniels or Paramount, they speak to the rampant commodification of the silent era's greatest stars. The public desired anything having to do with Bebe, and music companies (and other industries) were more than happy to step in and fill that need.

Audiences did not have to wait long for another Bebe Daniels feature: A few weeks after *The Dancin' Fool* came Cecil B. DeMille's domestic comedy *Why Change Your Wife?* Following the success of *Don't Change Your Husband* (1919), DeMille's first pairing with Gloria Swanson, the actor and director quickly became prolific, making six films together in less than three years.

The plot revolves around Robert Gordon (Thomas Meighan), a married man perpetually criticized by his old-fashioned wife Beth (Swanson). Robert eventually begins an affair with a dress shop girl, young, vibrant Sally Clark (Bebe). He leaves Beth to marry Sally but while on vacation his feeling for his first wife are rekindled, and after an intense standoff between the two wives a reformed Beth once again ends up with Robert.

Although the plot is far from sophisticated (some critics viewed it as merely a vehicle for DeMille to show Swanson and Daniels nearly nude[8]), the film was immensely successful in major markets like New York and Los Angeles. DeMille had a Midas touch and Swanson was fast becoming the nation's top sex symbol. *Why Change Your Wife?* was a hit and Bebe was the main beneficiary.

Her performance, however, was far from perfect. When attempting to be sexual, Bebe exhibits the same awkwardness she did as the King's Favorite in *Male and Female*. In one of her opening scenes, she must display a sheer negligee to Meighan, a potential customer. In doing so, she appears remarkably uncomfortable with her back and shoulders exposed; her performance becomes more natural as the movie progresses and her costumes are less revealing.

Part of this undoubtedly can be explained by nerves from playing opposite Thomas Meighan, 22 years her senior and one of the biggest stars in the industry. While he was also her on-screen partner in *Male and Female*, her role was significantly larger this time around and called for more acting and less posturing.

For the first half of the movie, Bebe plays the more sympathetic of Gordon's two love interests. Swanson's Beth Gordon is dowdy and nagging—so much so that the audience can rationalize Robert's decision to leave her for the sprightly young Sally. In the end, however, Beth abandons her outmoded ways and becomes the wife Robert wants. Sally shows her true colors with her closing declaration, "There's only one good thing about marriage anyway—and that's alimony."

Sally Clark is an interesting character. Not quite a vamp, although her dark features and home-wrecking ways are suggestive of the trope at times, Sally could almost be called a flapper—although the modern meaning of the term was not solidified until years later with stars like Clara Bow and Louise Brooks. Bebe seems almost torn between the two archetypal roles—vamp and flapper—that would define the her career for the first half of the 1920s. She simultaneously tries to be seductive and silly, experienced and innocent. The result leaves the viewer assured of Bebe's potential, but also reminded of her inexperience in dramatic pictures.

While this was by no means her best role, Bebe manages to steal many scenes from Swanson with her youthful exuberance (despite only being a year younger in real life). Bebe's highlights are, ironically, the scenes that she plays for laughs, regardless of her overwhelming desire for serious roles upon her departure from Rolin.

Everyone in the industry—most of all Cecil B. DeMille—knew that Bebe could be funny. It would be a shame, they thought, if her impeccable comedic timing, learned from and with Lloyd, was to be wasted on pure dramas. Whether she wanted to admit it or not, her future had been written for her. Despite her valiant protests, Bebe was to be a comedienne.

When Bebe finished production on *Sick Abed*, she had no further Paramount projects slated. So her heart sank when Jesse Lasky called for her on the last day of filming. "Surely there can be only one thing he wants to see me about," she thought. "This is the end—he's going to fire me. I've failed after all." She was so sure that this was to be the outcome of the meeting that she stalled all day, telling the studio messenger boy to inform Lasky that she was hard at work and could not be bothered. The truth was that she could not face rejection.

Eventually she could wait no longer:

> I went, draggingly, taking the most circuitous route, stopping on the way to speak to as many actors, stage-hands and electricians as possible. I walked into the dreaded office, head in the air, thumbs in my belt.... It is my gesture of defiance. I suppose we all have some little physical characteristic with which we face the storms of living. One thing I knew: I would not cry. I would not let a soul know the bitterness of my disappointment; having tried so hard, and now all for nothing.

She found Lasky sitting behind his huge desk, looking very much like the most important man in Hollywood.

"Mr. Lasky, you wanted to see me?"

"Well, yes," he replied casually. "Sit down. The fact is, Mr. DeMille and I have decided to...." He hesitated, and Bebe braced herself for the worst. Her courage was waning.

"To star you," he finished.

Bebe's poise, which she had managed to maintain until that point, suddenly left her. The first words out of her mouth where, "You're joking, Mr. Lasky. I'm no star."

As Bebe began to comprehend the news, DeMille stepped out from behind a screen where he had been hiding. "What did I tell you, Bebe?" he said with a smile.

The rest of the day was a blur for Daniels, who kept saying to herself, "I'm not fired—they're going to *star* me." Her four-year contract with DeMille was torn up after only six months, and a new five-year contract was drafted. But—it was quickly explained—her new contract would not be with Paramount, but with a newly formed subsidiary of the company.[9] And rather than the dramas of DeMille and his ilk, she would once again play in comedies.

Despite the disappointment she certainly faced in finding out she was to be making exclusively comedic pictures, Bebe—humble as ever—told a reporter, "I don't know whether I [am] quite ready for stardom or not—but I do hope I'll make good."[10] Whether she was ready or not, the stage was set for Bebe to become a star.

# 7

# Realart Pictures

> *Slowly but surely Realart is signing up as stars a collection of the loveliest girls in picturedom. The latest announcement is to the effect that Bebe Daniels has put her signature to a Realart contract.*
> —*Los Angeles Times,* June 2, 1920[1]

The year 1919—the same year of Bebe's split with Lloyd and Roach—also saw the establishment of a new motion picture production company, Realart Pictures. After it was founded by Adolph Zukor of Famous Players–Lasky as a production vehicle for Alice Brady, it was determined that Realart could not survive with Brady alone, and other stars, including Constance Binney, were signed.[2] Realart was headed by Arthur S. Kane and soon opened offices in Chicago, New York and Boston.

Realart very quickly shocked the world when Zukor signed Mary Miles Minter to a $1.3 million contract—at the time, the largest contract in Hollywood history.[3] Also added to the production company was Wanda Hawley, who had previously made films with Artcraft and Selznick Pictures.

Realart's first picture, *Erstwhile Susan*, premiered in November 1919, several months after the company was founded. Featuring Constance Binney in one of her first starring roles, it was quickly followed with vehicles for Minter and Brady. Hawley would make her debut with the company in May 1920. With several directorial efforts from the likes of William Desmond Taylor, Realart quickly established itself as one of the leading production companies in Hollywood.

When the time did come for Bebe to be added to the Realart roster, company president Morris Kohn declared, "The addition of Bebe Daniels means a step forward in motion picture production—one which will not be fully appreciated until her first picture is seen."[4] Bebe, the fifth major player to be signed by the fledgling Realart in a matter of months, would finally have a production company working to produce starring vehicles for her and her alone.

Her first Realart release originally carried the title *The Good Little Bad Girl*,[5] a nickname that would stick with her for years to come. Studios often attempted to portray her as a *femme fatale*, although her youthful innocence made it difficult for this to be taken too seriously. (One friend even defended her as a "bad little good girl."[6]) Paramount's branding of Bebe early on seems conflicted between the purely comedic, wholesome image she had developed with Roach and the vamp she played for DeMille. Bebe was not demure enough to be Mary Pickford but not mysterious enough to be Nazimova. This crisis of identity would plague her for years to come.

*The Good Little Bad Girl*, eventually renamed *You Never Can Tell*, also starred Jack Mulhall. The male lead was originally to be played by Conrad Nagel, who would eventually feature with Bebe in 1922's *Singed Wings*; however, production delays forced him out of the part.[7]

The screenplay was based on two *Saturday Evening Post* short stories, "You Never Can Tell" and "Class" by Grace Lovell Bryan.[8] The plot revolves around a hotel check room girl named Rowena Patricia Jones (Daniels) who plans on marrying a millionaire to support her struggling family. Attending a fashion show (Rowena has the same admiration for clothes as the real-life Daniels), she courts a flamboyant playboy (Edward Martindel) while at the same time shunning a visibly poor chauffeur (Mulhall). However, upon learning that her millionaire admirer is already married, the crestfallen Rowena is comforted by the masquerading chauffeur—who just to happens to be a millionaire himself, thereby allowing her to fulfill her dream of supporting her family.

For her first vehicle, *You Never Can Tell* was by all accounts a resounding success. One critic said that Bebe "handled the role ... to perfection,"[9] and the film had lengthy runs throughout the country. Vastly different from her seductive, vampish roles under DeMille, *You Never Can Tell* instead tapped into the coquettish charm of her later Harold Lloyd role, albeit with significantly more character development than she had ever before experienced. Although it is impossible to predict stardom from one movie, Bebe's first starring vehicle certainly seemed to suggest a fruitful career.

Bebe's Realart contract did not preclude her from appearing in other Paramount productions, at least initially. Between the release of *You Never Can Tell* and *Oh, Lady, Lady*, she was paired with Robert Warwick in *The Fourteenth Man*. A mixture of mystery, romance and comedy, the film capitalized on Daniels' quickly growing fame by placing her in a high-profile supporting role. However, without a major name attached to the project (director Joseph Henabery was a far cry from Cecil B. DeMille), the picture quickly faded into obscurity and remains one of Bebe's least-remembered projects.

Captain Douglas Gordon (Warwick) flees to New York after a fight at a Scottish inn, with a detective hot on his trail. He meets Marjory Seaton (Daniels), an eligible bachelorette whose affections are divided amongst several suitors. After a number of tribulations, including a prize fight between Captain Gordon and real-life boxer Kid McCoy, he is informed that a detective had been following him simply to inform him of a large inheritance, not to apprehend him for his actions. He and Seaton confess their love of one another.

F. Anstey's play *The Man from Blankley's*, on which *The Fourteenth Man* was based, was conceived as a comedy, and Henabery's direction played up this angle with varying degrees of success. Many critics found it to be amusing but insignificant. "Although this feature is not a wonderful one in any respect," wrote the *San Francisco Chronicle*, "it will pass the critical eye of the audiences because in it are combined thrills, romance and comedy—all blending well."[10] Bebe's supporting role failed to garner much critical attention, but given the slew of starring pictures Realart had in the queue for her, it hardly mattered. *The Fourteenth Man* was out of mind almost as quickly as it had been made, and audiences that wanted to see more of Bebe would soon have many more options.

At the start of September, Realart announced that they had 36 pictures in various stages of development, including the latest Daniels vehicle *Oh, Lady, Lady*. In an effort to ensure the studio's financial stability despite the variable quality of their pictures, theaters were instructed that these three dozen films had to be purchased on an "all-or-none" basis. This was a substantial risk for theaters, given that Realart was a fairly new company, but the rising stardom of actresses like Daniels and Mary Miles Minter meant that the new Realart program was largely successful.

*Oh, Lady, Lady* was adapted by Edith Kennedy from a musical comedy by Guy Bolton and P.G. Wodehouse. In an amusing plot, Bebe played May Barber, a country girl now acting under the name Rilla Rooke. While her former sweetheart Willoughby Finch (Walter Hiers) is about to be married, Barber falls in love with his best man, Hale Underwood (Harrison Ford). Barber's meddling ways cause concern that she may try to interfere with Finch's wedding, causing chaos amongst the involved parties. In the end, all is resolved for the two couples.

The adaptation of such a successful play seemed a safe bet for Realart, and critical response was as positive as could be expected. Bebe was praised as "altogether delightful"[11] and "entrancing,"[12] and the rest of the cast also received high marks. Harrison Ford was already a well-known leading man in Paramount productions, and Walter Hiers was prolific in a number of different genres. For only her second starring vehicle, *Oh, Lady, Lady* was another undoubted success and proved significant in establishing the young actress as a major force in Hollywood.

For the first time since becoming a bona fide movie star, Bebe returned to her birthplace of Dallas to spend two weeks around Christmas 1920.[13] Celebrating the completion of *Ducks and Drakes* and the release of *She Couldn't Help It*, the trip provided Daniels a rare chance for relaxation. (Throughout much of the 1920s she was making an average of a half-dozen films per year.) While there, she also made a number of public appearances to capitalize on her massive success.

The event was extremely important for the residents of Dallas, who did not typically have the chance to see movie stars in the flesh. One account describes just how frenzied her appearances were:

> "It's been the dream of my life to see Dallas—the place where I was born, but which I can not remember," Miss Bebe Daniels, screen star, said Wednesday shortly after her arrival here for a short visit. She was honored by a luncheon, a dinner and a dance Wednesday. Quite an entertainment program has been arranged for Thursday and one was planned for Friday, but had to be abandoned, for Miss Daniels must leave Friday at 2:05 p.m. for Los Angeles, to take up her film work again.
> 
> Four times Wednesday Miss Daniels appeared at the Old Mill Theater and each appearance was the occasion of an ovation. She made a short talk each time, telling how glad she is to be "back home," sang a song in her inimitable manner and smiled and kissed her hands to the applauding throngs.
> 
> An hour before her first scheduled appearance at 2:15 p.m. every seat in the Old Mill was taken. As the hour grew nearer the crowd got thicker and at 2 o'clock the outside corridor was jammed with movie fans, who had tickets but couldn't get in, while the line of those waiting extended down Elm Street for half a block.
> 
> Miss Daniels visited the Rotary Club luncheon Wednesday noon. If the weather permits she will go for an automobile ride Thursday morning during the course of which some moving pictures probably will be taken. She will appear at the Old Mill again two times Thursday and perhaps once on Friday.

> She will see *Oh, Lady, Lady*, in which she starred, for the first time, at the Queen Theater Friday morning.[14]

Her fortnight in Dallas proved to be a calm before the storm, as the first weeks of 1921 saw Bebe undertake the filming of both her next starring vehicle, *Two Weeks With Pay*, as well as her final collaboration with Cecil B. DeMille, *The Affairs of Anatol*.[15] However, January 1921 proved to be much more eventful than even Bebe herself could have predicted. Within weeks, she would earn one of her most enduring nicknames: the Speed Girl.

*She Couldn't Help It* was an adaptation of Miriam Michelson's 1904 novel *In The Bishop's Carriage* and the subsequent play by Channing Pollock. (There had already been a movie version, with Mary Pickford, in 1913.) The book is a moralistic tale of a young girl, Nance Olden, rescued from a life of petty crime when she finds herself inadvertently in the carriage of Bishop Van Wagenen. The book was only 16 years old and yet the plot was outdated and somewhat obscure by the 1920s. It seemed like an odd choice for Bebe's third Realart feature.

Despite the film's focus on the efforts of William Lattimer (Emory Johnson) to reform Bebe's Nance, much of its entertainment value came from Nance's jewel theft and other crimes. Bebe was being presented yet again as a "good little bad girl," a name which several newspaper reviewers used to describe her character. One writer deemed her "winsome, vivacious and beautiful ... one of the most popular of the later-day picture stars and an artist whose histrionic ability has forced her rapidly to the front."[16]

As her roles in *Everyman* and *Male and Female* were fresh in the minds of audiences, it came as something of a surprise that Bebe's new Realart roles were not overtly vampish in nature. "In this picture she is less vampish and more wistful than one expects her to be,"[17] mused the *Atlanta Constitution*, echoing the sentiments of many who were unsure just how to characterize Bebe. Within two years she had gone from Harold Lloyd's rough-and-tumble sidekick to exotic Oriental vamp to the "good little bad girl," sometimes combining various aspects of the three. Her popularity was rising, but her identity was increasingly undefined.

As Bebe's career followed a trajectory to fame, her life off-screen became increasingly important to fans. This hardly comes as a surprise, but for Bebe it presented something of a challenge. Without Harold Lloyd in her life, she was no longer half of America's favorite couple. Just a year earlier, she had been the embodiment of the American "Girl," but now she was searching for a new identity to embrace. Already it was clear that her "vamp" screen persona did not translate into her personal life, but her adoring fans were anxious to get to know the real Bebe.

Rather than deviate from the persona she had crafted while with Lloyd, she decided to embrace it. She was "The Good Little Bad Girl" on screen while at home she was as wholesome as ever. Her close relationship with her mother was well-documented, as was her childlike innocence that she managed to cling to in an increasingly scandal-ridden Hollywood. Bebe was, by nature, optimistic and full of life, and no amount of vampish roles could change that about her.

Although it may seem laughable to assume Bebe would have been anything but herself in the public eye, the early silent era was a time when many actors and actresses carried their movie personas into their private lives. For example, screen vamp Theda Bara allegedly kept crystal balls and tiger-skin rugs in her home where she would seduce unwitting young men. Those who knew Bara could see this was obviously a ruse intended to attract attention. Bebe avoided having to concoct a scandalous off-screen persona to elicit attention—for the time being. Within a few months, Paramount executive would have other plans for her.

But in December 1920, Bebe was viewed as nothing less than innocent and charming. A *Washington Post* article published that month was one of the first to examine her personal life, rather than merely evaluating her film performances:

> The question most asked by the average studio visitor is: "What kind of a girl is so and so—or what kind of a fellow is who's this?" Patrons of the pictures become so immersed in the characters of their favorite stars that they feel a very natural desire to know more about them, to learn if they are really what they seem to be.
>
> There is one instance, at least, where they will not be disappointed. Bebe Daniels, Realart star ... is the kind of a girl you would be delighted to know, whether you were 17 or 70, of either sex, and of any disposition or creed or character.
>
> First of all, she is genuine. Yes, the screen friends and admirers of the brunette beauty of the Realart ranks need never be alarmed. She will more than come up to their expectations. Bebe is a genuine girl, a fun-loving, wholesome, clean-minded, sweet and delightful girl—with a fund of good humor that is never at low ebb, an ability to talk on all kinds of subjects in a manner that is the acme of refinement and yet possesses a splendid balance. She is the favorite of all her associates and has always a pleasant word for everyone, from prop boy to director. They like to see Bebe on the set for they know that she is considerate, never temperamental—if that implies the exhibition of temper—and that she will do anything within reason that is required of her in portraying her role in a picture. Directors under whom she has worked all unite in voting her one of the most conscientious, willing and plucky little stars of the film world.
>
> Bebe Daniels lives at home with her mother. She loves motoring and likes to dress in pretty clothing. She is of Spanish descent and her ancestors were prominent people in South American life.
>
> She is ambitious to make a fine record on the screen and later to travel and see the world.
>
> Doubtless she will do both.
>
> Meanwhile, she is happy because she is a star and because she has so many friends among the people who see pictures.
>
> "I just love them all—every last one of them!" she says.
>
> That's a wholesale order, but Bebe is imbued with the spirit of human kindness and it means that she will go far in her work, because the public is the arbiter after all.[18]

There was one glaring omission from Bebe's public persona early in her dramatic career: romance. During this time, prominent relationships could make (or break) the career of a young actor; newspapers were filled with tales of Jack Pickford and Olive Thomas, Rudolph Valentino and Jean Acker, Charles Chaplin and Mildred Harris. Bebe got a taste of this during her much-publicized pairing with Harold Lloyd, when the two were considered one of Hollywood's favorite couples. For an aspiring starlet like Bebe, it seemed that a high-profile husband—or even suitor—might work wonders for her career in the absence of Mr. Lloyd.

Despite this (or perhaps because of the scandal associated with so many romances), Bebe was very careful to remain entirely focused on her craft. One interviewer found the teenage Daniels "totally uninterested in men,"[19] while another writer mused that, "at the age when most girls spend their waking and sleeping hours dreaming of their Prince Charmings, Bebe Daniels thinks only of her 'work.'"[20]

# 8

# Ten Days in Jail

*I know not whether Laws be right,*
*Or whether Laws be wrong;*
*All that we know who lie in gaol*
*Is that the wall is strong;*
*And that each day is like a year,*
*A year whose days are long.*
—Oscar Wilde's "The Ballad of Reading Gaol,"
quoted by Bebe Daniels in 1921

January 12, 1921—two days shy of Bebe's twenty-first birthday. Her mother and a boxer (sometimes identified as Marty Farrell, sometimes Jack Dempsey) were her passengers as she drove her Marmon Roadster along an Orange County highway, headed home to Los Angeles from San Diego. Despite a posted speed limit of 35 miles per hour, Bebe—the "good little bad girl"—was going 56½.[1] As fate would have it, motorcycle officer Vernon "Shorty" Myers was stationed behind a tree. Little did he know just who he was pulling over.

Initially, Bebe claimed that she was speeding because her radiator was leaking and she was trying to make it to the next town.[2] However, speeding was nothing new for Bebe. She once mused that she was "constantly being caught by speed cops for driving too fast."[3] Apparently, she had a well-connected uncle in the newspaper business who was on friendly terms with the Los Angeles Police Department; whenever she got a speeding ticket, she would simply phone her "Uncle Jack" and ask him to get her off. In this way, she was able to sustain her insatiable love for driving too fast.

What the teenage Daniels failed to realize, however, was that her Uncle Jack had no pull in Orange County. Assuming this run-in with the police would be no different than all the others, Bebe was dismayed to find out that Orange County was under the heavy-handed rule of Judge John Belshazzar Cox, notorious for imprisoning anyone going over 50 miles per hour.

Judge Cox was immediately placed in an interesting predicament. Not only was Bebe one of the most recognizable faces on the planet, she was also the first female to be arrested in Orange County for speeding. There was no precedent set, and the press immediately speculated about whether or not Cox would imprison a young girl.

Capitalizing on the scandal, local theater owner Ed Yost secured the debut of Bebe's *She Couldn't Help It* on January 18, just a week after the incident and the day before Daniels' arraignment. Yost scheduled three screenings in two days and expected "capacity houses."[4]

Theo Lacy, Jr., books Bebe Daniels in the Orange County Jail following her speeding arrest (courtesy Santa Ana Public Library).

Silly as it may seem today, there was also discussion about how Bebe would handle herself in court. She was still widely known as a "vamp" in her movies, and there was serious concern that she might try to seduce the judge and jury. In an article titled "Will Bebe Vamp Justice Cox?," Judge Cox replied, "They do say she's pretty and has vampish eyes.... I've seen her vamp weaker men than I in the pictures. I'm a strong man ... but if she tries to vamp me I don't know what will happen."[5]

A preliminary hearing was set for the morning of January 19. An estimated 1500 spectators crowded the courtroom and its vicinity, all hoping to catch a glimpse of Bebe (and perhaps even "study her vamping methods"[6]). Much to the disappointment of the crowd, she stayed in her car while her attorney W.I. Gilbert made an unsuccessful motion for a change of venue. A trial by jury was requested, a not guilty plea was filed and a March 17 court date was set.

Amidst the controversy, Bebe's next Realart film *Ducks and Drakes* saw a limited release at the end of February. Both story and script were penned by noted dramatist and playwright Elmer Harris. This film was the first of several collaborations between he and Bebe.

"A frisky, teasing, aggravating duckling whose pin feathers had just begun to sprout."[7] This is how Bebe's character, Teddy Simpson, was described by one reviewer. A flirtatious young debutante living with an uptight aunt, Teddy is engaged to Rob Winslow (Jack Holt). Nevertheless, Teddy phones other men who just happen to be fellow clubmen of her fiancé. The men, seeking to teach Teddy a lesson, lure her on a hunting trip where she is attacked by an "escaped convict" (in actuality, one of their friends). When Winslow expects to rescue her, he instead finds that she has escaped. Eventually, he manages to marry her and win her affections.

*Ducks and Drakes* was hailed as "another step up the ladder for Bebe Daniels,"[8] and she received some of her most positive reviews to date. As was the trend early in her career, the film played up her physical appearance just as much—if not more—than her acting ability. Bebe was outfitted with "gorgeous gowns and lingerie"[9] that many moviegoers considered risqué. One scene of Bebe bathing showed enough of her form to raise some eyebrows.

Bebe was well aware of the importance of costuming for a movie star, once stating, "If you're an extra player you have to starve to get your wardrobe; if a star, you're starved for ideas for it."[10] As far back as *Male and Female* Bebe was already being outfitted with exotic, revealing dresses; her leading lady roles for Realart allowed for even more impressive—and sometimes shocking—outfits. Regardless of how much skin the young vamp showed, Bebe always maintained a tastefulness and innocence in the eyes of the media and the public that few other actresses of her caliber could match.

News about Bebe's impending trial continued to appear in papers nationwide on almost a daily basis. Because new facts about the case were few and far between, reporters mostly stuck to playing up Bebe's vamping ability and "good little bad girl" public image. A minor development came when it was announced that the 30-person jury in the case would be comprised of half men and half women. The *Los Angeles Times* article breaking the news embodied the sensationalism that surrounded the case: "Miss Daniels' 'vamping' proclivities, if she has any, may avail her little in court, as woman's wiles do not work so well on her sisters as on her brothers."[11]

The major tension in the case came from the fact that Judge Cox's sternness had never been tested on a female criminal before, let alone someone with the public support that Daniels had. Although notorious for locking up any speeders he could catch, his will would be tested more than ever, it was speculated, in this case.

Finally the fateful day arrived. The Orange County Courthouse in downtown Santa Ana had never seen such a crowd. Farmers took the day off from tilling their soil to catch a glimpse of the star. Some felt pity for the girl, barely 20 years old, sitting in the courtroom with her mother and her attorney by her side. Others were not so sympathetic, voicing their opinions that a criminal was a criminal regardless of their gender or profession. The tension could have been cut with a knife.[12]

In the end, the best lawyer in the world could not have saved Bebe from the notorious Judge Cox. Despite a valiant effort to explain that her speeding was the result of trying to get to San Juan Capistrano to replace a bad radiator, Cox could not be swayed. As many had feared, she was sentenced to ten days in jail, the standard sentence for such an offense. The judge and jury were understanding enough to book her stay around her filming schedule, so she would not miss out on any work.

Judge Cox craved media attention more than a Hollywood star, it seemed. A veritable egomaniac, as evidenced by his behavior both during the trial and Bebe's jail stint, Cox was certain to extract as much press as possible from the incident. The saying goes that there's no such thing as bad publicity, and even though the judge was much-maligned for his treatment of the pitiable young starlet, his one-man crusade against speeding was immediately elevated to national prominence.

On Bebe's end, the verdict had an immediate effect on her personal life. Never one to find herself in the midst of a scandal, she would tell reporters that she could not sleep with the weight of the crime on her conscience. In lieu of a three-month appeals process that would only serve to draw out the affair, Bebe served the sentence. In mid–April, on the eve of her imprisonment, Bebe held a solemn "felicitation party"[13] at the Alexandria Hotel with her closest friends.

Bebe would not have to endure prison alone. Her mother, in a move characteristic of the lax rules imposed on Daniels' sentence, was allowed to accompany her the entire time. On April 16, 1921, Bebe was admitted to the Orange County Jail.

News reports of Bebe's time in jail were sarcastic towards the treatment she received. She was served three full meals a day by a formally dressed French waiter. She was permitted as many as 50 visitors per day; those who could not see her in person sent so many flowers that her room allegedly looked like a florist shop. Her cell was lavishly furnished by local proprietor William Spurgeon, who provided "a dainty dressing table, Oriental rugs, pretty drapes on the windows, a breakfast-room set and a Victrola with only 150 records."[14] (In later years, Spurgeon would recreate Bebe's cell in his department store's window-front, which became something of a minor tourist attraction.)

In the first few days alone, Bebe's callers included Max Linder, hot off the success of *Seven Years Bad Luck*, and Harold Lloyd. A characteristically humorous telegram from Roscoe "Fatty" Arbuckle simply read, "Dear Bebe, Houdini is in town. Can we help? Love."[15] The number of visitors was so high that Bebe even began keeping a guestbook (which allegedly held 792 names), inspiring her jailer to remark that it was "more like a summer hotel than a jail."[16] Several days into her jail stint, she was greeted by the familiar sound of Art Hickman's "Rose Room Tango." Standing on a chair to peer out her cell window, she saw Abe Lyman and his Orchestra, one of Los Angeles' most popular dance bands. She and Rudolph Valentino would often dance to their music at the Sunset Inn. (Contrary to popular belief, Lyman had not yet begun playing the famed Cocoanut Grove when he paid the imprisoned star a visit.)

In addition to entertaining visitors, Bebe passed her days reading and exercising, using the cell window for pull-ups. After a dinner that consisted of anything from "fillet steak, fried chicken, mushrooms, crayfish, lobster, fillet sole and sometimes even caviar,"[17] Bebe and her mother were permitted to take a walk outside, where the pitifully innocent Bebe would play on the swings and seesaw.

At last, after "the longest nine days of her life" (she was given a shortened sentence for good behavior), Bebe was released. The first to congratulate her was none other than Judge Cox, who presented her with a bouquet of roses and made sure that their final meeting was photographed and described in national newspapers.

The July issue of *Photoplay m*agazine featured an 3000-word article penned by Bebe while in prison. Uncharacteristically melodramatic in tone, one of the opening

**Abe Lyman's Orchestra serenading Bebe Daniels in her jail cell (courtesy Santa Ana Public Library).**

paragraphs reads, "Today—they have made of me a crook and a jail-bird—a member of the underworld."[18] Her motivation for writing the article, she stated, was to "bare my soul to the world that if it must judge me it may judge me as I really am." This desperate, overwrought tone comes across so heavily that one must wonder whether Realart's publicity department was in fact the author. So monotonous is the article in its desperate pleas for forgiveness that only a brief excerpt is necessary to understand its tone:

> I feel it but justice to myself that the world which has heard so much of this painful story should hear my own version. It seems but fitting for me, following the precedent set by other famous criminals, to tell you something of my youth, of my dear mother at whose knee I received a gentle and uplifting education. As I look back and think of my dear home, of the happy innocent days of my childhood—and then remember the voice of that judge, stern and impressive in spite of a Santa Ana accent, committing me to this jail I now inhabit, I can hardly realize it is I who am thus accused, accused, nay *convicted* of this thing. I think it must be a masquerade, a nightmare, from which I shall soon awaken to find myself not confined within these narrow prison walls, but safe, happy, laughing as I used to be before....
>
> Ah, how little the world wrecks the struggle of a woman's soul. How easy to say I was caught, tried by a jury of my peers, found guilty and imprisoned. Of the things that led up to this dark event, of the price I paid for my mistake, no one can ever know.
>
> For though the Persian rug beneath my feet may hide the cold stones of the prison walls, though the scent of flowers may drown the prison stench, though the white iron cot be replaced by a bed of ivory and rose, nothing can melt away the bars that stand between me and freedom. I am a convict! I am not free!

The story continues on in this same manner for several more pages. One must wonder whether the piece was intended to be taken seriously—although based on the outpouring of support Bebe received in the magazine the star's plight was taken to heart by many.

The incident that brought Bebe a new level of fame would prove not to have a lasting impact on her career. Within days of her release, she was once again gracing the silver screen with her latest production, and before the year was over she—and Realart—had capitalized on the incident with a new film called *The Speed*

**Bebe Daniels peers from the window of her jail cell.**

*Girl*. However, as her career grew over the next few years, the story that had once captivated moviegoers would fade into relative obscurity, reappearing as a footnote from time to time when Bebe was in the news. The Speed Girl would reflect on her imprisonment in her later years with a wry sense of humor, crediting her indictment with quelling her rebellious spirit as a young girl.

Based on a *Saturday Evening Post* short story by Nina Wilcox Putnam and released in May 1921, *Two Weeks with Pay* again paired Bebe with Jack Mulhall, who had supported her in her first starring role. Director Maurice Campbell was responsible for more than half of Bebe's Realart features. Bebe plays shop girl Pansy O'Donnell, taking a two-week vacation at the fashionable Fairview Hotel to advertise her employer, Ginsberg (George Periolat).

Upon her arrival, there are complications. First, she is involved in an automobile accident with presumed millionaire J. Livingston Smith (Mulhall). Then she is mistaken for movie star Marie La Tour. Instead of quashing the rumor, she plays along. Her double life inevitably leads her into trouble, and she is forced to make a high dive into the hotel pool as a publicity stunt. Smith comes to her rescue at the last minute; when she finds out he is not a millionaire but rather a garage owner, she consents to marry him.

*Two Weeks with Pay* was generally well-received, despite inconsistent pacing and a lack of genuinely funny gags. *Billboard* praised its star, starting that "Bebe Daniels, greatly improved, has poise, and is at her best when garbed in ultra-fashionable raiment,"[19] while another critic stated, "[W]hether a picture is particularly worthwhile or not makes little or no difference when the heroine is as pretty and charming as Bebe Daniels."[20] As early as 1921, Bebe was experiencing a trend that would become more pronounced later in her career: Even if a film was not of particularly remarkable quality, her own magnetism could usually prevent it from being a complete failure.

Bebe's co-star in *The March Hare* was Harry Myers, who went on to star in Chaplin's *City Lights* a decade later. At this time he was perhaps best known for his role in *A Connecticut Yankee in King Arthur's Court,* also released in 1921. As was the case with most Realart productions, the rest of the cast is fairly nondescript. The film served almost exclusively as a vehicle for Bebe. Perpetuating her "good-little-bad-girl" stereotype, she plays Lizbeth Ann Palmer, known to her family as the March Hare. The daughter of a Los Angeles millionaire, she travels to New York City to visit an aunt. Once there, she makes a bet that she can survive in the city on only 75 cents—unheard of for a frivolous young girl like herself.

*The March Hare* was undeniably one of the lightest roles in Bebe's career, described as an "effervescent comedy" that gave "full rein to her piquant, youthful personality."[21] Another reviewer described the film's "farcical fun" as "highly infectious"[22] These kinds of terms—"light," "harum-scarum," "breakneck"—abound in contemporary reviews. Knowing Bebe's desire for a dramatic career, it is easy to speculate the effect such roles had on her mentally. Having begun her post–Roach career with the highly dramatic films of Cecil B. DeMille, *The March Hare* and other Realart movies must have seemed like a demotion.

That said, Bebe did not compromise her integrity for such simplistic roles, as one

## 8. Ten Days in Jail     65

telling anecdote demonstrates. Assistant director Walter McLeon had this to say about Bebe's performance:

> Bebe Daniels is as game a little actress as there is in the world. When we were taking sand lot baseball scenes in her latest picture, *The March Hare*, the business called upon her to "slide home." Well—she slid! Then she picked herself up and went on with the action of the play without confessing that the stunt had nearly wrecked her. It was only when we wanted to make some interior scenes the following

**Bebe Daniels and co-star Jack Mulhall in *Two Weeks with Pay*.**

**Bebe Daniels and Mayme Kelso in *The March Hare*.**

day that we learned that her knees were so badly skinned that they showed through white silk stockings, and her arms so badly scratched that she could not wear evening dress for several days. Yet nobody heard a peep out of her over her bruises.[23]

Injuries, both in her line of work and her personal life, would become a recurring theme throughout much of Bebe's film career.

# 9

# The End of Realart

*A highly charged bombshell was exploded in the film industry Saturday with the disbandment of Realart by Adolph Zukor, on 24 hours' notice. Friday afternoon telegrams were sent to all the Realart exchanges notifying the employees their services would no longer be required, effective Saturday.*
—*Variety*, December 16, 1921[1]

*One Wild Week* featured a typically eccentric plot, as was standard for Bebe Daniels movies in the early 1920s. Pauline Hathaway lives a thankless life with her aunt until her 18th birthday when she is informed she has inherited a million dollars, provided her conduct is appropriate. While traveling to the city to visit Mrs. Brewster (Frances Raymond), a friend of her deceased mother, she is framed by a pickpocket and sentenced to 30 days. Pauline nearly loses her inheritance until Mrs. Brewster's nephew, Bruce Reynolds (Frank Kingsley), is able to clear her name.

By the middle of 1921, Bebe seemed to have hit her stride with regards to the quality of her Realart films. Following the great success of *The March Hare*, *One Wild Week* was by all accounts another one of her best works. One reviewer wrote that "alluring and roguish Bebe Daniels is the chief element of interest in *One Wild Week*, a feature which fits her so perfectly that it seems to have been made to order."[2] Her rambunctious adventures, suggested by the film's title, were a constant source of enjoyment for audiences; although wholly improbable, they were simple and entertaining.

*One Wild Week* can easily be considered one of Bebe's "good little bad girl" pictures, as the trope that came to define her was readily apparent. The *Chicago Daily Tribune* was quick to pick up on this: "Miss Daniels is at her best as a good girl possessed of the devil.... A producer displays great mental acumen when he casts her as the daughter of nice folks who hold the reins too tightly. All there is left for the director to do is to say 'Giddyap!' and young Bebe runs away with the picture."[3]

Realart's association with Famous Players–Lasky provided the major studio with a supply of beautiful young starlets. So when Jesse Lasky announced the studio's adaptation of *Anatol*, a 1893 play by controversial Austrian author Arthur Schnitzler, the cast included both Bebe and Wanda Hawley. Heading the cast were Paramount mainstays Wallace Reid as Anatol DeWitt Spencer and Gloria Swanson as Vivian Spencer, his wife.

*The Affairs of Anatol*, as the film came to be named, tells the stories of Anatol's

**Bebe Daniels and Carrie Clark Ward in the Realart production *One Wild Week*.**

various adventures after deciding that life with his wife is lacking in excitement. The deeply psychological play elicited praise from Sigmund Freud himself. DeMille chose to turn it into a more traditional domestic comedy. Nearly two hours in length, it clearly differs from his famed epics in many regards.

Bebe, in a much-diminished part compared to her Realart starring vehicles, does not appear until the 85-minute mark. She plays the same awkward vampish type she attempted to play in *Male and Female.* The difference between her first DeMille film and her last, however, is striking. The dramatic overtures of *Male and Female* are instead shed for subtle comedy in *The Affairs of Anatol.* Her character is remarkably similar in both films—particularly in appearance (both are dressed in opulent, exotic costumes suggestive of "Oriental" mysticism). But in one she is an archetypal seductress to a Babylonian king, in the other she is a parody of this trope.

Even her character's name, Satan Synne, is humorous in its lack of subtlety. Her calling card reads "The Devil's Cloister" (the name of her exotic lair), and the perfume she wears is "Le Secret du Diable." Even her dialogue is ridiculously over-the-top (she informs Anatol that a stuffed, heart-shaped pillow is "the heart of a Fool—who thought he knew Women!"). Her entire being is absurdist to the point where it successfully lampoons the very roles Bebe had seriously played a short time before.

In a self-aware turn of events it is revealed that Satan Synne is not the seductress she appears to be, but is rather trying to earn $3000 for her husband who was injured during the Great War. In the reveal, Bebe successfully sheds the absurd guise and becomes a real person. This masterful bit of acting—one of the most challenging Daniels had exhibited until that time—demonstrates why DeMille had so much confidence in her ability. Although she played a fairly diminutive role in the grand scheme of the film, Bebe's portrayal of Satan Synne is nevertheless one of the highlights of an overall entertaining picture.

As early as July 1921, Bebe was being referred to as "The Speed Girl" in advertisements and articles. When the filming of the upcoming movie of the same name wrapped the third week of August, anticipation had reached a fever pitch. Publications were quick to remind readers of Bebe's real-world drama from the beginning of the year, and *Photoplay* ran its long-form piece, supposedly penned by Daniels, about the incident.

Capitalizing on the arrest, Paramount launched a calculated media campaign aimed at highlighting the plight of a defenseless young girl versus the conservative establishment. Her speeding, the studio would purport, wasn't hurting anyone, yet she still couldn't avoid jail. With sensationalized accounts of her attempts to vamp the judge, she became something of an anti-hero to leagues of moviegoers. Advertisements billed the film as "Bebe at her daringest, dashingest, good-little-bad-little-girlishness."[4]

For Bebe though, the film was more than merely a media stunt. While it may seem futile to look for a deeper meaning in such a trite premise, the emergence of technology in postwar America was obviously something that the actress took seriously. She was an early adaptor to automotive technology, and by the end of the decade would be amongst the most prominent proponents of recreational aviation. With characteristic eloquence, Bebe described the premise behind the story:

> It is the age of speed. In their entertainment, their sports, their business, even in their love affairs, it seems the American man, woman and child demand ever a swifter pace. "Make it snappy—get there!" is the universal cry.
>
> Seriously, we may have to change all this at some not distant time and modify our speed—put on the brake a bit. But for the present there is no sign of abating, and the moving picture must, if it does anything, reflect life as it is.[5]

*The Speed Girl* certainly managed to "reflect life as it is." The fictionalized story basically mirrors the real-life story of Bebe's imprisonment, with some necessary embellishment. Daniels plays Betty Lee, a screen celebrity who is liable to act erratically. As the motivation for Betty's speeding, the actress discovers that the naval officer she is dating (Theodore von Eltz) must reach his ship in San Diego before it sets sail. As Betty's impishness is responsible for his truancy, she vows to get him there on time. As can be expected, the mad dash has disastrous results.

Betty, like Bebe, is sentenced to ten days in jail, and she decides to make the best of it. Almost immediately, her cell is transformed into a parlor where she can entertain her devoted fans. She strikes up a friendship with the judge who, just days earlier, seemed her mortal enemy (audiences were certainly expected to remember the camaraderie between Bebe and Judge Cox). There are romantic subplots, but at the end she weds the officer with whom she began the saga.

As would be expected for such a light comedy, response was generally positive.

Fans were excited to finally *see* Bebe behind the wheel after reading about it for months. The contrived story was simple but effective in providing a means for Bebe to assume the film's title role, and her supporting cast proved themselves above-average for such a picture. In theaters across the nation, *The Speed Girl* became one of Bebe's biggest successes to date, and also one of Realart's most popular films.

Interestingly, *The Speed Girl* seemed to position Bebe as a female analogue to Wallace Reid (with whom she had already acted twice). Reid made a series of extremely successful racing pictures, the most recent of which, *Too Much Speed*, was released only five months before Daniels' film. As both were fellow Paramount stars, it seems unlikely that this was coincidental. By 1921, the studio was looking for a replacement for Ann Little, who had appeared in *The Roaring Road* and *Excuse My Dust* with Reid. Perhaps Paramount was testing Bebe out as a foil for the equally reckless Reid.

Praise for *The Speed Girl* was not universal. "It makes monkeys out of [the police] ... personally, I consider it in exceedingly bad taste, if nothing worse,"[6] carped the *Chicago Daily Tribune*. *Variety* took their review a step further, stating that the film "furnishes first rate entertainment for the infantile. It is scarcely conceivable that any film fan of a mentality more mature than that could be amused by the feeble invention."[7] Such harsh criticism of one of Daniels' films was unprecedented; several of her productions had been dismissed as uninspired or juvenile, but such blatant animosity was completely unknown to the 20-year-old.

Not content with simply criticizing the quality of the picture, *Variety* then continued to question Bebe's motive for making the film. "The whole vapid rave might have been put on for no other purpose than to feed the vanity of the camera actress," they wrote; "if this kind of trash is salable why not have the stars write their own stories with no other end than self-exploitation?"[8]

The lengths to which *Variety* went to dismantle the film in their review is somewhat bizarre. At that time, a vast number of motion pictures were produced as nothing more than vehicles for their leading man or lady. While the *Speed Girl* plot was certainly unexceptional, there is nothing that made Bebe's role shameless. The same month that *The Speed Girl* debuted, Realart also released *The Love Charm* with Wanda Hawley, *Morals* with May McAvoy and *Hush Money* with Alice Brady—none of which elicited the same type of hostile reviews.

Fortunately for her career, the negative critique of Daniels would remain an isolated occurrence and the vast majority of audiences were delighted by the madcap film. Its widespread popularity helped to solidify Bebe's reputation as "the good little bad girl" and turned her stint in the Orange County Jail into one of the most successful and unconventional marketing stunts of the silent era.

Following the semi-autobiographical *The Speed Girl* came *Nancy from Nowhere* (1922), a Cinderella story with Daniels as an orphan adopted by an abusive couple. The only solace she finds is in her admirer, Jack Halliday (Edward Sutherland), who happens to be engaged—getting Nancy into hot water with *her* family as well. All seems lost for the young girl, and her foster parents are about to beat her once again, when Jack steps in at the last minute and rescues his new bride-to-be.

Bebe, for once it seemed, was praised for her performance. One critic wrote, "If we've got to have Cinderella at all, by all means let her be Bebe Daniels,"[9] while another superficially noted that "she looks prettier than she ever has looked before."[10] However, even Daniels' acting, a supporting cast led by Vera Lewis, and apt director Chester M. Franklin couldn't save such a hackneyed plot.

Critics and fans alike longed for a picture in which Bebe could live up to her full potential as an actress. She appeared to be on the right track with DeMille. Now her Realart contract seemed more like a crutch. Serendipitously, the company was very quickly nearing its end.

Early reports suggested that Bebe Daniels and May McAvoy were to star opposite Rudolph Valentino in 1922's *Blood and Sand*.[11] Valentino was beginning a new three-year contract with Paramount; for Bebe, the role would have been the biggest of her young career. McAvoy was to play the wife of a bullfighter (Valentino) and Daniels was announced as the seductive "Spanish vamp."[12]

Several months later it was revealed that the parts seemingly given to Daniels and McAvoy were to be played by Nita Naldi and Lila Lee, respectively. Bebe later recalled that her reason for turning down the role was part of a conscious move away from playing "vamps," for fear that audiences would subconsciously dislike her.[13] *Blood and Sand* went on to be one of the most successful pictures of 1922, with Valentino—hot off the successes of *The Four Horsemen of the Apocalypse* and *The Sheik*—reaching the zenith of his fame.

Daniels would presumably have benefitted greatly from the exposure of starring alongside Valentino (none of her 1922 films came close to matching the success of *Blood and Sand*), although personally the film would have represented a setback to her ambitions as an actress. Vampish roles were fine when her career was just beginning; as her fame grew, she understood the need to branch out. After all, the career of Hollywood's most famous vamp, Theda Bara, was notoriously short-lived. Bebe turned down this opportunity to share the screen with Valentino, but would eventually star with the Sheik in 1924's *Monsieur Beaucaire*.

Bebe's personal life continued to be followed by the press. In particular, her blunt, down-to-earth sense of humor was looked upon favorably. Always willing to speak her mind, Bebe was inclined to take on even established stars when she disagreed with them. One exemplary exchange was reproduced by the *Boston Daily Globe*:

> Bebe Daniels has a rare sense of humor. The other day at the Cocoanut Grove, Hollywood, a certain blonde star was talking to Mary Pickford and was showing off, loud enough for everyone to hear, about her trips to Europe. "It wad on my second trip to Europe that"—she began.
> Everyone was getting bored and Bebe looked over at Lila Lee. "O Lila, do you remember our seventh trip to Europe," said Bebe.
> "But wasn't the ninth funny?" said Lila, playing up.
> "Dear, will you ever forget in Rome when we called on the Catacombs and they weren't at home," gurgled Bebe.
> "And down in Egypt when you got the hieroglyphics all over your dress and we couldn't shake them off," continued the irrepressible Bebe.
> Meanwhile everyone in the Grove was laughing heartily and the blonde star had subsided. No one heard any more about her European trips.[14]

While the blonde recipient of Bebe's sharp tongue was coyly kept anonymous, readers could envision several actresses who fit the bill. Bebe's stardom as a dramatist was fairly young, but she was already distinguishing herself as an earnest voice of reason, uncorrupted by the toxicity of Hollywood.

Around this time, Bebe had her first public romance since her separation from Harold Lloyd—and this time a boxer was said to have won her affections. The rumors about Daniels and Jack Dempsey began as early as August 1921 (with one source claiming the two were "inseparable"[15]), but it wasn't until the first months of 1922 that the "knock-out" couple (boxing puns abounded) was a staple in the gossip columns.

In an unexpected turn of events, it was announced on February 11 that Bebe and Jack were engaged to be married almost immediately. While a specific informant was never named (instead, the news came from a "well-authenticated report"[16] or "the big champion's friends"[17]), the indiscriminate media were quick to spread the news.

Accompanying the news, which stated the wedding was to be held March 1, was a charming—but presumably fanciful—story describing how the engagement came to be. As one newspaper told it:

> According to the story told by Jack's friends, the champ was waiting for Miss Daniels in the vicinity of the studio, where she was working in a picture. When the little star emerged from the studio, a vine-like young man appeared with a strong British accent and an ingratiating smile that failed to win anything but a slap in the face. At that moment Dempsey walked into the set, so to speak, registering extreme irritation. After a few ill remarks on the part of the would-be masher, Dempsey slapped him across the stomach and there was a quick fade-cut for the vile-like young man.
> "My, but you're fast for a big fellow," Miss Daniels remarked.
> "I've got some little speed," Jack admitted modestly.[18]

At the time the news broke, Dempsey was traveling from Los Angeles to New York, while Daniels was on location in Arizona filming *North of the Rio Grande*. Therefore, Bebe's grandmother and Dempsey's mother and sister were the first to be quoted in the press. All of whom pled ignorance, while at the same making sure not to quell the free publicity being thrust upon their respective relatives.[19]

Several days later, when the boxer's train arrived in Chicago, he was met by a barrage of reporters, eager for more news. He affirmed that he and Bebe were close friends but quickly put an end to any rumors of engagement, emphatically stating, "Gosh, can't a fellow walk down the street with a girl without the gossips getting busy?"[20] Dempsey also added, wryly, that if Bebe were indeed to be married, "she'd pick someone better than I."[21]

It wasn't long before Bebe addressed the media, requesting that the papers "please deny that I am engaged to Jack Dempsey."[22] Although initially dumbfounded as to where such a rumor could have come from, she admitted more than a year later that she "wouldn't be surprised if a certain press agent working for Jack Dempsey knew something about the affair."[23]

Dempsey was no stranger to Hollywood during the early 1920s. Before meeting his eventual wife, actress Estelle Taylor, Dempsey's list of companions reads like a who's who of the film industry, Marion Davies, Mabel Normand and Peggy Hopkins Joyce chief amongst them. Despite this, his relationship with Bebe seems to have been more serious than these fleeting affairs. Later in life, Jack reflected that amongst all of the women he was seen with, "I got stuck on one or two. And one or two got stuck on me."[24] It is almost certain that he was referring to Bebe. Years later when Bebe recounted her "six big romances," Dempsey's name was nowhere to be found.[25]

An interesting denouement for Jack and Bebe's relationship can be found a decade after their alleged engagement, when one writer noted that Bebe still "finds Jack pleasant company at some of the informal Hollywood gatherings where they are members of the same crowd."[26] It appears that their friendship was not marred by the rumor that gripped the public for a fleeting moment.

As the Dempsey rumors began to fade, Bebe's second picture of 1922, *A Game Chicken*, was released on February 26. Filming, which wrapped the last week of January, was evidently taxing on Daniels, who was required to perform her own aquatic stunts three miles from shore.[27]

The film stars Bebe as Inez Hastings, a Cuban girl whose father runs the American bootleg trade in Havana. She falls in love with Rush Thompson (Pat O'Malley), a revenue officer tasked with tracking down her father. Despite the obvious obstacles in their relationship she continually makes efforts to be with him. In the climax, the two are trapped by bootleggers on a ship. Inez, in an attempt to aid Thompson, sets fire to the vessel, leaving them in danger until a government submarine rescues the couple. The movie opened to fairly positive reviews—many laced with references to her boxer lover—although even the most lukewarm reviews praised Bebe's performance above all else. Many were also quick to note that Inez's mixed heritage—her mother was Cuban, her father American—was indicative of Bebe's own past, and allowed her to play the part well. *A Game Chicken* was Bebe's last picture with Realart.

Around this time, Bebe's career was facing a major trial behind the scenes. After ten starring pictures with the production company, the Paramount affiliates (for whom Bebe and May McAvoy were the biggest box office attractions) ceased operations early in 1922. Soon after, it was announced that Famous Players–Lasky would reopen the former Realart studios as the Wilshire Paramount Studio.[28]

During its short lifespan (from the end of 1919 to the beginning of 1922), Realart Pictures produced 72 pictures, nearly all of them features for the core group of Daniels, Wanda Hawley, Constance Binney, Mary Miles Minter, Alice Brady and May McAvoy. The company was, in many ways, simply a vanity project for Famous Players–Lasky to produce light-hearted comedies with some of their prettiest contract actresses. They were often low-budget and had second-rate leading men and directors. None of the company's productions are today considered a classic of the silent era. Their movies—almost all of which are lost—are remembered, at best, for the early appearances of such celebrities as Daniels, Brady and McAvoy.

The legacy of Daniels' output with Realart is hard to ascertain. Only two of her ten films are thought to survive, and neither have been made available to the public since their initial release. To the casual film fan, therefore, the first years of the Roaring Twenties seem like something of a dead zone for Bebe's career, despite her prolific output. And while it is impossible to judge the quality of her Realart films (contemporary critics seemed to generally consider them entertaining, but not artistically significant), her time with the company nonetheless marked a very significant step in her career.

Looking back on her time with Realart, Bebe was more than a little critical of her pictures. "I realize just how poor and inane most all of my Realart pictures were," she stated in a 1923 interview.[29] *Bebe & Ben*, her authorized biography, makes little mention of her time with the company. But out of "poor and inane" pictures, Bebe was able to learn more about her career and herself than ever before.

While the studio was being assimilated into Paramount, the careers of those contracted by Realart were immediately being called into question. For several of Realart's actresses, it would prove to be the end of the line. Minter retired in 1923 following her proximity to the recent William Desmond Taylor scandal. Binney retired the same year, while Hawley had only limited success for the rest of her career.

For Bebe—a major success financially, if not artistically, for Realart—the closing of the studio proved to be a new beginning. Lloyd's choice of Bebe as a leading lady so early in her career was both a blessing and a curse for her. As one writer noted in 1926, "Bebe Daniels is unique in that she started as a leading woman."[30]

In many respects, her immediate success, from Lloyd to DeMille to a starring contract with Realart, ensured that Bebe never had to *learn* how to become a star; rather, she was simply granted the title without ever having to pay her dues. (As she whimsically put it, "I was hatched into stardom a trifle prematurely.") While incredible for her popularity, this career arc proved detrimental for her acting ability and mental state. Bebe, who showed as much promise as any young actress at the start of the 1920s, spent some of her most important years in second-rate productions that couldn't have been saved by even the greatest dramatics.

With the closing of Realart, Jesse Lasky immediately offered Bebe a starring contract with Paramount Pictures, seemingly a dream come true for the 21-year-old Daniels. Bebe, however, refused. She later rationalized her decision:

> When Realart gave up the ghost, Paramount gave me a starring contract. I went to Mr. Lasky, and asked to be relieved of starring for a while. I preferred to build up my battered reputation gradually. The critics had hacked huge chunks out of it. So I chose to work under the DeMilles and [George] Fitzmaurice and men of that type; I wanted to learn and grow and develop into a star by right of conquest.

Such a decision shows the maturity and poise that Bebe exuded for much of her career. Onscreen she was "the good little bad girl"; offscreen, she was making career choices that demonstrated a wisdom far beyond her years.

# 10

# New York

*When they start in dressing up a girl like Bebe Daniels, to make her look lusciously lovely as a whole flock of nymphs, they can't go far wrong from a box office standpoint.—Los Angeles Times, 1923*[1]

For her first picture following the demise of Realart, Bebe returned to her roots with the very type of film she first cut her teeth on in Hollywood: westerns. Her first foray into the genre in nearly a decade was *North of the Rio Grande* with leading man Jack Holt. A far cry from her cheap and quick Realart movies, it would have its ups and downs for Bebe.

Based on the novel *Val of Paradise* by prolific western novelist Vingie Eve Roe, *North of the Rio Grande* tells the story of Bob Haddington (Holt), a rancher who swears revenge on the man who killed his father. Along the way he falls in love with Val Hannon (Daniels), daughter of a wealthy landowner. In a strange turn of events, Bob is suspected of being a notorious rustler, while in fact Val's father John is both the rustler and the man who killed Bob's father. At the last possible moment, a mortally wounded Hannon confesses to his daughter, thereby allowing her to save her lover's life.

Despite the generic western storyline, the production stood out to Bebe as one of the most remarkable periods of her career. It was filmed on location in the desert northeast of Phoenix, Arizona. Unforeseen difficulties of the wilderness plagued the film. Accidents, some of which nearly ended Bebe's career (and life), abounded. The weeks she spent camping in the desert were entirely unlike anything she had experienced before.

Problems began when it was determined that Bebe's horse had to match Jack Holt's, leaving her to settle for an English-bred horse that was terribly ill-suited for the desert. Daniels was a skilled rider, but the task of commanding a temperamental horse through an alien landscape proved too much. At one point, Holt had to rescue both Bebe and another rider from falling over a cliff; during another scene, both Bebe and her horse had to learn how to jump over the cameraman while filming. Tragedy struck when one of the Native Americans cast in the film lost his life on location—a fact which was not mentioned in contemporary news reports.[2]

"Bebe Daniels Finds Thrill in Camp Life" read one headline, followed the opening line, "My work in Arizona was like one long, glorious vacation."[3] For a girl whose fondest childhood days were spent in the "wilds" of the San Fernando Valley, an extended stay in the Sonoran Desert seemed too good to be true.

"I had never slept in a tent before I reached Mormon Flats," she fondly reported to the press. She continued:

> My mother shared the little canvas covering with me. About midnight I was awakened by a splattering of rain in my face. Mother was calling to me. She complained that her cot was soaked. About half of my cot was in such a position as to escape the moisture which seeped through the tent. So Mother and I spent the rest of the night on a scant half of a little army cot.
>
> I rode about 25 or 30 miles a day, and the more I saw of that wonderful wealth of scenery the more I wanted to keep on riding. Besides, there is something about the great open spaces like that which make one want to ride and ride and look around at everything and think how glorious it is to be alive.
>
> All previous pictures have been of such a nature as to keep me pretty close to the studio and this is the first opportunity I have had to get away from Los Angeles in connection with my work. It also marks my first appearance in a Western type of story, with its fast action, daring horsemanship, cowboys and Indians.[4]

Her concluding statement seems strange, as her early teenage years were spent acting in nothing *but* westerns, but the sentiment remains: Her experience with *North of the Rio Grande* was eye-opening in that it demonstrated the opportunities that motion picture acting could present. Within the next few years, her productions would take her as far as New York City and the Caribbean.

One of the most harrowing incidents in the life of the young Miss Daniels came on May 18, 1922. Papers the next day were filled with the story of Charles Caprice, a 21-year-old man found in the living room of the Daniels residence with the "express purpose" of murdering the actress.[5]

Conflicting details about the case were quick to emerge, but certain facts were soon ascertained. Bebe had been receiving threatening letters for some time.[6] On the evening of the incident she was out with friends.[7] Phyllis Daniels placed the call to the police, who promptly arrived and arrested Caprice without resistance.

Caprice, a former Marine, claimed to have been hired by Pete McNamara, who he claimed ran a dope ring in San Francisco.[8] McNamara allegedly had incriminating information against Caprice, who was living "the life of a slave" under constant fear of being turned over to the police. The hit on Bebe was to be carried out for a sum of $25. When police arrived, the hit man claimed that he'd had a change of heart, and instead broke into the Daniels house to warn Bebe of the bounty placed on her head. He was in the psychiatric ward of the county hospital, awaiting mental evaluation, when the story first broke.

Connections were immediately made with the murder of William Desmond Taylor three months earlier. Amidst the overly sensational reports of the director's death were suggestions of a Hollywood narcotics ring; because of this, Caprice became one of the countless suspects in the Taylor case. While no connection was ever made, the similarity of the two incidents (Taylor was murdered inside his home) goes to demonstrate the dark undercurrent sweeping through Hollywood during the early 1920s.

This was, after all, the era of Olive Thomas and Fatty Arbuckle, and Bebe's story had all of the hallmarks of a sordid Hollywood scandal: a beautiful young damsel in distress, a crazed murderer-for-hire, and connections to a narcotics ring. The involvement of Daniels, who was fast developing a wild and reckless persona after her jail stint the previous year, made the story even more alluring to the masses.

Given all of this, it seems almost shocking that the case did not develop into something more. The last mention of Caprice in the papers came only nine days after the first; neither Bebe or her mother sought to press charges, and the county psychologist dismissed the would-be murderer as having a pseudoscientific disorder he called "movie mania."[9] In the span of a little more than a week the story had already come and gone, quickly disappearing into the annals of cinematic history.

In the absence of police reports or criminal charges, there is no hard evidence to suggest what actually happened that evening; even the existence of Charles Caprice cannot be independently confirmed outside of this handful of newspaper accounts. Yellow journalism ran rampant in Hollywood during the early days of the motion picture industry, and the idea that the entire story was concocted as a public relations stunt is not out of the realm of possibility. What is known for certain, however, is that unlike the other victims of the era's scandals—Thomas, Arbuckle, Taylor—Bebe was spared the scathing (and often fictitious) ire of Kenneth Anger decades later, ensuring that her reputation would remain pure and unadulterated.

As an interesting aside, the Caprice incident would not be the only attempt on Bebe's life. During the early months of 1926, she received an anonymous box of candies that, when tested, proved to be laced with poison. The sender was never caught.

*Nice People*,[10] part of Paramount's massive 41-film schedule for 1922, once again paired Bebe with Wallace Reid. The movie was adapted from Rachel Crothers' play of the same name by Clara Beranger and directed by her future husband, William DeMille. Daniels starred as Teddy Gloucester, the "only daughter of a rich and adoring father"; she was "educated to the taste of cocktails and the glow of pearls."[11] After an all-night party with copious amounts of alcohol, Teddy and her friend Scotty (Conrad Nagel) are stranded in a farmhouse during a violent storm.

A stranger named Billy Wade (Reid) also finds refuge in the farmhouse, just in time to protect Teddy from the drunken Scotty's unwanted advances. When Teddy's father finds her and Scotty alone the next morning, she becomes a pariah amongst her friends—formerly the titular "nice people." In the end, Teddy abandons her morally loose lifestyle and marries Billy to clear her name.

The story exudes the stereotype of the Roaring Twenties. As one reviewer wrote, "there are costume balls, licker on the hip, cigarettes galore, the sparking taint of smart and subtle deviltry and even a corncob pipe smoked by a wicked flapper of the jazz set."[12] Bebe and her fellow "flappers," most notably co-star Julia Faye, were remarkably modern in their portrayal, although the moralistic ending was firmly rooted in the past—a hallmark of the conservative DeMille brothers.

Reviews were generally positive, although many critics felt the film did not meet the high expectations set by the impressive cast and crew. *Photoplay* named it one of the top releases of the month and theaters across the nation found the film massively successful.

"*Nice People*, the last picture I made with Wally Reid, stays in my mind," Bebe wrote decades later. "All the time I had a sense of foreboding. He kept saying to me: 'I won't be alive a year from now.' We did not take him seriously because he always looked so fit. I did happen to know that before the film he did have some teeth extracted. This did not impress me as particularly serious, and I imagined he was just feeling the strain of motion picture work, being so popular and making so many films."[13]

Reid's morphine addiction, stemming from the treatment of injuries he sustained during the filming of 1919's *The Valley of the Giants*, was slowly consuming him. Never allowed a moment's rest by the studio, he sank deeper and deeper into the grip of the drug until it was the only thing keeping him alive. Treatment for addiction was still in its infancy, and Hollywood was hyper-cautious to keep a clean reputation. After the Olive Thomas, Virginia Rappe and William Desmond Taylor scandals, the movie industry could hardly afford to admit that one of its most beloved members was a junkie. There was no saving Wallace Reid.

Bebe continued: "I thought he was just a little over-tired, yet somehow a chill wind always seemed to touch me when he talked of dying. It wasn't just a casual remark so much as a positive statement, a prophecy. You had only to look at him, strong and obviously healthy, to feel that Death had many years before he would be calling for Wally."[14] Wallace Reid was dead four months after the release of *Nice People*.

Film footage of Bebe Daniels from her Realart and early Paramount years is exceedingly difficult to come by today so any fragment, no matter how short, is significant. All ten of her feature films from 1922 and 1923 are thought to be lost, so it is nearly impossible for modern audiences to get a sense of her screen presence from this period. After her vampish roles for DeMille, Daniels' acting transformed greatly—but without surviving footage, a fair assessment of her work is difficult to make.

Fortunately, a promotional film provides a fleeting snapshot of Bebe's screen persona. *A Trip to Paramountown*, released to theaters to advertise upcoming productions, showcases many of the studio's top stars. Anna Q. Nilsson, Rudolph Valentino and Gloria Swanson are amongst the short film's cast, but what might be the most interesting scene features Bebe and Wallace Reid. Shot during the production of *Nice People*, the footage is surreal and gimmicky. Reid is first shown playing with a toy car; seated in the driver seat is, through the magic of a split screen, a miniature Reid. In the next shot, Bebe is shown playing with a sentient Bebe Daniels doll, created through the same screen magic. Wearing a Spanish-style dress, the diminutive Bebe dances gracefully before being placed back into the *actual* Bebe's wardrobe. Her time on screen doesn't even last a minute.

*A Trip to Paramountown* was created as an advertisement rather than a piece of standalone art, yet today its historical importance is greater than the studio could have predicted. Intended to drum up anticipation for the coming season's attractions, it instead stands out today as a tantalizing glimpse into a formative time in Bebe's career. While *Nice People* will probably never be viewed again, it is fortunate that even such a small clip of Bebe playing to the camera managed to survive.

Cynthia Stockley's 1920 book *Pink Gods and Blue Demons* seemed to lend itself remarkably well to the silver screen: Sordid tales of South African diamond mines were exactly the kinds of stories that 1920s audiences flocked to see. Paramount purchased the rights to the book, truncating the title to *Pink Gods*, and cast Constance Binney and Anna Q. Nilsson in the leading female roles.

A month after Binney was announced for the film, the role was transferred to Bebe Daniels without explanation. *Pink Gods* would have served as Binney's first Paramount feature after the dissolution of Realart, proving the perfect vehicle for bona fide stardom. But behind the scenes, the actress was becoming increasingly disillusioned with motion pictures and opted to leave the industry. Although Binney would make two more films for minor studios, she quickly faded into obscurity at the same time that Bebe continued her meteoric rise.

Following the completion of *Nice People*, Bebe had only one day of vacation before *Pink Gods* began filming. As an escape from her grueling schedule, Bebe took the opportunity to "do some shopping, have some photographs taken, see some picture shows, and then go into the country with her grandmother to spend the day."[15] It comes as little surprise that Daniels would choose to spend the day with Little Mother; as her schedule became more hectic, it became increasingly important to her to spend time with her mother and grandmother.

Although *Pink Gods* was, by and large, fairly unremarkable, it did have one novel feature that helped it to stand out from other Paramount productions of the time. Noted Jazz Age artist B. Cory Kilvert was hired to create original images to accompany the film's titles—and they would be reproduced in their original colors.

Color films were by no means unheard of, but were still the exception rather than the rule. Paramount's *Joan the Woman* (1916) and *Treasure Island* (1920) featured colorized sequences, as did a few films from other companies. Already the Technicolor Motion Picture Corporation was in its infancy; two months after *Pink Gods'* release, Technicolor premiered the first color feature made in Hollywood, *The Toll of the Sea*.

Numerous methods of colorizing motion pictures were being devised during the silent era. The Dunning Pomeroy Process, which Paramount employed for *Pink Gods*, was still an extremely rudimentary and experimental technology. A decade later, a derivative of that process would be used to create the special effects in *King Kong*.

Kilvert explained the thought behind including color in *Pink Gods*:

> Since the motion pictures do not as yet seem to be able to get along without interpolated reading matter, it is our aim to have the titles carry along the action and visual idea of the scenes, with as little interruption as is possible. The process we are using allows the use of two colors, and my problem as a color artist is to device varied and harmonious combinations of different tints.
>
> Moreover, we have the pleasant feeling of being pioneers, for although color has been used in dramatic pictures, it has not been unqualifiedly successful.[16]

While *Pink Gods* itself would have little lasting impact on the development of color cinema (and is hardly considered a pioneering work), Kilvert's heart and mind were in the right place. Ultimately, the technology had not progressed far enough to enable color to be used effectively. *Pink Gods* would garner some attention for Kilvert's titles, but was quickly eclipsed by more groundbreaking films.

Near the end of October 1922, Bebe took her first extended leave from Hollywood for the filming of Edith Wharton's *Glimpses of the Moon*.[17] She had just finished *The World's Applause*, a William DeMille film that cast her as a Broadway star but failed to elicit much attention critically. One of her most anticipated pictures, *Glimpses of the Moon* also served as Bebe's first vacation in three years and her first trip to New York City.[18] Daniels was still in the midst of her transition from the silly scenarios she played in with Realart to more serious, dramatic work. A change of scenery, she figured, would do her some good.

*Glimpses of the Moon* interiors were filmed at Astoria Studios in Queens, opened several years earlier by Famous Players–Lasky and the hub of Paramount's East Coast productions. Sets included a lavish Louis XVI–style drawing room and a reproduction of the canals of Venice. The script was originally penned by F. Scott Fitzgerald[19]; however, at some point during production his work was scrapped and replaced by a new script adapted by E. Lloyd Sheldon and Edfrid Bingham.

The filming was delayed by one of the numerous health setbacks Bebe faced over the course of her career. After several months of pain, she was admitted to Roosevelt Hospital on the evening of Sunday, January 28, 1923. The following day an emergency appendectomy was performed by noted surgeon John F. Erdmann. Although the surgery was "most satisfactory,"[20] the story was still picked up nationally by news outlets. Some news sources claimed that, because of Bebe's health woes, her next starring role in *The Exciters* had been given to Agnes Ayres. But Bebe pulled through and played the role.

The vast amount of press coverage her appendectomy received speaks volumes to the star power she had during the early 1920s. There was hardly a more popular—or more highly regarded—name in all of the film industry, and any threat to her well-being was serious news.

Following her recovery, production of *Glimpses of the Moon* progressed rapidly, and the movie premiered on March 25. It was undoubtedly one of her most popular releases to date, largely due to the success of Wharton's novel the previous year. Bebe plays Susan Branch, a young girl financially supported by her wealthy friends. She falls in love with a struggling author (Bebe explained that the titular "glimpses of the moon" are "the moments when love first blossoms to find fulfillment, moments that bind lives together safe against temptation"[21]). He is also admired by Branch's chief supporter, Ursula Gillow (Nita Naldi). Despite a slew of domestic and financial issues, Susan and the author end up together.

Fresh off of the success of *Glimpses of the Moon*, Bebe took almost no time before returning to Florida to begin her next picture. At the time, Famous Players–Lasky was using more and more exotic locales for their pictures, and *The Exciters,* based on Martin Brown's successful Broadway play of the same name, was no exception. Again the interiors were filmed at Astoria Studios, the exteriors on location in Miami.[22]

It was announced that the male lead would be Bert Lytell,[23] and Richard Ordynski was slated to direct[24]; eventually they would be replaced by Antonio Moreno and Maurice Campbell, respectively. The remainder of the cast and crew was relatively nondescript, and contemporary advertisements make it clear that this film was little more than a vehicle for Moreno and Daniels.

Opening on June 3, 1923, *The Exciters* received tepid reviews. The movie was a laughable contrast to the serious nature of her previous work. Ronnie Rand (Bebe), a "peppery maid who craves excitement and gets it regardless of the consequences,"[25] faces the dilemma of having to marry by a certain date or lose her inheritance. Her choice of husband, Pierre Martel (Moreno), proves to be a criminal—which, instead of deterring her, excites her. His gang blackmails Ronnie and threatens to kill Pierre. The police save her, and it is revealed that her husband is not a crook but a U.S. Intelligence Service agent. In a twist, this news disappoints her greatly, although she nevertheless opts to settle down with him.

What *The Exciters* lacked in plot, it made up for with the cinematography of George Webber. Florida provided impressive backdrops for the near-constant action, and while the film might not have won Bebe any praise from the critics, it certainly thrilled many moviegoers who were already admirers of her.

Bebe closed out 1923 with the November release *His Children's Children*, adapted from a novel of the same name by popular author Arthur Train. Bebe began the production in July after she returned to New York from a publicity tour throughout the East Coast and Midwest. The film paired Bebe with director Sam Wood, who had previously directed her pair of Wallace Reid features in 1920. Paramount promised audiences that *His Children's Children* would be Wood's biggest production to date.

The plot concerns a monetary fortune, a dying grandfather, his unethical son and his three granddaughters. It's a generic society tale, the kind immensely popular in the early 1920s. George Fawcett played Peter B. Kayne, patriarch of the family; his son was portrayed by Hale Hamilton; the three girls were Bebe, Dorothy Mackaill and Katheryn Lean.

While the plot seems dated today's, critics were generally positive about the film. "It's a story with a moral, plus a lot of jazzy atmosphere and a laugh here and there," read the *Variety* review.[26] *Photoplay* deemed Hamilton and Fawcett's performances two of the best of the month, while remaining ambivalent about the picture as a whole. Few

**Bebe Daniels with James Rennie (left) and John Davidson (right) in the 1923** *His Children's Children.*

reviewers even mentioned Bebe specifically; for once she was overshadowed by the rest of her cast.

So 1923 ended not with a bang but with a whimper for Bebe. Stuck between genres—from serious dramas to light-hearted comedies—her career seemed to lack direction. No longer a fresh-faced starlet, Bebe was now a well-established Paramount contract player—but one without many critical successes to her name.

The start of 1924 brought her back yet again to the place where she had cut her teeth in the motion picture industry: the Wild West.

In August 1923 it was announced that Bebe would travel from New York to Flagstaff, Arizona, where she would "undertake another of those lively western girl roles for which she is so well suited by reason of her god horsemanship"[27] (*Los Angeles Times*). *Heritage of the Desert* would prove to be her last western. Featuring a quality cast comprised of Ernest Torrence, Noah Beery and Lloyd Hughes, it was released on January 23, 1924. Reviews were overwhelmingly positive. "Everybody with an ounce of red blood will come a-runnin' to see this picture,"[28] wrote one critic, and box office records indicate he was right in his assessment. Zane Grey's books always lent themselves well to cinematic adaptations, and Bebe's comfort in western subjects was apparent in her performance.

*Heritage of the Desert* was followed by *Daring Youth*, a thoroughly modern film that presented Bebe as a stereotypical 1920s flapper. A *Los Angeles Times* article described Daniels' role in the film and her evolution during the first half of the decade:

### Practices her Precept

Bebe Daniels sums up the road to film fame in two words.

"Be daring," advises the heroine of dozens of screen dramas. Many other qualifications, of course, are necessary. They fit in varying degrees, according to the aspirant's ability and ambitions. Without courage, however, it is hard to succeed.

Bebe says she knows this from her own experiences. For years she was the foil of comedies and no one stopped to consider whether she had ability or not. She was pretty and winsome and clever and pleased thousands of film fans. Then came her big chance in spectacular drama under the direction of Cecil DeMille. Miss Daniels appeared as an oriental siren. Not only did she wear the gorgeous robes with distinction, but she threw herself into the role with such fervor that she attracted the world's attention. Since then, the name of Bebe Daniels has appeared among the elect.

In *Daring Youth* ... Bebe has a brilliant role, entirely fitting her abilities. She plays the role of a young wife with advanced ideas of freedom. Even the marriage vows did not impress her with tho requirements of giving her entire life to husband. No, she would live her own life, giving him part of her time, and it is interesting to watch the outcome of this dangerous experiment.

... *Daring Youth* is a thrilling, and enjoyable photo-play.[29]

Bebe began working on her next film as soon as *Daring Youth* was completed. *Unguarded Women* went into production at Paramount's Long Island Studio. Filming and editing spanned a two-month period from the end of March until the end of May; the process was evidently painless for everyone except the leading man. "For five nights [Richard] Dix crawled through barbed wire entanglements, dodged bombs, climbed over trenches, splashed through mud holes and whatnot,"[30] read one report from the set. Dix commented on the strenuous nature of the film's flashbacks of World War I: "I was having a lovely time in this picture—all dressed up in evening clothes—and everything, until this war stuff came along."

Dix plays Douglas Albright, a Great War veteran who returns home a hero. But many of the accolades showered on him were actually earned by his best friend Captain Robert Banning (Joe King), whose death he witnessed on the front lines. Albright begins courting beautiful young Helen Castle (Mary Astor), whom he regales with war tales. Some months later he encounters Banning's widow Breta (Bebe) in China. Spurred by guilt and a sense of duty to his fallen friend, he forsakes his love for Castle to marry Breta.

The movie was well-received, although one writer noted that it "[did] not quite live up to the leering flamboyancy of its name."[31] Dix's performance was praised, as was that of 18-year-old Astor. Opinions on Bebe's performance were split, partly due to the fact that it was so different from the light fare she typically offered. Bebe was constantly yearning for more dramatic roles, but when Famous Players–Lasky gave them to her, they proved less popular than her comedic fluff.

Writing about *Unguarded Women*, *Los Angeles Times* critic Kenneth Taylor astutely noted, "Bebe Daniels fans will probably not like it at all, for it presents this young lady doing serious work of a kind never before associated with her. The role provides her with no opportunity for posing, or looking pretty, the first of which she has sometimes been guilty and the second of which she has usually accomplished."[32] In his final assessment of the film, which he considered to be thoroughly enjoyable, he stated that *Unguarded Women* "should prove attractive to all but out-and-out Bebe Daniels fans."

One can assume that such a tepid response to a purely dramatic role would have proved disheartening for Daniels, whose dream was to perform in such serious roles. Fortunately for Bebe, her next picture would likewise be dramatic, perhaps even histrionic. It would also pair her with one of the screen's greatest legends.

# 11

# Valentino

*Every man carries in his heart his own ideal of his real sweetheart. I married mine. So, too, every man carries in his thoughts his ideal screen sweetheart. Mine is Bebe Daniels.*

*In the course of my work before the camera I have played with most of the feminine stars of today. They are all charming, talented and delightful. It is never difficult to make screen love to any or all of them.*

*But Bebe brings to the screen a vivacity, a naturalness and a lovely spontaneity which made our one appearance together before the camera perhaps the most pleasant business memory I have.*

—Western star Jack Holt in *Photoplay*, July 1924[1]

One day late in 1923, Bebe found herself in Paramount executive Bob Kane's office. The mood of the meeting was more serious than Bebe was used to.

"Bebe, this is a little difficult," Kane began. "We know you're under a star contract, but we are wondering if you would contemplate being a supporting star. The picture is a particularly good one, and the circumstances are unusual."

Bebe's mind raced. There were only a handful of male leads who could command top billing over her, especially amongst the Paramount roster. Curiously she asked, "Who am I to support?"

"Valentino."[2]

Booth Tarkington is one of the most celebrated of American authors, although it must be conceded that awareness for his works has faded in the decades since his death. One of only three authors to be awarded the Pulitzer Prize for Fiction twice and one of the leading social commentators of his generation, Tarkington's works are analyzed and interpreted to this day.

Tarkington is best known for the award-winning *Alice Adams* and *The Magnificent Ambersons*, as well as the comical *Penrod*. His early works were nowhere near as successful. His second novel *Monsieur Beaucaire*, a historical tale set in 18th-century Europe, failed to attract much attention upon its release, although it was adapted into a successful play and opera in 1903 and 1919, respectively. With its extravagant costumes and opulent sets, it seemed the perfect candidate for a blockbuster. It came as no surprise when Famous Players–Lasky acquired the rights.

On Christmas Day 1923, Paramount announced the picture. But fans were not impressed by the studio's choice of source material; instead, anticipation was entirely focused on the return of Rudolph Valentino to the screen.

Following the production of 1922's *The Young Rajah*, Valentino entered into a very public dispute with Famous Players–Lasky over his weekly contract. The actor claimed the issue was creative control; cynics found it hard to sympathize given his exorbitant salary. While the details of Valentino's "one-man strike" against the production company have been recounted numerous times,[3] the outcome was his year-long hiatus from motion pictures.

During this year, Valentino and wife Natacha Rambova toured the United States promoting the Mineralava Beauty Clay Company. During this 88-city run, the Latin Lover grew in popularity. Absence was making the hearts of millions of girls grow fonder. The lack of new pictures from Rudy was, ironically, helping to revitalize a career stalled by several poorly received performances.

There was great excitement among his fans when it was announced that Famous Players–Lasky had struck a two-picture deal with him. "I think the signing of this contract is an excellent Christmas present to the motion picture public," announced Adolph Zukor. "[W]e purpose [*sic*] giving Mr. Valentino the finest productions possible from the best the industry affords."[4] Early news reports from the set promised it would be one of the most lavish productions of 1924.

Valentino took the role of Monsieur Beaucaire extremely seriously. George Ullman, his talent manager, documented this period of the star's life intimately in his biography *Valentino As I Knew Him*: "I was with [Valentino and Rambova] a great deal, and I could not help observing that Valentino so completely threw himself into the part he was playing that he was Beaucaire at home. To his wife his manners were those of the courtly Frenchman; even when talking business with me he was Beaucaire."[5] The lapse in acting had evidently not impacted his craft; but would the stodgy role enthrall the masses as the Sheik had just three years earlier?

"Seldom have I enjoyed a picture more than *Monsieur Beaucaire*," Bebe would declare decades later, "though at first it seemed to bristle with difficulties."[6] Working with the notoriously fickle Valentino was not amongst those difficulties; on the contrary, Daniels never had anything but the kindest remarks for him. "I had heard of the Valentino temperament, but have never met anyone less difficult to work with and more gracious to everybody in the studio, from the doorman up," she recalled. Perhaps it was his modest beginnings that left him with this humility. Whatever the case, Rudolph and Bebe—and Rambova—immediately took a liking to one another.

The abovementioned difficulties largely revolved around the production itself. Foremost amongst Bebe's troubles was having to learn the entire script in French, despite the fact that it was a silent film. Stanley Olcott was so demanding in his direction that he required the actors' lip movements to be correct to the period. While certainly a noble aspiration, the final effect is so subtle as to seem superfluous. Regarding the all–French script, Bebe remarked that "it was unique—and so were some of the accents, mine included!"[7]

*Monsieur Beaucaire* opened to mixed reviews. Even critics who enjoyed it admitted that it was a far cry from *The Sheik* and *The Four Horsemen of the Apocalypse*. Its stodgy setting did not allow Valentino to exhibit the same magnetism he had in previous films. For audiences used to seeing "The Latin Lover" as the sensual Sheik Ahmed Ben Hassan, his portrayal of the Duke de Chartres was immensely disappointing. By giving him such a tedious role, Paramount managed to strip him of everything that had made him popular.

Public sentiment towards *Monsieur Beaucaire* can perhaps best be gauged from the release of Stan Laurel's *Monsieur Don't Care* less than four months later.[8] The farcical short, a follow-up to 1922's *Mud and Sand* (from *Blood and Sand*), featured Laurel as "Rhubarb Vaselino." To all but the most devoted Valentino fans, the parody perfectly captured the excessive pomp of *Beaucaire*. There are no known surviving prints of *Monsieur Don't Care*, but still images of a powder-wigged Laurel biting Syd Crossley's leg demonstrate the absurdist nature of the biting lampoon.

At the end of May, as *Unguarded Women* was nearing completion and *Monsieur Beaucaire* was getting underway, it was announced that Bebe and Richard Dix would again be paired for *Sinners in Heaven*. Based on a novel by Clive Arden, it revolves around a pilot and his beautiful passenger, stranded on a remote island of cannibals. The two are worshipped as gods until their mortality is discovered. Through an unlikely series of events, they are rescued and wed.

Given the exotic setting, the production team (headed by director Alan Crosland) traveled to Nassau in the Bahamas.[9] Much of the excitement surrounding the film

**Bebe Daniels and Rudolph Valentino clothed in period attire in *Monsieur Beaucaire*.**

centered on the fact that Bebe had conformed to the Roaring Twenties ideal and bobbed her hair for the role.

Bebe provided interesting insight into the production: "The costumes they had sent out for Richard and me were far too bizarre for two people supposed to be shipwrecked on a desert island. So we put our thinking caps on, and with the help of the prop men and the natives we produced authentic-looking costumes from straw, treebark and local native materials."[10] This film does not survive today, but modern viewers can appreciate the improvisational costumes through still images.

*Sinners in Heaven* ranks among Bebe's more notable critical failures. Most writers dismissed it as cliched and uninspired, and took issue with the stars' performances. "[Dix] ought at least to refrain from appearing in any more South Sea island productions," read one review, while "[Bebe's] screen talent is sadly hampered by her hollow eyes and grass skirts."[11] This harsh review was by no means an anomaly; for someone as beloved as Bebe, such criticism was unexpected and unappreciated.

To close out 1924, Bebe made *Dangerous Money* and *Argentine Love* in rapid succession (and to polar opposite receptions). *Photoplay* panned the former as "just another flabby film story with William Powell, the scoundrel who tries to get Bebe's money,"[12] while praising Daniels as a "brilliant in this South American romance" in the latter.[13] Both would be overshadowed by her vastly superior films in the years to come.

A word must be said about Bebe's social life in New York City. While she was in Los Angeles, the first several years of the 1920s were anything but "Roaring" to the young Daniels. Once in a different environment (New York), she became a more visible public figure, often dancing or dining out—or even paying a visit to the local speakeasy.[14]

It was also in New York that Bebe happened to come across an old friend dating back to her earliest days of stardom: her former leading man, dance partner and lover, Harold Lloyd. Following their split, both in work and in love, the two had developed what Lloyd called a "real and deep friendship,"[15] so it comes as no surprise that the former sweethearts spent much of their time in the city together. Bebe later recalled acting very much like a tourist with Harold, saying, "We went to Grant's Tomb, Wall Street, and of course Broadway."[16]

Their time spent together came just during the months leading up to Harold's February 10, 1923, marriage to his second leading lady, Mildred Davis. While there is no reason to doubt the platonic nature of Harold and Bebe's relationship (and the former's devotion to his bride-to-be), their time spent together became fodder for media speculation. One interviewer, noting that Bebe's apartment was "flooded" with flowers, mused about the sender's identity. He concluded his feature on Bebe by stating, "The floral mystery was partially cleared up in my mind, however, when Bebe casually let drop the news that Harold Lloyd was also in New York, 'seeing'—Bebe claims—'the new shows.' Authorities differ."[17]

Also amongst Bebe's New York acquaintances were the Broadway duo Fred and Adele Astaire. Long before his famed pairings with Ginger Rogers, Fred and his sister were perhaps best known for their roles in Jerome Kern's *The Bunch and Judy* around the time of their acquaintance with Daniels. Fred would later recall the following about their time together:

> It was summer,[18] hot. When Adele and I had finished filming for the day, we used to pick up Bebe and we'd all drive through Central Park in an open horse-drawn cab. It was all a bit like those Central Park settings of romantic movies, and on the way we filled an ice bucket with bottles of soda pop. I can see us now—cooling off in the heat, drinking our ice cold soda pop—singing, laughing.... They were great days."[19]

Bebe developed many other high-profile friendships. There were murmurings that she was romantically linked to John Gilbert (a number of other starlets were also said to be dating "the great lover of the silver screen"[20]), as well as a long-standing friendship with William Randolph Hearst and Marion Davies. Bebe remained close to Davies for much of her life, and the two shared a mutual companion and advocate in Louella Parsons.

Although Bebe told several stories about Hearst and Davies in *Life with The Lyons* (including her visits to Hearst Castle), one humorous story recounted by Marion Davies demonstrates perfectly the playful nature of their friendship:

> Bebe Daniels and I were very good friends. She said, "I can sew." And I could sew, too. So she said, "I'll bet you can't sew a dress."
> I said, "I certainly can."
> She said, "I'm going out the night after tomorrow, and I'd like to have a white satin dress with some sort of a long fringe. Something that looks graceful."
> I said, "Have you got a pattern?"
> "Don't tell me you work by pattern? I thought you could make dresses."
> "I used to, when I was a youngster. I used to make my dolls' dresses."
> "Well, that was very good training. If you can make a doll's dress you can make anything." So I really worked on it, like mad. I got it all ready for her and I sent it down. I didn't know if she wore it or not, but the very next day a dress arrived from her with a note. It said, "Thanks very much for the white satin dress. I wore it and it was a great success. So here's one I made for you last night, when I came back from the party."
> It was the most spectacular gown, with rhinestones sewn all over it. I thought she must have stayed up all night. Then I saw a label: I. MAGNIN AND COMPANY.
> I called her up and said, "I hope you feel all right after working so hard after the party."
> She said, "Well, I came home from the party at one o'clock."
> "What happened? Did the dress I made for you fall apart?"
> She said no. She said, "I worked on yours from two until the wee small hours of the morning."
> I said, "I'm sure. You sewed all those spangles on by hand?"
> She said yes.
> I said, "Did you sew the I. Magnin label on, too?"
> She said, "What??!! I've been loused up."[21]

Such was the whimsical, free-spirited nature of Hollywood in the 1920s—perfectly suited for Bebe Daniels' own *joie de vivre*.

# 12

## Romping Back into Comedies

> *If a modern song of blue skies, joy and merriment were to turn into a human being its name would probably be Bebe Daniels.* —1925 Paramount Studios advertisement

A brown-eyed girl in her early twenties entered the lobby of the Biltmore Hotel in New York sometime during the early months of 1925. She timidly approached the front desk and, after some hesitation, told the concierge, "I want a job as telephone operator." She said her name was Betty Clay.

The hotel staff asked about her qualifications and experience. She had none. Somehow, though, she got the job, and the following morning, she began work.

Betty initially held her own amidst the other operators. They were quick to grow suspicious, however, when their coworker began receiving orchids from unnamed admirers. Perhaps the biggest red flag that Betty was not actually what she seemed to be: She was seen leaving work in a limousine.

What no one realized—or, more likely, what the hotel coyly turned a blind eye to—was that Betty Clay, telephone operator for only three days, was none other than Bebe Daniels preparing for her next role. *The Crowded Hour*, filmed at Paramount Astoria, called upon Bebe to play Peggy Laurence, a telephone operator-turned-Red Cross worker who follows her love interest to France during World War I. *Photoplay* reported that the scheme to work as an actual telephone operator was "Bebe's own idea, and she certainly relished it."[1]

The source material for the movie was the Edgar Selwyn-Channing Pollock play of the same name, which had a 139-performance Broadway run beginning in November 1918. Given the warm reception to the play, particularly Jane Cowl's performance in the role Bebe would eventually play, anticipation for the movie was high.

However, *The Crowded Hour*'s plot—or lack thereof—was almost universally cited. The movie should have been "crowded with more plot and story," one magazine dryly mused. What may have worked on Broadway nearly a decade earlier clearly did not translate well to celluloid. Director E. Mason Hopper managed to salvage what he could from the limited source material, however, and the cast, particularly leading man Kenneth Harlan and ex-vaudevillian T. Roy Barnes, was well-received by critics. There were also accolades for the leading lady's performance. *Billboard* called it "one of the most excellent portrayals this reviewer has ever seen [Bebe] give,"[2] while *Photoplay* considered it "proof that she is equal to the demands of a big dramatic role."[3] These reviews are indicative of the frustration felt by many towards the vehicles Paramount was giving Daniels. Perhaps no review represents this viewpoint better than *Los Angeles Times* critic Grace Kingsley's desperate plea for better material for Bebe:

> If Bebe Daniels ever gets a really great story, she is going to become the screen's greatest actress.... Why don't those Lasky people turn Bebe loose to do her greatest in some great, world-famed story, instead of wasting her on even such above-mediocre things as this one? There is nothing she cannot do in the way of emotional acting. She proves it now. Every trace of the old self-consciousness has vanished. She has more dramatic fire than any other actress, even more than the fiery Pola.[4]

Such appeals to Lasky and associates would be met in due time. For the time being, however, Bebe's career continued to languish. *The Crowded Hour* was quickly followed with *The Manicure Girl*, a somewhat generic rags-to-riches story that finds Maria Maretti (Daniels) torn between a wealthy playboy and her own poor fiancé. Bebe was once again paired with director Frank Tuttle; it was their third feature together.

Bebe, who played the titular beauty parlor employee, was once again praised for her redeeming performance in an uninspired film. Tuttle's rapport with Daniels, undoubtedly built up during the filming of *Miss Bluebeard* and *A Kiss in the Dark*, helped her performance stand out in a film that was in many ways unremarkable. Years before he would direct blockbusters with Clara Bow and Bing Crosby, Tuttle was still finding his footing in Hollywood; like Bebe, he could not salvage a subpar script, and consequently *The Manicure Girl* is rightly forgotten amidst an otherwise remarkable filmography.

The film's many laughs and quick pace, though, were not enough to save it from being lost amongst a slew of other features. In 1925 Paramount was releasing full-length films at a rate of more than six a month, and despite Bebe's box office appeal, few of her films proved to be more than minor successes. In an exceedingly crowded market, the lack of adequate roles made it impossibly difficult for Bebe to rise above the crowd and achieve what many felt was her true potential.

*The Manicure Girl* was not a total loss, however, as marketing opportunities abounded for advertisers. "There's a Manicure Girl in every home where there's Glazo," read a series of advertisements produced by the nail polish company that were placed in 30,000 of Glazo's dealers nationwide. Some theaters offered moviegoers free manicures in their lobbies with the purchase of a ticket.

Amidst her moderate successes of 1925, Bebe found time to return to L.A. and enjoy her Los Feliz home for the first time. As the house had sat unoccupied (although lavishly furnished) since its acquisition, Bebe threw a joint homecoming and housewarming for Hollywood's elite. One of the attendees, popular gossip columnist Cal York, told his readers that the party had "all that warmth and conviviality that only Bebe knows how to manage."[5] Given her hospitality and penchant for event planning, it seemed a shame to many of her California friends that so much of Bebe's time was spent filming in New York.

Eddie Sutherland's early life was remarkably similar to Bebe's. Born of an actress and a stage manager, he began his screen career during the heyday of slapstick, the mid–1910s, as a Keystone Cop. The two were products of the same early era of Hollywood, cut from the same cloth before the industry changed dramatically in the 1920s.

Possibly at the urging of Charlie Chaplin, Sutherland decided to focus on directing instead of acting. Bebe and Eddie's paths crossed when he was selected by Paramount to direct her in his second feature film. (His first, *Coming Through*, featured his uncle Thomas Meighan and Lila Lee.) Sutherland went on to receive acclaim for directing W.C. Fields and Wallace Beery, so for Sutherland and Daniels both, *Wild, Wild Susan* proved to be little more than a stepping stone towards greater heights.

A convoluted story adapted from a *Liberty Magazine* short story, *Wild, Wild Susan* stars Bebe as Susan Van Dusen, a New York socialite who applies to a detective agency to add excitement to her monotonous life. She falls in love with novelist-turned-taxi driver Tom Waterbury (Rod La Rocque), who has the detective agency offer Susan a reward for tracking *him* down (knowing it will prove impossible as he himself is in hiding). Through a series of twists and turns that find Susan in an abandoned house with a gang of criminals, she learns that the entire incident was a charade arranged by her family to bring her and Tom together.

While by no means a hit, *Wild, Wild Susan* was met with substantially more praise than her previous films. Noted humorist "Bugs" Baer penned the movie's titles, which many critics complimented. Sutherland, though inexperienced, exhibited a directorial skill beyond his years, and he quickly became a staple at Paramount Astoria studios.

Amidst a slew of contemporaneous blockbusters, including Mary Pickford's *Little Annie Rooney* and Erich von Stroheim's *The Merry Widow*, it is surprising that *Wild, Wild Susan* managed to garner any attention at all. Bebe was involved in a number of thrilling stunts that elicited coverage in the papers, including a jump from the SS *Leviathan* to a gangplank as the ocean liner drifts away from the dock. *Photoplay* considered it one of the best releases of the month and *Motion Picture News* called it "beauteous Bebe at her best."[6] But Hollywood's former "Good Little Bad Girl" would now need more than cheap thrills to be a hit.

In the 1920s plastic surgery was still very much in its infancy, often reserved for disfigured World War I veterans. The belief that cosmetic surgery could (and should) be used for matters purely aesthetic was not widely held, and as such the majority of people who underwent such procedures were careful to hide the truth. Debates were raging over appropriate skirt and hair lengths; to a public that was still largely conservative, the thought of unnecessarily doctoring one's own facial structure seemed utterly absurd.

It came as a shock, then, when it was announced that Bebe would be undergoing nasal surgery at the Jewish Hospital in Cincinnati. Within hours of the operation, she vehemently denied that the surgery "had for its object the correction of her nose."[7] Instead, she claimed that the routine surgery was merely to remove a small growth in the nasal cavity. Although the news that her surgery was medical rather than cosmetic was widely reported, few people were incapable of seeing through her blatantly fictitious façade.

Dr. Samuel Iglauer, who operated on Bebe, was well-known for his nasal reconstructive surgery. (A year and a half later, he performed almost the exact same procedure on Mae Murray.) So ubiquitous was his name with regards to plastic surgery that the humorous word "Iglauerizing" was invented to describe "a transformation of the nose."[8] His involvement in Bebe's surgery was a definite indication that her "nasal growth" story was merely a cover.

Photographs of Bebe before and after May 1925 show a definite change. Just what compelled her to have her nose "bobbed and made shorter[9]" is unknown. (As one writer crudely phrased it, she "had her Hittite nose Grecianized by plastic surgery in the interest of her art."[10]) Perhaps changing standards of beauty in the notoriously superficial 1920s convinced her that plastic surgery was necessary to grow in popularity. Negative sentiment towards the surgery never materialized, and within days the majority of moviegoers had already forgotten the entire story.

"The elevator sequence in *Wild, Wild Susan* is one of the funniest things I ever did," Bebe told an interviewer shortly after the film's release.[11] "Susan runs the elevator up and down, and doesn't know how to manage it." The newspaper feature opened with a line that certainly seemed shocking to anyone who had followed Bebe's career: "Bebe Daniels is going romping back into comedies."

Prior to this, Bebe had repeatedly expressed her preference for drama over comedy. She had abandoned her leading man and romantic interest Harold Lloyd in favor of a dramatic contract with Cecil B. DeMille. She was vociferously critical of her Realart output when awarded dramatic roles with Paramount. After the success of *Monsieur Beaucaire*—which proved that she had the talent necessary to share the screen with someone like Valentino—it seemed unlikely that Bebe would ever transition *back* into trite comedies.

But here she was—in the *Los Angeles Times*, no less—declaring to the world that "the majority of pictures which I make hereafter ... will be gag comedies." It seems almost impossible to imagine that this decision was made by Bebe herself; certainly there was pressure from Paramount higher-ups coaxing Daniels to return to her roots.

Her next feature, *Lovers in Quarantine*, carried this new philosophy to an extreme—for better or for worse. According to one reviewer, the movie was made "on the principle that if the 'gags' are good, the plot or direction does not matter."[12] "Absolutely the most entertaining picture in which fascinating Bebe Daniels has flashed her winsome smile up-to-date,"[13] read another. The film's heavy reliance on gag comedy was looked upon as a refreshing "return to form" for Bebe, who knew how to make audiences laugh whether she liked to admit it or not. The story finds impulsive Diana Gordon (Bebe) falling in love with Tony Blunt (Harrison Ford), who in turn is in love with Diana's older sister Pamela (Eden Gray). While Tony plans to elope with Pamela, he doesn't count on Diana's intervention. Eventually the two find themselves quarantined on a steamer, where they acknowledge their love for one another and are formally engaged.

*Lovers in Quarantine* was the last pairing of Bebe with Frank Tuttle, whose impact on her career should not be understated. While far from her best comedies—those were still to come—their work together nevertheless paved the way for Bebe's comedic triumphs in the coming years. To reach her true potential, however, Bebe would need a new director with a fresh vision for her films. She would meet such a director early the following year: Clarence G. Badger, the man who perfected female-fronted silent comedies.

Before her first film with Badger, however, Bebe would finish 1925 by once again working with William C. DeMille, director of *Nice People* and *The World's Applause*. Although not nearly as renowned as his brother, William was a formidable director and writer in his own right. For *The Splendid Crime*, he took on every aspect of the film—from writing and production to direction and even subtitling—by himself. And to help make his picture a success, he called upon an actress who he "long ago believed possible of great dramatic achievements,"[14] Bebe Daniels.

Produced under the working title *Magpie*, this crime melodrama was a change of pace for Bebe. While some critics chose to praise DeMille's adept direction, others decried the serious tone of the movie (which, while not without some humor, was nevertheless a drastic departure from *Lovers in Quarantine* and *Wild, Wild Susan*). Bebe plays Diana, a beautiful young burglar set straight by the young millionaire she is attempting to rob. Diana is able to redeem herself by taking the blame for said millionaire's crimes, and eventually they make good to one another. Neil Hamilton and Anne Cornwall play Bebe's victims, and were heralded as leading a strong supporting cast.

The only constant through much of Bebe's career, it seems, was the public's clamoring for better starring vehicles. "Few cinema talents for comedy have been so consistently wasted as those of Miss Daniels,"[15] one writer said of *The Splendid Crime*. When Bebe was in dramas, people wanted her in comedies. When Bebe was in comedies, people wanted her in *better* comedies. All Paramount had to do, it seemed, was listen to the pleas of moviegoers and critics alike. Eventually they would get their wish.

Bebe Daniels' life behind the scenes at Paramount was just as fascinating as her time in front of the cameras. Although not often recounted today, Bebe was one of the few women at the studio who was granted control of her own film production unit. The announcement, made by Jesse Lasky at the end of 1925, read as follows:

### Bebe Daniels to Head Own Unit

Bebe Daniels is to head her own producing unit to make big feature comedies for Paramount, under the terms of a new agreement announced last week by Jesse L. Lasky. The arrangement is designed to provide Miss Daniels with facilities for the full expression of her gift for comedy.

The organization which she will head as star is now being assembled at the Paramount studios in Long Island. The unit will have special scenarists as well as comedy constructors or gag men. Her first work under the new regime will be *Miss Brewster's Millions*.

**Bebe Daniels and Neil Hamilton in *The Splendid Crime*.**

**A mid–1920s postcard depicts Bebe Daniels's home in the Los Feliz neighborhood of Los Angeles.**

> In announcing the formation of the Bebe Daniels unit Mr. Lasky said: "Miss Daniels is the foremost comedienne of the screen and Paramount is going to take full advantage of her unequalled ability. We are completing plans that will place her comedy productions on a plane with those of the outstanding male stars who have forged to the front ranks in this particular field. She has proved her worth as a dramatic actress as well, but she so easily excels as a comedienne and the demand for comedies with a feminine star so great that it would be inexcusably poor business not to make this move. Hector Turnbull, associate Paramount producer, will he in charge of the unit."[16]

Even at the peak of their fame, neither Louise Brooks nor Clara Bow, Paramount's other top-grossing female stars, were awarded the luxury of their own production unit. In an era before female studio executives, this made Daniels one of the highest-ranking women at Paramount. In future discussions of feminism in early Hollywood, Bebe's remarkable prominence during the second half of the 1920s must be explored more fully.

# 13

# Engagement Rumors

> *Bebe Daniels is the sort of person [we] would unanimously brand as a "good egg." She's entirely free from that painful air of great importance, and unlike many of her profession, does not, upon meeting you, take a deep breath and begin, "Now at the age of five, I had been a pronounced success for nearly twelve years, etc., etc., etc."*
> —Atlanta Constitution, July 19, 1925

Marriage rumors once again began swirling around Bebe late in 1925. It was in October of that year that famed writer Michael Arlen traveled from England to Hollywood to try his hand at screenplays. Quickly the two were linked romantically by the press after they were seen attending such events as the premiere of King Vidor's *The Big Parade*.[1]

Arlen, born in Armenia, moved to England as a child; his writing career began there. His 1924 novel *The Green Hat*, immensely successful, made him something of a celebrity. It was with this newfound fame that he began traveling to America. His first trip to Hollywood was met with excitement from the media nationwide. Upon his arrival, he nearly immediately took up an intimate friendship with Bebe.

Daniels and Arlen's inner circle of friends included Mr. and Mrs. Frank Borzage, Pola Negri, Charlie Chaplin and Rudolph Valentino.[2] At a gathering arranged by Arlen, it was noted that Bebe "was easily the best dancer there—and that of course is saying a tremendous lot."[3]

Soon the press began predicting a wedding, with one particularly flowery *Los Angeles Times* article bearing the headline "Michael and Bebe to Wed, Rumors Say."[4] While recognizing that hard evidence may be lacking, the writer ensures that "the fact is clear that Michael Arlen escorts the adorable Bebe very often," a sure sign of his impending marriage to the "dark-eyed beauty of Cinemaland."

As with most Hollywood gossip, the marriage never happened. Arlen's time in America was always short, and by the end of 1925 the couple's names were no longer linked together. Years later, Bebe described their romance as a case of "love at first sight," before confessing that "he needed the loving care of a mother, not a wife."[5] Their relationship is nothing more than a footnote in either of their lives.

George Barr McCutcheon's 1902 novel *Brewster's Millions*, about a man who must spend a million dollars within a year in order to earn an even larger inheritance, lends itself well to the silver screen, as evidenced by the numerous adaptations made over the years. Bebe's version, fittingly retitled *Miss Brewster's Millions*, was the third cinematic adaptation of the story, following one by Cecil B. DeMille and one starring Roscoe "Fatty" Arbuckle.

The storyline was perfect for the types of light comedies that Bebe was quickly cornering the market on. Paramount added veteran director Clarence Badger to the project, and the result was a Bebe Daniels film almost indistinguishable from her other projects at this time. Some felt it had "been a long time since Bebe Daniels had such a pleasant picture,"[6] while other critics found the movie on a par with her Hal Roach two-reelers in terms of its silliness and disposability.[7]

Production of the film resulted in one of her numerous on-the-job injuries, as described in *Photoplay*:

> Bebe Daniels was saved from serious injury the other day by her hair.
> Not by a hair's breadth, however, but by her luxuriant crop of black hair. Her latest picture—a female version of *Brewster's Millions* with Bebe as Miss Brewster who crashes into pictures—called for her to do some daredevil stunts that made her Lloydian exploits, in the days when she and Harold appeared together in comedies, diminish in proportion to the value of the mark.
> Bebe wouldn't have a double. When the script called for her to transfer from a speeding motor to a bicycle, Bebe did. But the bicycle swerved and Bebe landed on her precious head. After first aid was given at the Lasky Hospital, Bebe was taken home where she remained for several days before returning to the pictures.[8]

Even in the her least serious roles, Bebe was uncompromising in her devotion to the craft of acting. It seems merely a stroke of luck that none of her injuries amounted to anything serious.

Another notable event took place during the filming of *Miss Brewster's Millions*, this one humorous. As part of her wanton spending to earn her larger inheritance, Miss Brewster purchases a worthless movie studio—which, for the purposes of the movie, was simply Paramount's studio on Sunset Boulevard redressed as "The Excelsior Studios." Several people, allegedly, were confused at the appearance of such a substantial new studio seemingly overnight.[9]

While not her best work by any means, the pairing of Clarence Badger and Bebe proved to be significant. Over the next several years Badger directed Bebe seven more times, culminating with some of her most critically acclaimed movies. Although he is mostly remembered for *It* and *Red Hair*, his blockbuster collaborations with Clara Bow, the impact that the director had on his other subject through 1928 proved invaluable.

*Miss Brewster's Millions* was followed very quickly by two of Bebe's more sensational productions, *The Palm Beach Girl* and *Volcano!*. She was working at breakneck speed with Paramount; since the dissolution of Realart, she had made 22 pictures in four years. Although she maintained her residences in Los Feliz and Santa Monica, Bebe was spending much of her time in New York—while filming at Paramount Astoria—and on location, as more and more of her films called for exotic locales.

Announced at the end of 1925, *The Palm Beach Girl* became one of Paramount's most anticipated movies. Bebe left Los Angeles in February 1926 to begin work on the production; amongst those who gathered at the train station to bid her farewell were Jack Pickford, Warner Baxter, Ford Sterling, Anna Q. Nilsson, Betty Compson and Pauline Garon.[10]

## 13. Engagement Rumors

Before traveling to Palm Beach to film the exteriors, Bebe first returned to New York to shoot at the Paramount studio. Production evidently progressed very rapidly: The movie made its debut on May 17, three months almost to the day after filming had commenced. The male lead was Lawrence Gray, who had received his big break the year before when he starred opposite Gloria Swanson.

The plot was as simple and trite as had come to be expected from Bebe's films. She plays Emily Bennett, an "irrepressible imp from Iowa"[11] visiting relatives in Florida. Bennett manages to overcome her fear of the water with a speedboat owned by Jack Trotter (Gray). The climax features a hapless Bebe, alone in Jack's boat, speeding across the finish line—not only winning the race she unknowingly found herself in, but also winning the heart of the boat's owner.

"This isn't the best picture Bebe Daniels has had—but it's lively and entertaining, and you'll like the cast,"[12] said one critic. The sentiment was echoed across the country—poor material, to be sure, but Bebe did what she could to save it from being a total disaster. It was a common tactic for studios to waste their worst material on their biggest stars, knowing that their drawing power alone could make the films successful.

*Volcano!*, released the following month but filmed before *The Palm Beach Girl*, received similarly tepid reviews. The plot seems bizarre by today's standards: Zabette de Chavalons (Bebe), a French girl, integrates herself into Martinique's native population. She falls in love with Stéphane Séquineau (Ricardo Cortez), but the two cannot wed as a mixed marriage would be detrimental to his reputation. Finally, against the backdrop of an exploding volcano, he learns of her true French heritage and the two end up happily together.

*Volcano!*, shot during September 1925, marked Bebe's long-awaited return to Paramount's Hollywood studios after a two-year absence in New York. It was during this hiatus that she was called back to New York for *The Palm Beach Girl*, presumably during *Volcano!*'s laborious post-production.

This delay in production was caused by the one factor that made *Volcano!* such a spectacle: the volcanic explosion itself. "Enough to send any audience out talking about the picture," one reviewer wrote, and featuring sets that "stand up with anything DeMille ever did."[13] Furthermore, the sequence was hand-tinted, showing the eruption of Mount Pelee in "natural colors" and increasing its dramatic effect on the audience. Bebe's films were typically without large pageantry; director William K. Howard, at the beginning of his legendary career, decided to pair the star with special effects worthy of her dynamism. The result brought *Volcano!* more exposure than most of her films until that time.

During the mid–1920s, college films were all the rage in Hollywood. The prototype was Harold Lloyd's 1925 feature *The Freshman*, which was immensely successful and paved the way for similar movies. These productions, which invariably emphasized athletics over academics, soon flooded Hollywood. Clara Bow starred in *The Plastic Age*, George Walsh in *The Kick-Off*, Richard Dix in *The Quarterback*, Red Grange in *The Halfback*, Rod LaRocque in *Brave Heart* and Buster Keaton in *College,* to name a few. Playing off of stereotypes of the football star in his letterman jacket and the sorority girl cheering him from the sidelines, these pictures represented easy money for studios and cheap thrills for audiences.

With this phenomenon so prevalent in Hollywood, it seems fitting that Bebe's next picture would be called *The Campus Flirt*. Her leading man was newcomer James Hall, billed as one of the most promising young actors to grace the screen in quite some time. Although his career would prove to be limited, *The Campus Flirt* marked the first of five screen pairings between he and Bebe.

Patricia Mansfield (Daniels), the spoiled daughter of aristocrats, must fend for herself at the archetypal Colton College. Along the way she faces the dual challenge of winning the affections of her love interest (Hall) and helping her school win a track meet. Her coach was played real-life track star Charley Paddock.

While the majority of college pictures were being shot at the University of Southern California (due to its stately architecture and proximity to Hollywood), most of *The Campus Flirt* was filmed at the University of California, Berkeley. Titles were drawn by famed cartoonist Rube Goldberg. The film is also notable as the first screen appearance of vaudeville star El Brendel.

*The Campus Flirt* received fairly positive reviews and proved to be one of Bebe's biggest box office draws to that point—although it was noted that the film was a guaranteed success "for no other reason than its star appears in running pants."[14] Bebe's athletic attire, as well as a competent production team headed once again by Clarence Badger, made it a safe bet for Paramount.

While filming *The Campus Flirt,* Bebe "fell in love" once again—not with co-star Hall but with her "coach," Charley Paddock. At a time when newspapers were starved for any trace of romance in Bebe's life, the sudden news of the couple's engagement made national headlines.

Paddock was born on August 11, 1900, in Gainesville, Texas, only a short distance away from where Bebe was born six months later. Raised in Pasadena, he served in the Marines during the First World War, then became one of the world's most famous track stars. Claiming both the 100- and 200-meter titles at the 1919 Inter-Allied Games, Paddock achieved worldwide fame—and the title of "the fasted man alive"—when he claimed two golds and a silver at the 1920 Olympic Games in Antwerp, Belgium.

Although less successful four years later in Paris, Charley was still a major pop culture figure—and given his all-American good looks, it made perfect sense for him to try his hand at motion pictures (like so many other athletes at the time). His pairing with Daniels seemed serendipitous.

After only five weeks on set together, Bebe announced their engagement. *Motion Picture Magazine* ran a sentimental account of their romance:

> All the favorite bachelors of Hollywood have been running after Bebe Daniels for years. But it took a professional runner to catch up with her. You have all heard of Charlie Paddock ... after his triumphs in the West, it was inevitable that he would be offered a part in the movies, always hospitable to celebrated figures.
> 
> His first role was with Bebe in *The Campus Flirt*. He made the most of this and saw that Bebe got safely home from the studios every night without being way-laid by any of the aforementioned bachelors.
> 
> Then one day it rained. Charlie carried Bebe across a mud puddle to her dressing room. That settled it. Charlie, like Sir Walter Raleigh, knows how queens feel about mud puddles. And when soon after this he asked Bebe to marry him, she said she would.
> 
> The only thing that makes us skeptical is that Bebe insists upon a twelve months' engagement. Who ever heard of anyone staying engaged for a year in Hollywood? To the same person, we mean.[15]

While the story sounds about as believable as Jack Dempsey's run-in with a would-be suitor, the news itself was valid. In a statement to the press, Bebe called Charley "one of the finest men I have ever met," but explained that the wedding would not take place for at least a year due to prior commitments by both parties.[16]

Articles focused less on Bebe's choice of husband and more on the fact that *anyone* could win the affections of the "unobtainable" young star. Several failed engagements made many wary of the news, although the fact that news of the announcement came directly from Bebe gave it credence. Finally, it seemed, the Speed Girl would settle down—with none other than the fastest man alive.

*The Campus Flirt*, perhaps more than any previous picture, lifted Bebe to new heights of stardom. While not critically acclaimed by any means, it was financially successful enough that Jesse Lasky, through his West Coast operative B.P. Schulberg, tore up Bebe's original contract with the studio—still with two years left on it—and awarded her a new five-year contract. This agreement guaranteed Bebe higher-quality material (something many of her fans had been pining for) and ensured that she would remain one of Paramount's leading comediennes. Schulberg said,

[*The Campus Flirt*] has securely established Bebe Daniels as filmdom's outstanding comedienne. She has definitely proved that in high-class light comedy she has found her real forte, and it will be our purpose to continue to give her the best vehicles of this type that are to be secured anywhere."[17]

A portrait of a sporty Bebe Daniels on the set of 1926's *The Campus Flirt*.

By this point, Bebe must have known that her aspirations of becoming a respected dramatic actress were all but gone. The public had spoken with their pocketbooks, and the studio listened. Bebe was *funny*, they insisted, and Lasky and Zukor were determined to keep repeating the successful formula. This problem has plagued countless other actors and actresses throughout the years. Clara Bow, riding high on "It Girl" roles, tried to cross over into serious cinema with *Ladies of the Mob*, which was by most accounts a complete flop.

One other thing must be said about Bebe's new

contract: It guaranteed new pictures for Paramount through 1931. In 1926, a five-year contract seemed like a safe bet to everyone involved; after all, Hollywood had been booming since the teens, and the sky seemed to be the limit for stars and studios alike. Little did anyone expect that a Warner Bros. picture called *The Jazz Singer* would soon change the business forever.

Amidst the Paddock marriage rumors, news of her new contract and the release of *The Campus Flirt*, Bebe was awarded a rare vacation before abruptly being called upon to begin her next picture—the last under her old contract.[18] *Stranded in Paris* was based on the German novel *Jenny's Escapade* by Hans Bachwitz and Fritz Jakobstetter, published earlier that year.

Bebe was once again cast opposite James Hall to play Julie McFadden, an adventurous American shop girl who wins a trip to Paris. Along the way she falls in love, while also finding herself in a number of humorous predicaments that she must use her quick wit to get out of. Many critics were very favorable in their assessments of her performance, and it was said that the role of McFadden was "chosen to fit the personality of Bebe Daniels."[19] Ford Sterling also received praise for his supporting performance.

A ca. 1926 portrait of Bebe Daniels showing her fashionable bobbed hair.

*Stranded in Paris* was a high note to end the year on. Bebe, never one to rest, had already begun filming her next picture before *Stranded in Paris* had even been released. B.P. Schulberg announced in early November that her first film under her new contract was to be *A Kiss in a Taxi*.

Bebe had reached new heights in 1926. After her self-imposed departure from starring roles, she was rightfully receiving top billing once again. This was as much due to her own fame as it was to the relative anonymity of her leading men. No longer was she competing with the likes of Wallace Reid and Rudolph Valentino. Lawrence Gray, Ricardo Cortez and James Hall were all competent actors, but it was very clear that Bebe was the main attraction.

This, in turn, was part of a conscious effort by studios to separate male and female stars from their pictures. Why waste Bebe Daniels *and* Richard Dix, for example, on

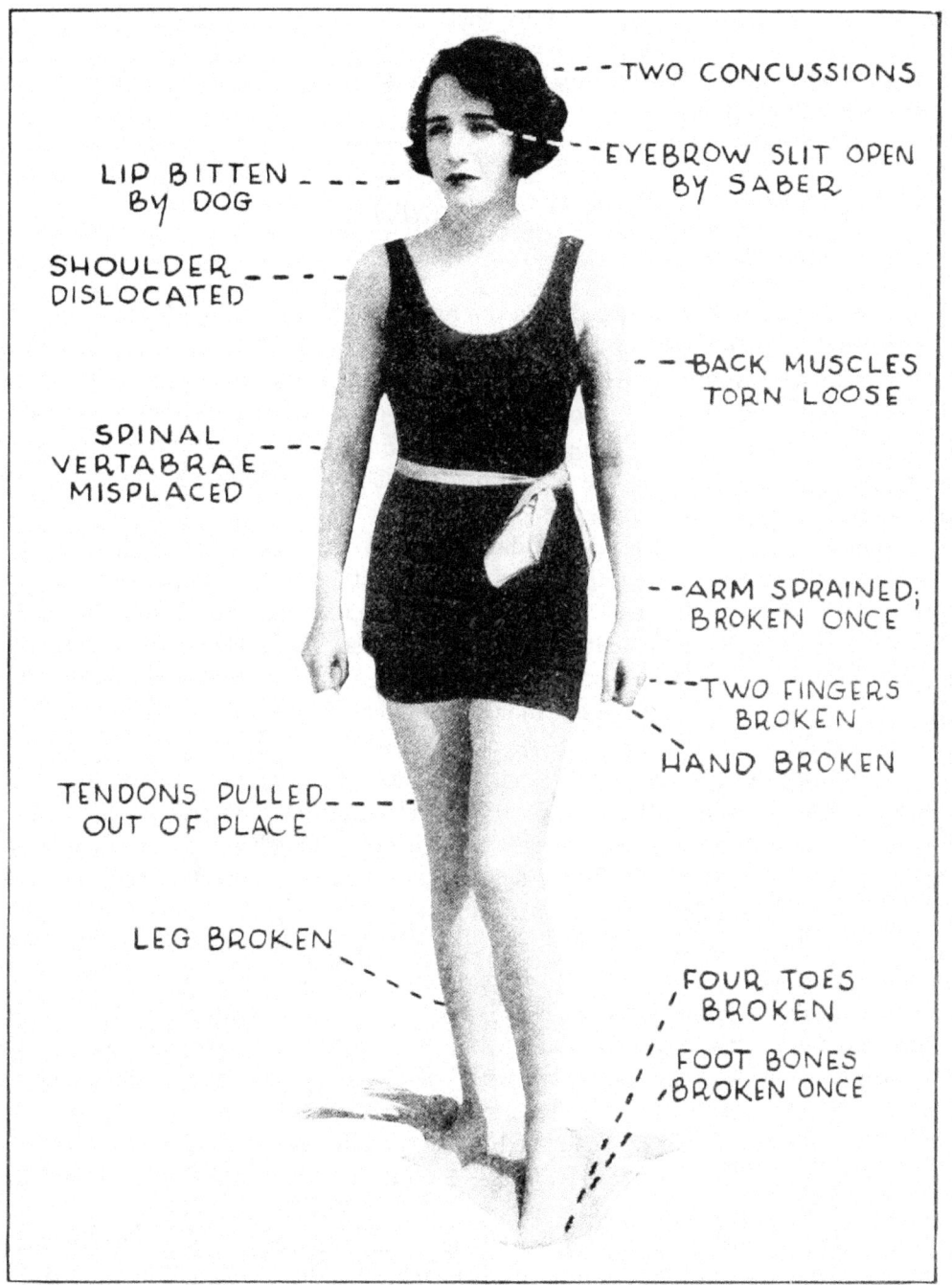

**This diagram documenting Bebe Daniels's numerous on-screen injuries appeared in *Photoplay* magazine in 1926.**

the same picture, when separate productions for both Daniels and Dix would hypothetically double the studio's profits? The same held true for all of Paramount's female stars—primary amongst them Bebe, Louise Brooks and Clara Bow—all of whom were almost exclusively paired with lesser-known actors from this point on.

New contract in hand and once again teamed with Clarence Badger (widely considered responsible for much of *The Campus Flirt*'s success), Bebe seemed poised to take over Hollywood in 1927.

## *Whatever Happened to Bebe Daniels and Charley Paddock?*

This question was undoubtedly on the minds of the 25-year-old's fans when the papers failed to produce any more news about the couple. The alleged engagement seemed to hold so much promise for the bachelorette Daniels—when would a wedding date be announced? Or, on the contrary, was the entire story a charade intended to drum up press for the forthcoming *The Campus Flirt*? In retrospect it certainly seems like it was, although as late as November of 1926, Charley confirmed the engagement (albeit reluctantly) to a newspaper reporter.[20]

What is difficult to understand today is how invested the public was in Daniels's personal life. Even her own mother would admit that "what the public wants to read about Bebe is that she is married."[21] Her innocent reputation, free from serious misconduct (the "speed girl" incident was amusing to most), made her a popular figure for masses of moviegoers to root for. Unlike a Barbara La Marr or Mabel Normand, Bebe was never linked to any front-page scandals, and the masses wanted nothing more than for her to find a nice husband and settle down.

Therefore, if her engagement to Charley Paddock was an orchestrated press stunt, it would almost guarantee that *The Campus Flirt* would be a major success for Paramount. Audiences, fueled by the thought that they could catch a glimpse of the future Mr. and Mrs. Paddock together for the first time, would flock to theaters in droves. And based on the success of the film, the plan worked.

That's not to say there was never any chemistry between Bebe and Charley. Years later, she would reflect that "out of our friendship grew a fine understanding which continues to this day."[22] However, as early as January of 1927, newspapers were very quick to inform the public that Bebe's affections were no longer directed towards the Olympian; instead, she was infatuated with one of Hollywood's most scandalous figures.

There exist few people in the entire history of Hollywood with a public perception more innocent and demure than "America's Sweetheart," Mary Pickford. Her brother, however, could not have been more different. Jack Pickford's entire life was addled by substance abuse (both alcohol and hard drugs), failed marriages, and other assorted scandals. Although a prolific actor in his own right, it is these scandals rather than his creative output that he is mostly remembered for today.

His evasion of military service during World War I almost earned him a dishonorable discharge, and his first marriage to former Ziegfeld girl Olive Thomas ended when the 25-year-old took a lethal dose of mercury bichloride in a Parisian hotel room (the official report said accidental overdose, but rumors persist to this day).

Jack Pickford's next unsuccessful marriage came to another of Ziegfeld's beauties—Marilyn Miller—in 1922. By all accounts abusive relationship from the start the couple separated four years later, but weren't granted a divorce until the end of 1927. The lack of a formal divorce did not prevent Jack from playing the field once again. It was under these circumstances that his name came to be linked with Bebe Daniels's.

Given Bebe's reputation, it seems baffling that she would chose to associate with a known alcoholic, drug addict, and wife-beater like Pickford. However, all signs pointed to *their* eventual marriage as soon as Jack and Marilyn's was terminated.[23] Once again the public buzzed at the thought of the beloved "Miss" Daniels finally becoming a "Mrs."

In June 1927—exactly a year after the filming of *The Campus Flirt*, where Daniels and Paddock first met—the *Los Angeles Times* ran the headline: "BEBE ENDS TROTH TO PADDOCK AS PICKFORD AFFAIR IS HINTED."[24] This was news to no one in Hollywood, although the presence of an official statement from Bebe's camp made her romance with Pickford seem more palatable than if she was still in limbo with Paddock. Serious talk of marriage between Pickford and Daniels once again filled the papers, with only one thing seemingly standing in the way—his marriage to Miller.

Meanwhile, in one of Hollywood's greatest twists of fate, Marilyn Miller was herself pursuing a serious relationship with a man she hoped to marry as soon as the divorce from Pickford was finalized. Her husband of choice? Ben Lyon—who had only met Bebe on several occasions at that point.

Curiously, news of Daniels's relationship with Jack Pickford faded from the public view as quickly as it had appeared. Perhaps it was all simply a rouse to provide an explanation for the end of Bebe and Charley's engagement (which, in and of itself, may have been a publicity stunt). While it certainly a cynical viewpoint to adopt, information about Bebe's personal life was a commodity to newspapers and movie magazines. News of her lovers proved good copy, increasing her stardom and box office pull. Paramount certainly knew this, and it is not beyond the realm of possibility that Bebe's private "affairs" were nothing more than orchestrations by the studio to get her name on the front pages.

Although Jack and Marilyn went to France to finalize their divorce, the couple returned with the marriage intact (for the time being, at least). Fortuitously, not only did this prevent Bebe from marrying Pickford, but it also stopped Marilyn Miller from pursuing her romance with Ben Lyon.

Bebe cryptically had this to say about the relationship: "Jack Pickford was romantic and generous when it came to sending roses but he was too practical and insisted on wearing overshoes and carrying an umbrella."[25] Indeed, if Jack's penchant for overshoes proved to be a deal-breaker, it may simply have never been much of a relationship to begin with.

While much has been written about Bebe's professional career, a word must also be said about her personal life during the Paramount years. Bebe the young girl was very similar to Bebe the actress, "[throwing] herself into everything she does so violently!" her mother once exclaimed.[26] Her hobbies, from reading to drawing to golfing, all shared one common trait—an intensity that Bebe exhibited from a very young age.

In 1925 Bebe's chosen form of recreation proved to be golf, despite the fact that she said she "despised" the sport only several years earlier. But whereas many young girls played golf for fun or relaxation, Bebe set her sights on becoming a champion. Competing for numerous amateur cups and spending every free moment of her time on the links, she was determined not just to be good, but to be the best.

As evidence of her impulsive nature, one man recalled the time he "sighted a girl standing in the middle of a muddy hole. Her skirt was torn and frescoed with mud—her shoes were smeared with mire—her hair blew in the breeze—and she was wielding her mashie with a persistent hand. It was Bebe."[27] Keeping in mind her tom-girlish upbringing and the way she threw herself entirely into anything she attempted, this story hardly seems surprising.

The next year saw Bebe revisiting her childhood love of horseback riding. As her mother told it, "she decided to be the best horseback rider in the world—until she got discouraged by reading about some woman who could climb under her horse and up onto the other side while he was galloping, and abandoned that for ukulele lessons."[28]

Another of Bebe's unsung talents was her artistic skill—noted by one interviewer early in her career when she showed him "some clever pen and ink sketches that reveal a decided talent."[29] During her last years in England, Bebe still kept a painting that she did as a young girl hanging on her wall, which she would proudly show to visitors.

All of these hobbies suggest a whimsical, childlike innocence in Bebe's personal life. Never jaded by her continually growing fame—or salary—Bebe threw herself into simple recreation much the way any young girl world. Perhaps it was her baptism by fire into motion picture stardom at the age of 14 that kept her frozen in a perpetual state of youth. Robbed of her teenage years as a "normal" girl, she instead waited until she had the means to make up for the fun she had missed out on.

Perhaps because of this, Bebe always had a particular fondness for children, and even when she was one of Paramount's top stars she would entertain young neighbors at her Los Feliz home. A writeup in *Motion Picture Magazine* opened thusly: "'*Visiting hours 10 to 11 a.m. Please meet in the patio.*' That's the neat little placard that hangs beside the bell on Bebe Daniels' beautiful Commonwealth Avenue home in Hollywood. But if you are over fourteen, you're out of luck, for you can't join the gay gatherings that take place in the Daniels' patio."[30] Her hospitality—and legendary three-layer cake—led to her acceptance as one of the neighborhood boys.

# 14

# Dashing Screen Star

*Beautiful Bebe Daniels fills a unique and very lucrative niche in exhibitors' programs. She is the only comedienne on the screen today who can at the same time supply laughs and "it"—a combination which the public loves.*
—Paramount's Program for 1928–1929

By 1927, Bebe was no longer the starlet she once was. While 26 was not old, per se, the fact that Bebe had broken into motion pictures so young gave people the impression she was older than she was. While her new contract seemed to guarantee starring roles until 1931, the coming year still served as something of a crucible for her. She was one of *the* most popular actresses, and her pictures were very successful commercially, but they usually fell short in the eyes of critics. No one doubted Bebe's talent as an actress; after all, she had been hand-picked by Cecil B. DeMille when she was still a teenager.

Bebe was desperately in need of high quality material to showcase her talent. *The Campus Flirt* came close, but films such as *Volcano!* and *The Palm Beach Girl* did little if anything to advance her career. Fortunately, 1927 would bring her just the roles she needed.

First, a word must be said about the year in general. Nineteen twenty-seven proved to be a watershed year for Hollywood. *Sunrise*, widely considered by many today to be one of the greatest films of all time, made both F.W. Murnau and Janet Gaynor stars, while *7th Heaven* paired the latter with Murnau protégé Frank Borzage. The science fiction epic *Metropolis* continues to captivate audiences with its remarkable special effects. Clara Bow conquered the box offices not only with *It*, her trademark movie, but with *Wings*—the picture that edged out *Sunrise* for the first Academy Award for Best Picture.

Many of the most popular silent movies in the 21st century were released in 1927, suggesting that the medium had reached an artistic—or at least commercial—pinnacle that year. And all of this before audiences could watch (and hear!) Al Jolson singing "Blue Skies" in October. With the exception of perhaps 1939, there exists no more important year in the history of Hollywood.

Although Bebe's output decreased from previous years (she had not released only four pictures in a year since 1923), the roles she did play helped validate her as both an adept actress and financial success. And while none of those four pictures rank amongst the top-grossing movies for 1927, they nevertheless represent the new heights being reached by directors, producers and actors alike.

Bebe began 1927 in the same city where she ended 1926: Paris. *A Kiss in a Taxi*, her second consecutive picture set in the City of Love, opened on February 22. It was adapted from the 1925 Broadway play of the same name, which in turn was adapted by Clifford Grey from the 1924 French play *Le Monsieur de cinq heures* by Maurice Hennequin and Pierre Veber. The Broadway version was a success, running for more than 100 performances. The Paramount production promised to capture the play's uniquely French character.

Following in the tradition of *The Campus Flirt* and hinting towards further flirtatious roles, *A Kiss in a Taxi* featured Bebe as Ginette, a French waitress whose kiss is a conquest for the poor young artists frequenting the Café Pierre. To ward of their advances, she throws glassware at them. She falls in love with Lucien (Douglas Gilmore), whose father forbids their marriage. After an incident at work, Ginette finds herself in a taxi with an unfamiliar gentleman, Lambert (Henry Kolker), who forces a kiss on her. After a confusing scandal with her new "lover," the situation is cleared up and she is reunited with Lucien. Also in the cast was famed silent comedian Chester Conklin, playing a wealthy character named Maraval (and receiving second billing under Daniels).

Reception was positive, although many critics noted that the film was inferior to the play. "From the first moment when a short-skirted Bebe appears," wrote the *Boston Daily Globe*, "throwing plates and wine glasses to protect herself from the kisses of her admirers, to the final scene when she wins Lucien and teaches a much-needed lesson to the worst 'chicken-chaser' in Paris, there are plenty of good laughs."[1] This seemed to be the film's reputation—a perfectly entertaining collection of gags, but not very cohesive on the whole. The film would, within a matter of months, be eclipsed by some of Daniels' greatest successes.

After conquering the track in *The Campus Flirt*, the athletic Daniels turned her sights to a sport that she already had propensity towards: horseback riding. Based on the French play by René Fauchois, *Mademoiselle Jockey* was one of Paramount's most heavily promoted releases at the start of 1927. Tom J. Geraghty, screenwriter of *Wild, Wild Susan*, adapted the play for the screen,[2] while Clarence Badger signed on to direct.[3] It had all the makings of a blockbuster.

Pre-production was so far along on *Miss Jockey* (as the film came to be known) that Paramount ran a full-page *Motion Picture News* advertisement promoting it. "You know Bebe," it read. "She's the one comedienne on the screen with 'it.' In *Miss Jockey* she's a madcap miss whose cradle was a saddle. How she takes the men and horses over the jumps! And wins the big race to save the lad she loves—and how!"

The story of a young girl riding horses from the time she could walk certainly calls to mind Bebe's adolescent years. Production was set to start as early as February 1927, when Paramount announced that *Miss Jockey* would be temporarily postponed in favor of *Señorita*. After the completion of *Señorita*, Bebe began work on *Swim Girl, Swim*, followed by *She's a Sheik*. The end of the year was fast approaching, and *Miss Jockey* was nowhere to be found in Paramount's lineup.

The reason for the film's eventual abandonment was never explained. Perhaps after running in *The Campus Flirt*, fencing in *Señorita* and swimming in *Swim Girl, Swim*,

Paramount felt that people had tired of Bebe's athletic prowess. Or it may be that the plot was simply too similar to the way she won Charley Paddock's love by winning a race. Whatever the case, all that remains of *Miss Jockey* today is a magazine advertisement intended to prime the public for yet another of the former Speed Girl's daring races.

*Advice to Lovers*, another announced title on Paramount's 1927 lineup, also never even entered production. With a script written by Samuel Hopkins Adams and Joseph Jackson, it would have starred Bebe as "a dashing debutante editing the lovelorn column."[4] A full-page magazine ad depicting Bebe in various sporty outfits provides more information about the film's proposed plot: "A brilliant comedy special with Bebe as a vivacious society girl taking the place of an old male fossil who runs the 'Advice to Lovers' column on a newspaper." This was, however, a time when films were often sold on titles alone, and contemporary advertisements are littered with films that were never actually produced. Just what advice Daniels would have provided to hopeful lovers will never be known.

Between 1926 and 1928, every film that Clarence G. Badger directed starred either Clara Bow or Bebe Daniels, Paramount's two leading box office draws. Studio executives knew that well-made vehicles for these two women would fare better than anything else they could offer, so it was of the utmost importance to find directors who could work with them. Badger, it quickly became apparent, fit the bill perfectly.

His style was unique in its simplicity. Unlike the methodology of men like Frank Borzage and King Vidor, Badger was characterized by a straightforwardness that few other directors could match. Badger films were accessible to the masses, extremely easy to watch without having to do much thinking. Bow and Daniels were allowed to shine, without Badger's artistic vision interfering. Although he was never critically acclaimed, nearly every silent feature he directed was a commercial success—something much more important to Lasky, Zukor and Schulberg.

Badger knew exactly what the public wanted to see from Bebe and Clara, and he delivered it time and time again. By directing her in exciting, vibrant pictures that appealed to the youthful spirit of the Jazz Age, he was perhaps the single most important figure in Bebe's resurgence. Following the dour *Monsieur Beaucaire* and the utterly forgettable *Miss Bluebeard*, Daniels' career appeared to be out of gas. Within two years, she was nearing the pinnacle of her success.

While Badger's impact on Bebe's career was important, credit must also be given to Lloyd Corrigan. Now best remembered for his directing and acting, Corrigan began his career as one of Paramount's leading screenwriters. Of the dozen films he wrote for the studio between 1926 and 1928, Badger directed ten (and of these ten, Bebe starred in eight). Whereas Badger was the great populist director of the silent age, providing accessible pictures to the masses, it was Corrigan who had his finger on the pulse of the movie going public. Badger knew how to make a successful picture if handed a good script—which is exactly what Corrigan knew how to write.

For Bebe's next feature film, Paramount decided to retread old ground. "Splash!" read the newspaper advertisements. "She's in again! Speedy Bebe in a laugh-a-second, flashy action comedy—right in the swim!"[5] A college picture featuring athletic stunts, *Swim Girl, Swim* was by no means inventive, calling to mind *The Campus Flirt* (and the unproduced *Miss Jockey*). The announcement that Badger (who had directed four of Bebe's last seven films) would helm the project was further evidence that Paramount executives were playing it safe with this production.

The essence of *Swim Girl, Swim* did not differ greatly from *The Campus Flirt*. Bebe once again plays a co-ed, this time the awkward Alice Smith, who is wholly engrossed in her studies. Alice is known as "Bugs" to her classmates because of her fascination with entomology which she shares with Prof. Spangle (William Austin). At Dana College, where pretty girls abound, the unconventional Alice is unable to attract the attention of popular jock Jerry Marvin (James Hall).

To get Marvin's attention, she enters a channel-swimming contest despite her lack of ability in the water. Midway through the race she is rescued by Spangle's boat, which inadvertently takes her near the finish line. When the boat collides with another vessel, she is thrown into the water and "finishes" the race before her competitors.

Her seemingly incredible performance wins the affections of Marvin, who introduces her to the famed real-life swimmer Gertrude Ederle. (In 1926, Ederle became the first woman to swim the English Channel.) Gertrude begins training Alice, whose guilty conscience forces her to tell Jerry the truth. He rejects her and, in defiance, Smith enters another race. This time, with Ederle's expert coaching, she wins not only the competition but also her lover's hand once again.

Bebe Daniels (in white) in *Swim Girl, Swim*, with (from left) James Hall, Gertrude Ederle, and William Austin.

Ederle's addition to the cast was significant as it marked her first film appearance after her momentous feat the year before. Upon her return to America, she had been engaged in a series of public appearances on the vaudeville circuit; *Swim Girl, Swim* brought her to an even larger audience. The 1920s were an age where both athletes (like Babe Ruth and Jack Dempsey) and feats of endurance (like Lindbergh's flight) were celebrated like never before; Ederle's swim tapped into both cultural phenomena and instantly made her a household name. One critic noted that Ederle "actually gets applause when she makes her first appearance on the film."[6]

Reception to the film was almost unanimously favorable. "Never has Bebe ... been seen to better advantage than in *Swim Girl, Swim*,"[7] read one review which largely captured public sentiment. *The Campus Flirt* had introduced collegiate Bebe to the world; *Swim Girl, Swim* perfected this trope for her. Able to adequately transition between the roles of timid schoolgirl and dashing athlete, Bebe's wholesomeness made her perfectly suited to college pictures.

"Bebe Daniels seems determined to make a collection of dashing athletic characterizations,"[8] *Los Angeles Times* reporter Grace Kingsley wrote when *She's a Sheik* was first announced. Although the premise (and setting) differed greatly from *The Campus Flirt* and *Swim Girl, Swim*, the common feature Kingsley referred to was the physicality

From left, Phyllis Griffin Daniels, Bebe Daniels, and Eva de la Plaza Griffin in 1928. On the table is "Mr. Snoopy-Horse," one of the actress's numerous pets.

that all of Bebe's movies now shared. Every scenario she found herself in forced Bebe to run, swim or fight her way to the inevitably romantic conclusion. Bebe's unique style of comedy captured the fast-paced era's zeitgeist.

Whereas *Señorita* was a tongue-in-cheek homage to Fairbanks' swashbuckling roles, *She's a Sheik* drew from Valentino's *The Sheik* and *The Son of the Sheik* as inspiration. Bebe played Zaida, granddaughter of an Arabian sheik, determined to take a Christian husband. The object of her affections is Captain Colton (Richard Arlen), whom she has kidnapped with the intent of seducing him. Despite her best efforts Colton remains uninterested—until he finally submits to jealousy after seeing the advances of his foreign rival, Kada (William Powell).

Arlen, a bit player for six years, had recent risen to prominence with a co-starring role in *Wings*. Prior to the start of production on *She's a Sheik*, he had also appeared opposite Esther Ralston in *Figure's Don't Lie*, which added to his rapidly rising popularity. Powell, who first appeared with Bebe in *Señorita*, was cast as the villain, as was so often the case early in his career. Arlen and Powell would soon reprise their roles as Bebe's love interest and villain, respectively, in *Feel My Pulse*.

*She's a Sheik* was filmed at the Guadalupe Dunes in Santa Barbara County, several hours north of Los Angeles. A popular filming location, these very same dunes were also used by Cecil B. DeMille in 1923's *The Ten Commandments*. By all accounts, camaraderie abounded on set. In the evenings Arlen would impress the cast and crew with his cowboy rope tricks while Powell would perform sleight-of-hand magic. Bebe, it was observed, spent every free moment playing mumble-peg, the knife-throwing game so popular with schoolchildren of a century ago.[9] Always child-like in her innocence, she seems to have found a very compatible cast in this production.

A 1928 advertisement by the American Tobacco Co. depicting Bebe Daniels.

Bebe very quickly followed *She's a Sheik* with *Feel My Pulse*. Gregory La Cava, a prolific director of short comedies from the first part of the decade, was assigned the project; after several successful pictures with Richard Dix and W.C. Fields, he had become one of Paramount's go-to directors.

In *Feel My Pulse*, Bebe plays Barbara Manning, a hypochondriac sheltered from the real world. Finally she leaves the confines of her home to visit a sanitarium she has inherited, expecting to find peace and quiet for her perceived illnesses. It quickly becomes a running gag that Barbara is actually in impeccable physical shape. After being accompanied by an undercover newspaper reporter (Richard Arlen), she finds that her institution has been overtaken by bootleggers (led by William Powell). In the film's climactic battle scene, she holds the bootleggers captive with feats of amazing bravery and athleticism, thereby assuring herself that she is not as sickly as she once thought.

After a string of acclaimed films to close out 1927, *Feel My Pulse* opened with a whimper. The *Los Angeles Times* deemed the picture "not so good,"[10] blaming an absurdist plot and missed opportunities for humor. The *New York Times* agreed, asserting that the plot's possibilities "have been sacrificed for boisterous comedy"[11]—to decidedly mixed effect. Some publications were quick to point out that Bebe provided a number of legitimate laughs, but the vast majority agreed that the film was a big step down from her previous works.

*Feel My Pulse* is unique in being the only one of Bebe's late-era Paramount features to have seen widespread availability in recent years. Numerous companies have released it (with varying degrees of print quality), allowing a wide audience to experience Bebe at the height of her fame and creative output. While *Feel My Pulse* certainly wasn't her best film from the late 1920s, it is in many ways exemplary of her unique brand of production—a strong female lead unwittingly caught up in physical stunts, while at the same time managing to charm the male lead into loving her. It is by a simple stroke of luck that *Feel My Pulse* survives today while so many of her other, equivalent films are irretrievably lost. But rather than mourn the disappearance of so many Paramount silents, we should celebrate the fact that even one remains intact and readily available.

Although Bebe's career was punctuated by numerous injuries and accidents, one incident on the set of *The Fifty-Fifty Girl* brought her closer to death than ever before. The scene called for the interior of a Pullman coach to be recreated on the back of an open truck, thereby simulating the appearance of a moving train. While she was filming a love scene with co-star James Hall in Pasadena,[12] the top of the compartment got caught on a low-hanging branch, dislodging the entire structure and leaving "a mass of tangled wreckage."[13] Although the truck was traveling at a slow speed, the result of the accident was disastrous.

James Hall was thrown clear of the compartment, suffering only a fractured wrist, while Clarence Badger and his cameraman both walked away unscathed. The unconscious Daniels' injuries were clearly the worst of the lot, and she was rushed to the Pasadena Emergency Hospital. Badger later related that she "struck the pavement on her back as she was catapulted into the street," while "the heavy debris fell on top of her."[14] Dr. L.W. Skelton announced that the actress suffered from "a severely sprained back, possible internal injuries and a possible fracture in the pelvis region."[15]

Bebe Daniels with Richard Arlen in the 1928 feature, *Feel My Pulse*.

Her prognosis improved almost immediately. X-rays showed that she was free from internal injuries and broken bones, and that her most serious condition was her sprained back. She was transferred to the Hollywood Hospital to be closer to her home and her mother. From her hospital bed, she reflected on her injuries. "I guess it's all in a day's work," she said. "I figure it's part of the job. I am feeling much better now and am glad to get back to work."[16] Not even two weeks after she was nearly crushed to death, she was back at Paramount finishing *The Fifty-Fifty Girl*. "The word is that she donned her makeup with the good old Bebe enthusiasm which nothing can quench for long,"[17] one columnist noted.

A decade of being injured in the line of duty rightfully had a strenuous effect on Bebe. But rather than let it interfere with her creative output, she decided to turn her bad luck into a publicity stunt. Coinciding with the release of *The Fifty-Fifty Girl*, Bebe announced that she was searching for a unique good luck charm to help protect her from future on-screen accidents. Almost immediately she was receiving over 100 pieces of mail per day from admirers, each offering up personal talismans. The contest winner would receive either an evening gown, if female, or a finger ring, if male, from Bebe.

Some of the charms offered were nothing short of bizarre. "One Los Angeles woman sent in a tiny pin carved to represent the head of a kitten," the *Los Angeles Times* reported, while another "offered to let the star have the tiny skull of a sparrow, picked up in Scotland, which had brought the owner good luck for years. A veteran of the World War, who had gone through four years of fighting unscratched, sent in his precious pocket piece which he had carried for fifteen years."[18] Despite the vast amount of mail she was receiving, Bebe read each letter.

After 5,000 letters were received, the hard-luck actress announced that the contest was coming to a close. "I am amazed at the response," she said, "and overwhelmed at the amount of interest manifested in my welfare. They have been so gracious and sincere in sending the little tokens that it makes my work in selecting one very difficult."[19] Finally, the six-week contest came to a close when Lillian Callahan, a 15-year-old from Long Beach, was selected for her gift to Bebe. Her good luck charm, a "tiny emblem typifying the spirit of Christianity,"[20] was credited with saving her family's lives during a recent automobile accident. As promised, the girl received an evening gown the next day, personally selected by Bebe.

As the contest came to a close, Bebe graciously addressed the thousands of fans who had written to her. "If the kind thoughts they expressed to me in the letters have any potency for good," she said in a statement to the press, "those little imps of bad luck that have been chasing me for the last few years will never get within a hundred miles of the studio in the future."[21] Maybe the good luck charm worked, or maybe Bebe's roles became less physically demanding, but during her remaining time in Hollywood the actress would not suffer another major injury.

On May 12, in the midst of Bebe's superstitious publicity stunt, *The Fifty-Fifty Girl* was released. Bebe was pleased with the reception it received. Once again her high-energy performance was found to be thoroughly entertaining. The *New York Times* found the movie "amusing enough with comedy for the merry and with thrills for the nervous—and a happy ending for everyone."[22] Indeed, this line not only captures the essence of *The Fifty-Fifty Girl*, but the vast majority of Daniels' comedies from the late 1920s.

As Bebe's athletic pictures became more and more popular, the actress became something of a figurehead for physical fitness. Much like today's moviegoers look to actors and actresses for lifestyle advice, so too did silent film fans look to their favorites for guidance. It came as no surprise when Bebe's secret to her athleticism was demanded. But rather than supplying a miracle regimen or well-guarded workout routine, she replied simply and directly about her unassuming fitness habits:

> During the past year or so most of my screen productions have required an athletic type of heroine and I am asked constantly how I keep myself fit.
> Most of the questions concern my athletic endeavors between pictures for it is well known that, while a picture is actually in the making, a player must go through a training period similar to that of an athlete preparing for almost any line of sport.
> When I am not actually at work I do cut down exercise to a great extent with the belief that a good rest is very beneficial. However, during the summer, when I am at the seashore, I spend most of my spare moments swimming in the surf.
> I am under the impression that light exercise, taken regularly, is the greatest thing in the world for a woman's health. Just ten minutes a day, immediately upon arising in the morning and then again just before retiring will do wonders.[23]

*Hot News*, although not a story involving athletics, would nevertheless prove to be one of Bebe's most physically demanding movies. Originally announced as *The News*

*Reel Girl*, it was the last collaboration between Bebe and Badger, marking the end of a remarkable partnership that brought both parties universal success. It was also Daniels' first film with Neil Hamilton, who would co-star in her next two films as well. The original scenario was conceived by Monte Brice and Harlan Thompson; it was praised by Paramount executives for its unusual and whimsical nature.

Bebe stars as Pat Clancy, an aspiring camera operator for her father's newspaper *The Sun*. Unwilling to work with a camera girl, the paper's top cameraman Scoop Morgan (Hamilton) quits for a job at the rival *Mercury*. A heated rivalry between the two ensues, each vying for a scoop for their outlet. While covering a jewel heist, Pat and Scoop are kidnapped by James Clayton (Paul Lukas); when they are rescued, the two acknowledge their love for one another. The story was cliched yet amusing. It also embraced a feminist ideology that was only beginning to burgeon during the 1920s.

By its very nature, *Hot News* was primarily a collection of harrowing vignettes rather than a cohesive whole. The various news stories covered by Pat and Scoop provide the bulk of the movie's entertainment value. These distressing situations included "careening through the air in a breeches buoy, a sinking ship at one end of the line and her deadliest rival at the other, a fight with a jewel thief on his yacht at sea, a mad escape in a speeding automobile, a clash with a supersensitive rajah at a garden party and a love scene on the Statue of Liberty's eyelashes."[24] For an actress as physical as Daniels, the plot provided ample opportunity for stunts without concocting another sports story.

One particularly humorous scene involved 300 babies; every mother wants *their* child included in the newsreel, thereby sparking a mob scene. The movie's varied scenarios made filming very enjoyable for Bebe. In an interview upon the film's release, the actress

Neil Hamilton and Bebe Daniels embrace in 1928's *Hot News*.

declared, "Next to working in an ammunition factory, I think the most dangerous job in the world is that of a newsreel cameraman!" She continued:

> We are not apt to realize the great dangers these fearless men go through in order to get the scenes we see from our comfortable seats in the theater. They risk their lives in remote sections of the world, filming shipwrecks, erupting volcanoes, wild animals, airplanes, riots, and even scenes of great beauty from almost inaccessible places.
>
> Speaking of inaccessible places reminds me of a scene in *Hot News* which took Neil Hamilton, my leading man, and myself to the most hair-raising place either of us has ever been.
>
> We sat on the little finger of the Statue of Liberty, holding ourselves in position with one hand and grasping our motion picture cameras in the other! It was a great thrill for us, but I suppose that a real newsreel cameraman would have taken it as a matter of routine duty and thought nothing of it.[25]

*Hot News* was fairly well-received, with the major caveat that its plot was "utterly implausible."[26] "One's immediate impression is to like this picture, despite an inability to believe most of the incidents which compose the hodgepodge of thrilling adventures,"[27] read one of the more complimentary reviews. But the critics almost didn't matter: Bebe was at the peak of her drawing power in 1928, and so long as she was presented in a sensational production, people would flock to see it.

# 15

# The End of an Era

> *Bebe Daniels, Paramount comedienne, is still squawking loudly in an effort to break her contract with the company and thus get out of making the three silent pictures she is scheduled to make under her present Paramount contract. Bebe wants to make "talkies," but B.P. Schulberg insists that she keep "silent" and fulfill her contract to make another trio of silent comedies.*
> —*Billboard*, December 1, 1928[1]

Before the inevitability of talkies became apparent, Paramount had big plans for Bebe into 1929. *Take Me Home* was announced as the first of four starring vehicles for her, each promised to be produced at great expense befitting an actress of her caliber. *The Fifty-Fifty Girl* and *Hot News* were just harbingers of her future accomplishments, Paramount was trying to say. Her greatest heights lay ahead of her. The motion picture industry was hers to conquer.

Few could have predicted how fact talkies would render silents obsolete—particularly not someone like B.P. Schulberg, who (because of personal interests) always favored Clara over Bebe anyway. Ultimately, only two of the four pictures promised to Bebe were produced before the company parted ways with their "unique and very lucrative" client. The coming year would prove to be the most strenuous and trying of Bebe's career. It would also prove to be the most triumphant, both professionally and personally.

But in May 1928, no one could have known that. All that was known was that Marshall Neilan was to begin directing Bebe in *Take Me Home* imminently.

Chorus girl Peggy Lane (Bebe) and Broadway star Derelys Devore (Lilyan Tashman) both fall for country boy-turned-actor David North (Neil Hamilton). The plot of *Take Me Home* was simple enough, and the cast was above-average. Bebe was paired with Hamilton for the second film in a row, Tashman proved an adept villainess, and Joe E. Brown led the supporting players. And while Neilan's style was drastically different from that of Clarence Badger, he did well by the story and its star.

When Peggy inadvertently thwarts Derelys' advances towards David, Derelys has her fired. The climax comes in a backstage confrontation between the two women in which Derelys is injured minutes before that night's performance. Peggy takes her place and wins not only the approval of the audience but also David's hand in marriage.

The somewhat cliched ending calls to mind Lloyd Bacon's 1933 classic *42nd Street*—only in that film, the roles are reversed and Bebe is no longer the up-and-coming

## 15. The End of an Era

youngster. However predictable it may have been, moviegoers and critics alike were generally positive about the film. Bebe "departs successfully from her usual acrobatics in this natural comedy of back-stage life," read *Photoplay*'s review.[2] It wasn't the typical fare people had come to expect from Bebe, but it was enjoyed nonetheless.

Midway through the filming of *Take Me Home*, Bebe came down with a serious case of influenza and production came to an immediate halt. She was admitted to the hospital for what was expected to be a week-long stay; it ended up taking her nearly six weeks to fully regain her health.

During her recovery, Bebe kept up a strange schedule. She would pass her days resting in her dressing room at Paramount and spend her nights under the care of a nurse at the hospital. "You see," Bebe explained, "that was the only way I could rest. As soon as people learned I was back at the studio, they began to call at my house in the evening to extend felicitations. It was almost a case of being killed by kindness."[3]

As the silent era came to a close, so too did Bebe's time as a bachelorette. But before she would actually settle down, she had one last lover to add to her ever-growing list.

Thomas Hitchcock, Jr., was born on February 11, 1900, in South Carolina. His father was a famed polo player and horse trainer, and Tommy Jr. quickly followed in his footsteps. After serving in World War I and attending both Harvard and Oxford, Hitchcock made a name for himself when he led the United States to victory in the International Polo Cup. He very quickly became to polo what Babe Ruth was to baseball, Bobby Jones to golf and Bill Tilden to tennis.

While Bebe was vacationing in New York in September 1928, the first reports of her engagement to Hitchcock were leaked to the press. Bebe, the papers remarked, was "starry-eyed and happy ... that she has said 'yes' to Tommy Hitchcock, Jr., who is equally as famous as she is."[4] At the time, Hitchcock was hard at work preparing for the first Cup of the Americas between the U.S. and Argentina and did not immediately respond to the rumors. For several days, the media had a field day with Bebe's latest engagement rumor.

Hitchcock in many ways embodied the Roaring Twenties (some claim he was the inspiration for F. Scott Fitzgerald's Tom Buchanan). He was in the same vein as All-American athletes Jack Dempsey and Charley Paddock and the match between he and Bebe certainly made sense: He was clean-cut, a war hero and Ivy League graduate who had mastered the most aristocratic of sports. He had an untarnished reputation—in contrast to his predecessor, Jack Pickford—and the proposed engagement was met with much rejoicing.

The media-savvy Bebe would not let such a rumor persist unless there was some truth to it and she cut short her New York vacation to return to Los Angeles. "It's all wrong," she told the *Los Angeles Times*. "Matrimony is just what I'm not thinking a thing about at the present time. So I have no prospective fiancés."[5] As for Hitchcock, the polo star led the U.S. to victory over Argentina and married Margaret Mellon only three months after his alleged engagement to Daniels.

By the end of 1928, the public was beginning to tire of Bebe's seemingly constant engagement rumors. Instead of the boy who cried wolf, Bebe was becoming the girl who cried marriage. Even when the rumors did not come directly from Daniels (as was the case with Hitchcock), she always seemed to let them linger just long enough to benefit from the free publicity before setting the record straight. Even Will Rogers applied his characteristic wit to Bebe's never-ending search for a husband:

> Our clever little movie star, Bebe Daniels, doesn't overlook many sporting events. On the eve of the international polo games here she has just denied that she is to marry Tommy Hitchcock. Just before the tennis match she denied an engagement to Tilden, and during the Olympics she publicly denied a betrothal to Charley Paddock. On Nov. 4 I hope she has the good judgment to refuse both Smith and Hoover, and when Christmas rolls around, if she is going to marry Santa Claus, why keep it a whispering secret.[6]

From Harold Lloyd through Tommy Hitchcock, the public wanted Bebe to find a suitable husband. But when the same news story broke time and time again, with only the love interest's name changed, it was a matter of time before people grew weary of Bebe's personal life. Fortunately, her next lover would prove to be the last.

The release of *What a Night!* marked not only the end of 1928, but also the end of a chapter in Bebe's life. The story has been told countless times: The advent of talkies mercilessly ended the careers of countless silent stars. Actors like Douglas Fairbanks and Clara Bow just couldn't adapt to the new format, and a new crop of stars took their places. It was a tumultuous, volatile time that reinvented the industry in immeasurable ways.

Bebe is often considered to be a near-casualty of the rise of talking pictures. After a remarkable string of commercial and critical successes in the late 1920s, Paramount, it seemed, simply had no more use for her. Bebe claimed that the studio was putting her in subpar productions, giving her little chance of recapturing her former glory. Paramount responded to this by saying that "her salary under contract was so big that they had to skimp on her pictures to make money."[7] A deadlock ensued, and ultimately Bebe needed Paramount more than they needed her.

B.P. Schulberg, as infamous as Bebe was famous, was responsible for her decline at the studio. It was his belief that in the future only Broadway stars would be able to adapt to talkies. Despite her pleas for a voice test, Schulberg continually refused to give her a role in a talkie. In the end, she was forced to buy out the last six months (and three movies) of her contract for $175,000. For the first time in her adult life, she was without a motion picture contract.

Some sources claim that Bebe was considered a "has-been"[8] by the time her Paramount contract was terminated. While she was certainly not at the height of her fame by the end of 1928, calling her a has-been is unequivocally untrue. In the 1929 edition of *Photoplay*'s annual popularity contest, she placed fourth behind Clara Bow, Colleen Moore and Billie Dove. Even past her prime, Bebe still finished ahead of Mary Pickford, Marion Davies, Joan Crawford and Greta Garbo.

Bebe was not so much a "has-been" but rather a victim of Paramount's cutthroat practices. Having been intentionally given subpar material to finish her silent film career, fans were under the impression that Bebe's career was waning because of her own ineptitude. The fact is that no actress of the late 1920s—even a Clara Bow or Louise Brooks— could have salvaged the films Paramount was producing. Bebe had not failed to transition from silents to talkies; her studio had decided that she did not have a future in Hollywood and purposely set out to make this true. It was a self-fulfilling prophecy, and one which would leave Paramount regretting their short-sightedness.

Just like the last time she had been without a contract (after leaving Rolin in 1919), Bebe began to panic. She wrote about being full of despair and hopelessness, a feeling that her mother shared. Although she tried to convince herself that a rest was much-needed, she still craved nothing more than to be back in pictures. All she wanted was a chance at a voice test, something which Paramount had never offered. Fortunately, she would not have to wait long.

William LeBaron, production head of newly founded RKO Pictures, asked Bebe to come to his office one day in early 1929. He knew Daniels from his time at Paramount, where he had seen all of her silent pictures with the studio. When she sat down to talk to him, he was very direct with his point: "Bebe, how would you like to sign with us for four pictures?"

Bebe was shocked. At that time, B.P. Schulberg was actively pursuing Bebe to come work for Paramount once again—not as an actress, but as a writer. Given her success heading her own production unit, this did not come as a surprise, but Daniels was convinced she had a future in front of the cameras.

"But, Bill," she replied, "Schulberg says I can't talk!"

LeBaron simply laughed.

"Don't you at least want me to take a voice test before I sign a contract?" she continued.

"No. If you want to take one afterwards for your own curiosity you can do it. But you don't have to do it for us."

And just like that, Bebe was back in the movie industry.[9]

At Paramount, Bebe had been contracted alongside stars such as Clara Bow and Louise Brooks and worked with such noted directors as Clarence Badger. At RKO, the caliber of talent was significantly lower. Daniels and former co-star Richard Dix led a lineup that also included Olive Borden, Sally Blane and Betty Compson (all respected actresses, but a far cry from Paramount's roster). It was not the same environment that Bebe had grown accustomed to working in. But RKO was willing to take a risk with her when no one else would, and she relished the opportunity.

Bebe Daniels and Ben Lyon first met in 1924. While in New York with her close friend, director Eddie Sutherland, the two were introduced at the Montmartre Cafe. Sutherland would often talk Bebe up to his male friends, while Bebe would do the same for Eddie amongst her female circle. It was in this innocuous way that Lyon entered Bebe's life.

At first, Bebe was far from impressed with Ben. "I recall now," she later wrote, "that I thought he was terribly conceited, and all he did was talk about himself and his next picture. Later on I found out it was the result of two things—enthusiasm, and his subconscious desire to impress people."[10] It was another two years before Bebe and Ben again crossed paths, this time in a Florida restaurant during the making of *The Palm Beach Girl*. Bebe encountered a heavily bearded Ben (he had grown it out for *Bluebeard's Seven Wives*) and did not recognize him as the "conceited" man she had met in New York City. He asked her for a dance, yet again he failed to impress her. Any hope Ben had to win over Bebe was put on hold until late in 1928, when the two again met in Hollywood. This time, the results were different.

# 16

# Mrs. Bebe Daniels Lyon

*Bebe Daniels, Star, to Become Bride: Engagement to Ben Lyon Is to Be Announced, Is Hollywood Rumor.*[1] —*Washington Post*, January 1929

Through much of 1929, the media focused heavily on the impending marriage between Bebe Daniels and Ben Lyon. Their engagement, the culmination of a decade of romances for Bebe, was looked upon favorably by many who felt that the all–American Lyon was a perfect match for her. Perhaps the most sensationalized coverage of the engagement came from *Photoplay*, who ran articles that epitomize the frenzy surrounding the announcement:

> The news of the engagement of Ben Lyon and Bebe Daniels has busted us all up, and we'll never be the same again—no, never!
> Whenever we needed a hot squib about the romance of a pretty heart-cracker we could always pin the yarn to Bebe.
> We've had her all but hitched to a dozen eligibles—Harold Lloyd, Jack Dempsey, Charlie Paddock, Jack Pickford and a dozen others.
> Now we have to quit.
> The Lyon angle is just as tough.
> Ben has been the real sheik of the lots, though we talked more about Rudy.
> Dozens of women have loved him, though he was never more than mildly ruffled. Barbara La Marr was very fond of him. Gloria Swanson is one of his best friends. Marilyn Miller certainly cared in a big way at one time, and we thought he was losing sleep over Marion Nixon.
> Now we are all wrong. Whenever we need an attractive bachelor now it will be Gilbert or Nils Asther. This is Warning No. 1.[2]

The next month, the magazine ran a follow-up containing specific details of their relationship:

> Ben Lyon and Bebe Daniels are going to tackle matrimony from a new angle. They are learning to make the necessary compromises before instead of after taking the vows.
> Bebe has always been a bridge hound, while Ben never cared a hoot about the game.
> But now he has bought every obtainable book on the subject, and is boning hard so he can make a fourth in the games around the old Lyon fireside.
> Bebe, not to be licked, is taking up flying, so that she can indulge Ben's hobby, too. As a matter of fact, she is actually taking up piloting.
> With this give and take spirit, the Daniels-Lyon marriage should not be one of these Hollywood flowers that bloom in spring, tra-la, and fade away in the fall, boo-hoo![3]

Although some were understandably wary of the news (after all, an extended engagement had been announced for Bebe and Paddock), it quickly became apparent that this time Bebe was serious. The couple were often seen together in public, and rather than deflecting interview questions she embraced her love for Ben straightforwardly. Following several phony relationships that proved to be little more than publicity stunts, Daniels went above and beyond to prove that this time her engagement was for real.

Based on newspaper headlines from the first half of 1929, one would be justified in thinking that Bebe was an aviatrix rather than a motion picture actress. Following the premature termination of her Paramount contract but before the massively successful release of *Rio Rita*, Bebe began to take flying just as seriously as her acting—if not more so.

Bebe and Ben quickly became two of the most public faces of aviation, and the newly engaged couple were often spotted at Southern California air meets. When Nevada Airlines began regular air service between Los Angeles and Reno, Bebe christened the company's first two Lockheed Vegas, Aries and Aquarius.[4] It was Ben himself who gave Bebe her first lessons, helping her to develop into a pilot in her own right.

There was even brief talk about Bebe entering the Women's Air Derby (better known as the Powder Puff Derby) in August 1929. The first female-only air race in the U.S., it was a milestone in both aviation and the women's liberation movement. For an actress of Bebe's caliber to compete alongside the likes of Amelia Earhart, Ruth Nichols and Louise Thaden (to name a few of the other Derby participants) would have been nothing short of monumental.

Bebe's intent to enter the Santa Monica-to-Cleveland race was well-documented by the press. "They wired me that Bebe Daniels had entered and I didn't know she was a flier,"[5] remarked Earhart. Ultimately, it was Daniels' lack of experience that kept her out of the race. Bebe did not come close to meeting the race's strict requirements. Her career as a competitive aviatrix was over before it had even started.

Fencing was also part of Bebe's life in the late 1920s and early 1930s. She initially took it up because of her role in *Señorita*; it developed into a full-fledged hobby and eclipsed swimming, tennis and golf as Bebe's sport of choice. Numerous newspaper accounts detail her extensive training in the field. Bebe was always one to devote herself whole-heartedly to athletics. Her "sporty" pictures provided Bebe with the perfect excuse to stay in top physical shape.

On May 11, 1929, Bebe took part in one of the most time-honored Hollywood traditions. At that time the forecourt of Grauman's Chinese Theater was still relatively barren, with only 11 sets of cement footprints and handprints. Bebe's prints, the twelfth addition to Sid's ever-growing collection, joined those of Colleen Moore, Gloria Swanson and Pola Negri. "To Sid—Our King of Showmen," reads the inscription above petite feet and hands. Two days later, Marion Davies placed her hands in the plot immediately above Daniels'.

The inclusion of Bebe in the most famous pantheon of Hollywood stars speaks to her popularity during the 1920s. Nowhere to be found in the forecourt are Clara Bow, Louise Brooks, Greta Garbo and Billie Dove, all of them better remembered today than Bebe. Daniels was considered a sufficiently important presence in Hollywood by Sid Grauman to have her immortalized, while the others were not. This fact alone helps to contextualize the public's adoration of Bebe at the peak of her career.

*Rio Rita* became one of Florenz Ziegfeld's greatest successes on Broadway when it opened February 2, 1927. Its run of 494 performances was considered remarkable for the time, and with the advent of talking pictures it seemed natural for a film version to follow. The young and unproven Radio Pictures decided to take a gamble financially on the movie, with the mindset that their version would reproduce Ziegfeld's stage spectacle as nearly as possible. (Ziegfeld was actively involved in the film's production.) It was certainly a risk, but one from which RKO could greatly benefit.

Conflicting reports came out of RKO that Bebe had alternately been cast in and cut from the film production of *Rio Rita*. In total 35 actresses auditioned for the part, including Ethlynne Terry (who starred as Rita in the original Broadway production). Almost a month after Bebe was announced as Rita, *Billboard* reported: "Miss Daniels' exit from *Rio Rita* is understood to have occurred when the film moguls, to their horror, discovered that while Bebe is undoubtedly a wow as a comedienne, on the other hand she is no [Italian soprano Amelita] Galli-Curci when it comes to warbling."[6]

The spectacular production required many hours of preparation. Daniels recalled that 126 men labored full-time to construct the various elaborate sets, while a team of dressmakers worked nonstop for weeks to create the film's 600 costumes.[7] For a new studio, $678,000[8] was a gigantic sum to invest in a musical, but in the grand scheme of Hollywood this was a remarkably low budget. *Gold Diggers of Broadway*, *The Broadway Melody* and *On with the Show*, three of 1929's other major musicals, each cost between two and three million. *Rio Rita* was doubly risky in that it threatened to bankrupt the studio, while also competing against films with much larger budgets.

Problems plagued the production, which was filmed in only 24 days, between June 26 and July 20. RKO was unprepared to make such an opulent film in such a short space of time. As the studio did not have their own color camera for the Technicolor sequences, they had to borrow one from Warners, forcing director Luther Reed to film at night when Warner Bros. was closed. Daniels, John Boles and the rest of the cast were unfamiliar with shooting sound pictures, leading to an intensive period of trial and error. It was soon learned that any little noise, from costumes rustling to women waving fans, was amplified. Scenes were reshot, precious time and money were wasted, and there was little hope for the success of *Rio Rita*.

However, there were high points behind the scenes. Harry Tierney and Joseph McCarthy, who wrote the songs for the 1927 musical, were brought to Hollywood to craft new songs for the film. Amongst their new numbers were "Sweetheart, We Need Each Other" and "You're Always in My Arms (But Only In My Dreams)," the latter becoming one of the best selling records of 1929. Additionally, Wheeler and Woolsey (the only holdovers from the original Broadway cast) promised to provide a major draw in their first film. Although the studio and the lead actress were both unproven (at least in terms of talkies), anticipation was nevertheless high.

Bebe's Rita Ferguson, a Mexican beauty, is pursued by two men. The first, Texas Ranger Jim Stewart (Boles), is chasing an infamous bandit known only as "The Kinkajou." The second, General Ravinoff (Georges Renavent), is a Mexican warlord with obvious criminal ties. Rita learns that her brother is suspected of being the Kinkajou, and Ravinoff blackmails her into marrying him in exchange for protecting her brother's identity.

The film's Technicolor climax takes place on Ravinoff's barge, where he and Rita are to be married. Ranger Jim cuts the ship's ropes and the vessel floats north of the border, allowing Texas Rangers to storm the barge and arrest Ravinoff—the true Kinkajou. With Ravinoff incarcerated, Rita and Stewart are able to embrace their love for one another. (Wheeler and Woolsey, the film's other stars, are merely involved in a humorous subplot that has little bearing on the film as a whole.)

On October 6, *Rio Rita* had its New York City premiere. In attendance were Ziegfeld and all the film's stars. Word quickly spread across the nation about the success of Bebe's first talkie. Any questions of her ability were quickly quelled, while the film was heralded as nothing short of a marvel. The *Los Angeles Times*, in anticipation of the film's West Coast debut, wrote: "Rivaling the success of any picture, we hear, which has ever been produced, *Rio Rita* ... opened in New York Sunday night at the Earl Carroll Theater. Critics are unanimous in its praise, some going as far as to say it is the best talker so far produced."[9]

One writer noted that "cyclonic success descended upon Bebe"[10] that evening, proving definitively that her Hollywood career would not be cut short by the end of the silent era. Her voice, which she had worked so hard to improve in order to get the role of Rita, garnered particular acclaim.

Bebe's *Rio Rita* triumph was poignantly described by Louella O. Parsons. While her lifelong friendship with Bebe suggests that the columnist almost certainly lacked objectivity, it is nevertheless an important document championing Daniels' remarkable introduction to talkies:

### Bebe Upsets Gossipers, Makes Talkie Grade

The most prevalent gossip in Hollywood a scant 12 months ago was that Bebe Daniels was through in pictures.

Everywhere one went the same whisper was heard until it became one of those open Hollywood "secrets."

"Too bad. Bebe is such a dear but her voice doesn't register," was the sentiment expressed again and again. Everyone loves Bebe and no one wanted to see her made a victim of these star-extinguishing talkies.

Bebe herself said nothing. She bought a few more pieces of property. She entertained just as lavishly and when some of the inquisitive politely inquired what she intended to do she answered, "I'll let you know when I know myself."

The cheerful and almost flippant indifference of

**Bebe Daniels and her co-star John Boles as they appeared in their first talkie, *Rio Rita*.**

Phyllis Daniel's independent daughter was put down to sheer bravado. The report everywhere was the same. Paramount had given Miss Daniels four or five voice tests and she was just a total loss over the microphone. Her fate, it was prophesied, would be the fate of Corinne Griffith, Norma Talmadge, Billie Dove and many other big stars.

The movies were in for a new era and for a complete change of star personnel. Bebe was through—why, she couldn't even get a job in the quickies.

The fact that Bebe had never actually had a voice test at Paramount made no difference. The gossip continued. No one stopped to consider that after a succession of home-made stories, incredibly amateurish and made against Bebe's judgment, her contract with Paramount was terminated by mutual consent. No one in the Paramount organization believed that it was worth the trouble to test her voice. They thought it a waste of film.

Fortunately, William Le Baron, the head of RKO who had long watched Bebe's career at Paramount, was not influenced by these rumors. He made a voice test, and it only needed one to convince him he had a prima donna right in Hollywood. Moreover, he had found the very girl for *Rio Rita*.

He was right. Bebe in *Rio Rita* is the surprise of the year. No Broadway actress, imported to Hollywood, compares with this child of the movies, grown up and trained in the silent pictures.

A few of Hollywood's hardened cynics, still incredulous, intimated that perhaps a double was used. Bebe soon put an end to this rumor by singing in public and making records.

Irving Berlin, who heard her sing at the home of the George Fitzmaurices' one night, remarked that she would be a sensation on Broadway in a musical comedy.[11]

As a result of the success of *Rio Rita*, Bebe quickly signed a recording contract with RCA Victor. The day after the film's release, September 16, she entered the studio to record two of her solo songs from the movie, "You're Always in My Arms (But Only in My Dreams)" and "If You're In Love, You'll Waltz."[12] Proving that her voice was more than adequate for musicals, her first attempt at recorded music was very successful. *Photoplay* mused, "It isn't the first time that a motion picture star has had her voice 'canned,' but Bebe will probably emerge with the most success to date."[13]

In the wake of *Rio Rita*, *Love Comes Along* seemed almost austere by comparison. Whereas the former cost $678,000 to produce, Bebe's first film of 1930 cost only $220,000.[14] Gone were the lavish gowns and striking sets, replaced with a vague seaport and an equally bland plot. One critic wrote, "[T]his piece ... is in no way as pretentious an affair as its predecessor."[15] Its obscure source material was *Conchita* by Edward Knoblock, an unfinished play from almost a decade prior.

On the remote island of Caparoja, seaman Johnny (Lloyd Hughes) encounters Peggy (Daniels), an American actress who is stranded and survives by performing in a tavern. Their love affair—set against local customs, arranged marriages and other stumbling blocks—makes up the majority of the fast-paced plot, and at the conclusion they predictably are united.

When the film was released in January 1930, audiences noted the drastic drop in quality from *Rio Rita* to *Love Comes Along*. While Bebe's performance was by no means poor (she was even called the film's "one shining light"[16]), the entire production was fated to be panned from the start. The only element of *Rio Rita* that RKO retained, it seemed, was vocal numbers for Bebe (of which there were four). The two most popular, "Until Love Comes Along" and "Night Winds," were released by Victor to moderate success. Even in a subpar picture people still enjoyed hearing Daniels sing, and her musical performances stand out as the saving grace of *Love Comes Along*.

During the early months of 1930, Bebe kept just as busy in her personal life as she did on the RKO lot. Whether serving as a bridesmaid for Bessie Love, appearing at the annual San Francisco Policeman's Ball, or attending dinner parties at the home of Mr. and Mrs. Harold Lloyd, her name was constantly appearing in the papers. When NBC launched a weekly radio program dedicated to screen stars, Daniels was announced as the show's inaugural guest (singing "You're Always in My Arms" from *Rio Rita*).

Contrary to popular belief, Bebe's popularity in the first years of talkies rivaled her fame even at the height of the silent era. In the *Exhibitors Herald World* poll released at the start of 1930, Bebe ranked sixth in popularity amongst actresses. Clara Bow, Colleen Moore, Nancy Carroll, Joan Crawford and Greta Garbo were considered more marketable at the box office, a formidable lineup of stars to be included in. Although *Rio Rita* served as her defining performance for years to come, even her critical and commercial misses at the start of the decade helped keep her on the minds of many moviegoers.

While Bebe's "engagement" to Charley Paddock had turned out to be a publicity stunt to promote *The Campus Flirt*, Bebe's impending marriage to Ben Lyon provided a legitimate reason for anticipation surrounding *Alias French Gertie*. For audiences clamoring to learn more about the personal lives of the couple, it provided an opportunity to see Daniels and Lyon interact onscreen. Although a scripted drama would not portray their lives like they were in real life, a sense of their chemistry could nevertheless be gleaned.

A small-scale drama, *Alias French Gertie* was more akin to *Love Comes Along* than *Rio Rita* in terms of production value. The basic plot—two jewel thieves team up after escaping from the police during a heist—was based on Bayard Veiller's unproduced play *The Chatterbox*, which also served as the inspiration for the 1925 silent *Smooth as Satin*. Joining Daniels and Lyon in the extremely small cast were Robert Emmett O'Connor (as a detective who inspires the thieves to go straight) and John Ince and Daisy Belmore as the couple's neighbors. Inexpensive and quickly made, the film would have to rely on its stars' performances for its success.

Unfortunately, even Bebe could not make a hit of the picture. Reviews were almost universally critical—although, it must be noted, fault was found with the script rather than the actors. It seemed as though the critics *wanted* to like Bebe and Ben in their first co-starring vehicle, but couldn't bring themselves to endorse the film. "That invariably engaging player, Miss Bebe Daniels, is badly treated in *Alias French Gertie*.... [I]t is so obvious and undistinguished that you can only wonder why so likable a star is wasted in it," wrote the *New York Herald Tribune*. "If you are a Daniels fan, the picture will probably remind you ominously of unhappy days in the late silent cinema when the same young lady was being tragically wasted in bad slapstick comedy equally unworthy of her."[17]

Some critics did point out that Bebe's charm and pleasing accents made the film somewhat enjoyable, as did Ben's reliable acting. But the film nevertheless was a box office disaster, and marked a serious misstep in the notoriously fickle history of RKO Pictures. Even with a proven talent such as Bebe Daniels at their disposal, the inexperienced studio could not duplicate the success they had experienced with her in 1929. As one critic aptly wrote: "Brutal as it is to say so at the beginning of her wedding week … this witness must express disappointment at Bebe Daniels' second failure to live up to the promise of *Rio Rita*. They can't seem to find another rich part for her."[18]

On June 14, 1930, Bebe Daniels married Ben Lyon.

The wedding was held at the Beverly Wilshire Hotel, completed only two years earlier but already a center of Hollywood high society. The event was international news. Bebe's fans, who had followed the ups and downs of her personal life for over a decade, could hardly believe that she was finally tying the knot.

The small private ceremony was attended only by family and close friends. The Reverend James H. Lash, pastor of the First Congregational Church of Hollywood, officiated. "It was a warm and wonderful feeling," Bebe would later say about the day.

Bebe's bridesmaids were "eight of the fairest blondes and brunettes and redheads in filmdom's leading circle."[19] There was Diana Kane, wife of director George Fitzmaurice; Mae Sunday, ex-wife of Billy Sunday, Jr.; reporter-novelist Adela Rogers St. Johns; Rita Kaufman, wife of Paramount executive Albert Kaufman; and actresses Constance Talmadge, Lila Lee, Betty Compson and Marie Mosquini. Serving as Bebe's matron of honor was her dearest friend Louella Parsons.

Serving as the ushers were eight of Ben's close friends and business associates: George Fitzmaurice, RKO producer Henry Hobart, actors Sam Hardy and Richard "Skeets" Gallagher, agent Frank Joyce, Dr. Harry Martin (husband of Louella Parsons),

Bebe Daniels and Ben Lyon on their wedding day, June 14, 1930.

Wallace Davis (fiancé of Mae Sunday) and Howard Hughes. Lyon's best man was his best friend and business partner, Hal Howe.

Bebe's dress was, in her own words, "tight-fitting with a long train of hand-woven ivory satin and Italian lace, with a lace veil yards long."[20] In keeping with the old tradition, Bebe had with her Mary Pickford's lace handkerchief ("something borrowed") and wore a blue locket that belonged to Little Mother ("something blue"). Her bouquet consisted of white orchids and lilies of the valley.

Following the ceremony was a reception for several hundred of the couple's friends and associates. In attendance were nearly all of Hollywood's biggest names: Mary Pickford and Douglas Fairbanks, Norma Talmadge, Richard Dix, Irving Berlin, Clara Bow, Corrine Griffith, Colleen Moore, Rod La Rocque, Bessie Love, William Haines, Lionel Barrymore, Dolores Del Rio, Gloria Swanson, and May McAvoy. Even Bebe's former lover Jack Dempsey attended with wife Estelle Taylor. (Conspicuously absent were Mr. and Mrs. Harold Lloyd.)

The wedding was widely considered by the press to be one of the most beautiful in Hollywood up to that time. Such a lavish yet tasteful ceremony was fitting for the film colony's favorite daughter. With as clean a reputation as had ever survived the scandal-ridden movie industry during the 1920s, Bebe's marriage Ben Lyon was looked at as just the kind of success story that Hollywood needed to clear its reputation. Bebe, in her virginal white gown, stood out from a slew of other stars marred by claims of immorality.

Ben's gift to his bride was a diamond necklace that she wore the entire day. Bebe gave Ben a brand new tennis court at their home. The couple left the reception early to sneak off to their secret honeymoon destination. There was much speculation in the press about where the couple would go, further fueled by the fact that Ben had a pilot's license and could fly anywhere they liked.

It was eventually revealed that the couple merely drove up the coast to the Santa Barbara Biltmore. Upon their arrival at the hotel's bridal suite, the newlyweds were met with a most disorganized scene. As Bebe recalled it, "furniture was upturned, pictures taken off the walls, rugs rolled up, flowers out of their vases and strewn over the floor. Even the bed had been 'apple-pied.'"[21] While the hotel management was apologizing profusely for the mess, Ben noticed a note lying amongst the chaos. "CONGRATULATIONS.—JOAN BENNETT," it read.

And thus, with a practical joke so characteristics of those early days of Hollywood, did Bebe and Ben's marriage begin.

# 17

# Leaving RKO

> *I think the world is always a little indifferent to heroes who are too perfect, and to roles in pictures which show them that way. You note that the great lovers of history didn't go in for perfection in a big way. The men who have been notoriously successful with women were the Don Juans, the Casanovas, the Solomons and Marc Antonys, and none of them had what you might call a blameless escutcheon.*
> —Bebe Daniels, *New York Herald Tribune*, March 15, 1931[1]

After the lackluster *Love Comes Along* and *Alias French Gertie*, Radio Pictures shamelessly set out to recapture the success of *Rio Rita*. *Dixiana*, their next vehicle for the newly-married Bebe, was set in the South. The setting may be the biggest difference between *Dixiana* and *Rio Rita*. Luther Reed directed both, Wheeler & Woolsey and Dorothy Lee co-starred in both, and Harry Tierney composed the music for both. In an attempt to impress audiences, RKO spent almost $70,000 more on the production of *Dixiana* than they did on *Rio Rita*. On paper, *Dixiana* was shaping up to be the most lavish movie musical to date.

There were, however, a couple of items that RKO did not take into account. The first was the issue of the male lead. With John Boles engaged in other productions, Radio Pictures had to look elsewhere for an actor capable of singing the film's challenging musical numbers. As RKO did not have such an actor at their disposal, they had to turn to other sources—namely, the Metropolitan Opera, where they discovered Everett Marshall. Making his film debut, Marshall certainly had the voice for the part, but his charisma onscreen was so lacking that his inclusion in the film was considered a critical misstep.

RKO also could not have anticipated the public's growing disinterest in movie musicals. As the reality of the Great Depression sunk into the hearts of moviegoers, the idea of lavish sets (designed by Max Rée), opulent gowns and a celebration of Antebellum high society seems almost irreverent in retrospect. When talkies were new and exciting and disposable income flowed freely, *Rio Rita* had been a hit. But in the somber wake of the stock market crash, such a picture was ill-fated from the start.

There is even evidence to suggest that Bebe opposed *Dixiana* from its inception, instead wanting to bring to the screen *Carmen* with John Boles.[2] Although RKO had been the sole studio willing to take a chance on her voice, by the middle of 1930 she had had several failures with them and was beginning to grow restless. Even though *Dixiana* had potential to once again capitalize on her talents, the actress was savvy enough to question its production. A job was a job, though, and she made the picture with no further qualms.

Perhaps because of *Dixiana*'s diminishing target audience, RKO launched a massive publicity campaign to promote it. The upcoming feature was purported to be a sordid tale of sex and jealousy, which was in direct contrast to the film's sterile, staged atmosphere. A *Photoplay* advertisement demonstrates the hyperbolic language used to publicize *Dixiana*:

> In staggering magnificence ... in *thundering emotions* comes "DIXIANA" *to hold the world spellbound*! ALL THAT IS LIFE HAS BEEN ENGULFED IN THIS AMAZING PRODUCTION! Romance.... Fiery Drama.... Bouncing Comedy.... Revelry.... Stupendous Spectacle! The story of Two Men ... and a Woman who set men's hearts aflame ... *amid the Mad Abandon and Fevered Passions of Mardi Gras!*[3]

For the *Dixiana* premiere, RKO arranged a spectacle befitting the grandiose film. Personal invitations for the evening of July 22 were extended to the governors of all southern states, while carrier pigeons were used to deliver invites to local mayors. The Orpheum Theatre in downtown Los Angeles (site of many RKO premieres) had recently been equipped with technology for talking pictures, and a crowd of more than 2000 flocked to see Daniels' latest extravaganza. All of the film's principals were in attendance, plus a choir singing African American spirituals. While *Dixiana*'s response may have been tepid, for one night Bebe was the toast of the town.

One of the few aspects of *Dixiana* that was truly successful was its use of Technicolor in the final two reels. "Technicolor has put a light in [Bebe's] eyes and a flush in her cheek—has given warmth and meaning to her every glance and gesture,"[4] read the film's advertisement copy. The use of Technicolor did help to differentiate *Dixiana* from contemporary productions. Although color had been utilized to a small extent in *Rio Rita*, *Dixiana* represented the culmination of another year's worth of technological advances, and as such the results are spectacular (one researcher called it "some of the best Technicolor surviving from that era").[5]

For a long time, the film's Technicolor sequences were thought to be lost. In the 1950s *Dixiana* became a television staple, although the story came to an unexplainable halt because that footage was missing. Fortunately, the 21 minutes of Technicolor scenes were meticulously restored from the original camera negatives by the UCLA Film and Television Archives, allowing audiences to once again experience *Dixiana* as a cohesive whole.

Just as *Love Comes Along* served as a bare-bones followup to *Rio Rita*, *Lawful Larceny* too was a modest affair after the spectacle of *Dixiana*. Despite the unspectacular production values and lack of musical numbers for Daniels, a case can be made that *Lawful Larceny* was the most critically acclaimed of any of Bebe's RKO films, and certainly demonstrated her acting ability most tastefully.

*Lawful Larceny*, based on a play by Samuel Shipman, was unique in that Lowell Sherman was not only allowed to reprise his role from the 1922 Broadway production, but was also hired to direct the film. Sherman was one of the few men at the time who made a habit of directing his own films. Bebe had her first experience with Sherman six years earlier, when he had played King Louis XV of France in Valentino's *Monsieur Beaucaire*.

Bebe's role was drastically different from those in her previous talkies. "From the underworld character she interpreted in *Alias French Gertie* and the singing southern beauty she portrayed in the operetta *Dixiana*," wrote the *Los Angeles Times*, "she undergoes a complete transition and plays a vengeful wife in *Lawful Larceny*."[6] Her versatility during her time with RKO was remarkable, particularly when compared with her often-similar silent performances just a few years earlier.

Marion Corsey, the "vengeful wife" played by Bebe, discovers at the start of the film that her husband (Kenneth Thomson) has been conned out of his money by beautiful Vivian Hepburn (Olive Tell). Mrs. Corsey takes it upon herself to retrieve the stolen funds by embezzling Vivian's love interest, Guy Tarlow (Sherman). Through a series of twists (that include the local judge being romantically interested in Vivian), she ultimately recovers her husband's small fortune. The entire incident, however, takes its toll on their marriage, and the film ends ambiguously regarding their future together.

Daniels' performance and the film as a whole were very well-received by critics—and this time, without the pomp and circumstance necessary to *Rio Rita*'s massive success. "Her entire performance—her reading of her lines, her costuming and her poise—is the most convincing she has had in her present cycle of screen success,"[7] wrote one critic, and *Chicago Tribune* critic Mae Tinee named it one of the six best releases of the month. Although no one knew it at the time, *Lawful Larceny* would be Daniels' last picture with RKO—and it was certainly a high note to end on.

By the time *Lawful Larceny* was released, the first golden age of movie musicals had already come and gone. *Dixiana* had tried to recapture the magic of *Rio Rita* with inferior results, leaving RKO hesitant to invest massive sums in the genre again. As historian Richard Barrios wrote, "musicals were dying, operettas most of all,"[8] and the studio was quick to adjust to this changing demographic.

In May 1930, RKO had announced *Heart of the Rockies* as Bebe's next musical spectacular. Conceived on the assumption that *Dixiana* would match the success of *Rio Rita*, the proposed credits for *Heart of the Rockies* were virtually indistinguishable from *Dixiana*'s. Everett Marshall was again to be starred opposite Daniels, Harry Tierney would compose the film's songs, Anne Caldwell would write the story, and Luther Reed would direct. It was a powerful team in the abstract, although one whose whole was perhaps not as great as the sum of its parts.

Plot details are scant regarding *Heart of the Rockies* as the film never actually made it into production, but promotional material called it "An empire in the clouds dramatized in pageantry, song and story."[9] Filming was scheduled to take place in September in Banff, Canada.[10] Production was cancelled at some point prior to this. It was also rumored at one point that Irene Dunne would instead be cast in Bebe's role, although this too never materialized.

*Heart of the Rockies* would have represented the final picture under Bebe's original contract with RKO, although its cancellation put the fulfillment of said contract into jeopardy. The second half of 1930 was an uncertain time for Daniels' future; RKO was suffering financial difficulties at the same time they were transitioning away from musical features (films such as 1931's *Cimarron*, while massively successful, were also extremely expensive). Although she was RKO's top-grossing female star, they simply could provide her with adequate vehicles.

## 17. Leaving RKO

With her RKO contract terminated early, demand for Bebe Daniels began to spread throughout Hollywood. MGM attempted to sign her to a one-picture deal in August. Somewhat surprisingly, William LeBaron announced in October that Radio Pictures had resigned Daniels to a long-term contract, promising "two special productions a year of the caliber of *Dixiana* and *Rio Rita*."[11] Further confusing matters was the news that Bebe had agreed to film *Reaching for the Moon* with Douglas Fairbanks at United Artists. Daniels had gone from not having a contract the year before to suddenly being barraged with offers from various studios.

The situation was resolved on Christmas Eve, when multiple sources came forth claiming that Bebe had signed a five-year deal with Warner Bros., with the caveat that she could continue working for RKO for the first year (she would ultimately not invoke this part of the contract). At Warners Bebe joined her husband, as well as silent-era stalwarts George Arliss and John Barrymore. Compared to the variable quality of RKO's pictures, Warner Brothers could provide Bebe with vehicles befitting a star of her caliber (in theory, at least), and a five-year contract would all but ensure her continued prosperity in Hollywood.

Following the success of *Rio Rita* and the potential shown by *Dixiana*, it seemed natural for Bebe's next film after *Lawful Larceny* to be another musical. This time United Artists recruited Irving Berlin to write the film's score *and* the story. The entire production proved to be a complete debacle.

*Reaching for the Moon* began life as *Love in a Cottage*. Berlin's story centered on Larry Day (Douglas Fairbanks), a Wall Street broker who has much better luck with finances than he does women. Stuck aboard an ocean liner with aviatrix Vivian Benton (Bebe), he must heed the advice of his valet (Edward Everett Horton) to win her affection. In the end Day loses his fortune, but wins Vivian's hand in marriage.

Bebe's seamless transition to talkies was the antithesis of Fairbanks' career path. Whereas Bebe was found to have a voice perfectly suited to both talking and singing, Douglas' voice was remarkably unappealing. His farewell to silent, 1929's *The Iron Mask*, was also his last major success. Although the movie did feature two brief talking sequences cut on Vitaphone disks, it was not until the Pickford-Fairbanks co-starring vehicle *The Taming of the Shrew* that audiences really heard the King of Hollywood speak. The vast majority were not impressed.

While silent Douglas Fairbanks comes across as heroic, daring and unmistakably masculine, his talking counterpart in *Reaching for the Moon* is whiny and unpleasant. While he looks like the Zorro and Robin Hood of days gone by, he loses most of his charm with his ill-fitting voice (a fact exacerbated by the film's weak script). There was talk during production that it would be his last motion picture; he would go on to make three more, all of them unsuccessful.

Bebe—now sporting blonde hair for the first time in her life—steals the show. Her dialogue is witty and sharp, and her nonchalance towards Larry Day is subtle in a way that directly contrasts Fairbanks' overly broad performance. In short, Bebe comes across as likable while Douglas simply does not.

The film is notable as the solo debut of a young actor by the name of Bing Crosby, who performs its only musical number, "When the Folks High Up Do the Mean Down Low," alongside Bebe and June MacCloy. In the context of a larger musical the song would have made sense, but in the absence of Berlin's other songs the scene seems random and unnecessary.

The film premiered at New York City's Criterion Theater on December 29, 1930, with such entertainment icons as Jack Dempsey and Claudette Colbert in the audience. Public opinion of *Reaching for the Moon* was divided. *Photoplay* hailed Fairbanks' performance as one of the best of the month, and *Motion Picture Magazine* called the film "perfectly mad and utterly delightful."[12] On the other hand, the *Wall Street Journal* dismissed it as "a hodgepodge of satire, farce, romance, and musical comedy."[13] Modern critics have sided with the latter opinion more often than not.[14]

Perhaps the movie's harshest detractor was Irving Berlin. Decades after its release, he said, "I had just come back from Hollywood. I'd written a lot of songs for a picture called *Reaching for the Moon.* This was after the stock market crash. Musicals were the rage out there and all of a sudden they weren't. Out went the songs. I developed the damnedest feeling of inferiority."[15]

Ultimately, *Reaching for the Moon* suffered because of limitations put on production more than anything else. It was originally slated to be filmed in Technicolor; this idea was scrapped because of budget concerns.[16] The dance numbers were initially supposed to be choreographed by Busby Berkeley,[17] and the role of Vivian's best friend Kitty was first offered to Ginger Rogers instead of June MacCloy.[18] Missing these key pieces, the movie failed.

The final blow was a falling-out between Berlin and director Edmund Goulding. Berlin had originally composed 14 original songs for *Reaching for the Moon*, six of which were filmed and included in an press screening before the movie's release. Other songs were included in early drafts of the script, but ultimately cut by Goulding. What could have been Berlin's first triumph of the silver screen was hacked to pieces before the public ever could enjoy it.

Musicals had taken studios by storm in 1929—in large part thanks to Bebe's *Rio Rita*—but by late 1930 they had fallen out of vogue, where they would remain until 1933's *42nd Street* brought them back to prominence. When *Reaching for the Moon* was first conceived, it made perfect sense for it to be a musical; several months into production, it became a risk that Goulding was not willing to take.

Today, *Reaching for the Moon* is most fondly remembered for its lavish sets, which represent a high-water mark in art deco design. Its confusing plot, subpar script and near-complete lack of Berlin's original compositions are—perhaps rightfully—overlooked.

Following productions for RKO and United Artists, Bebe moved to Warner Bros.— her third studio in as many films. There she was reunited with Ben, who had already made *A Soldier's Plaything*, *The Hot Heiress* and *Misbehaving Ladies* for the company (or its subsidiary, First National). Not surprisingly, Warners cast them in their first picture together since their much-celebrated wedding.

Ben was quick to make certain that this wouldn't be come a trend. "We were in *Alias French Gertie* together before we were married, too," he explained, "but in a general way we feel it isn't advisable to appear in too many pictures in this way. Don't you agree? But she's very easy to make love to."[19] He was apparently serious about this fact; *My Past* would prove to be the last American picture in which they would star together.

Based on the popular 1930 novel *Ex-Mistresses*—published anonymously, it was said, because the story was so scandalous—*My Past* retains many of the book's risqué moments. Perhaps the most shocking to contemporary audiences is the scene where Bebe removes her bathing suit and playfully encourages Ben to swim after her. While the sexual undercurrent through the entire movie seems fairly tame by today's standards, at the time the movie was advertised as "Adults Only By Order of Censor Board."

The "past" referred to in the title is that of John Thornley (Lewis Stone), a successful businessman who has admired showgirl Doree Macy (Daniels) for years. Macy begins an affair with Thornley's partner Robert Byrne (Lyon) with the understanding that he and his wife have separated for good. When this proves to be untrue, Doree is devastated and refuses to forgive him. Selflessly, Thornley sacrifices any hope he had for a life with Doree and strands the two alone in Europe—allowing them to rekindle the love they briefly shared.

*My Past* had a soft opening in Washington, D.C., in the middle of February; the following month it began playing in New York and Los Angeles. Reviews were generally positive, although the film was far from a blockbuster. Audiences were contented seeing Daniels and Lyon on the screen together again, and the tumultuous love story was played convincingly by both. The film was certainly a success, and showed promise for Bebe's future with Warner Bros.

*My Past* features one of Bebe's best performances. She had honed her skills in talking pictures while at RKO, so her early Warner Bros. films feature an actress at the top of her craft. Her interplay with her husband—so obviously natural and uncontrived—differentiates this film from others made around the same time. While she could act well opposite (say) John Boles or Lloyd Hughes, she was very clearly most comfortable with Ben Lyon. In the pantheon of pre–Code talkies, *My Past* deserves more praise than it has historically received.

# 18

# Barbara Bebe Daniels

*Ben is so tender and true, and there is no jealousy between us. We are more happy about each other's successes than we are about our own. And isn't Barbara wonderful? She's such a good baby, so sweet, and look how firm her baby flesh is! She sleeps all through the night, too, and never cries. Oh, we're going to have a wonderful Christmas.*
—Bebe Daniels, *Los Angeles Times*, December 27, 1931[1]

Bebe's first picture of 1931 was not a starring feature. Instead, both Bebe and Ben participated in the charitable production *The Stolen Jools*, created to raise funds for the National Variety Artists Tuberculosis Sanitarium. Although produced by Paramount, the charitable nature of the film allowed for stars from Warner Bros., MGM and RKO to take part. The cast, therefore, is something of a who's-who of Hollywood during the early 1930s.

The film's thin plot centers around Norma Shearer's jewels being stolen at the Screen Stars Annual Ball. The police encounter Wallace Beery, Buster Keaton, Edward G. Robinson, Laurel and Hardy, Joan Crawford, William Haines, Gary Cooper, Maurice Chevalier, Loretta Young and Douglas Fairbanks, Jr., amongst many others. One scene, running a mere 20 seconds, finds Bebe and Ben relaxing at home, working on a crossword puzzle. Their saccharine conversation ends abruptly when a shadowy figure is seen lurking outside their window:

BEBE: Ben?
BEN: Hmm?
BEBE: What's a three-letter word for perfection?
BEN: You, darling.
BEBE: Flatterer.
BEN: Hey, Bebe. What's a five-letter word for me?
BEBE: Jewel, sweetheart.

Their inclusion in such a star-studded production demonstrates their remarkable popularity into the talkie era. *The Stolen Jools* provided audiences with their first glimpse of Bebe and Ben together on-screen following their highly publicized wedding.

The 1941 adaptation of Dashiell Hammett's *The Maltese Falcon*, starring Humphrey Bogart and Mary Astor, is one of the most acclaimed films in Hollywood history. It was the third time that the story had been brought to the screen. The first, released a year after Hammett's novel debuted, starred Ricardo Cortez as Spade and Bebe as Ruth Wonderly (aka Brigid O'Shaughnessy). Following the plot and dialogue of the book almost exactly, that version film has become somewhat notorious for containing many "lewd" pre–Code elements that the later adaptations of the novel could not exclude.

*The Maltese Falcon* was initially purchased by Warner Bros. as a vehicle for John Barrymore. The male lead was given to Cortez when it was announced that Barrymore would not be starring in any modern films (historical pictures such as *General Crack* were proving to be his forte). The strong female lead called for a gifted actress, and Bebe, in her first part under her new long-term Warners contract, seemed a natural choice. Working titles for the film included *All Women, Bad Women* and *Woman of the World*; the studio ultimately returned to the novel's title.

The plot is now famous: Detective Sam Spade (Cortez) is conned by Ruth Wonderly (Daniels) into searching for the mysterious "Maltese Falcon"—a statuette of a black bird that is apparently immensely desirable. Also hot on its trail are Dr. Joel Cairo (Otto Matieson) and Casper Gutman (Dudley Digges), adding to Spade's confusion about the bird's value. Complicating the hunt is Spade's love affair with Wonderly, which threatens to cloud his judgment as a detective. In the end he produces evidence that incriminates her for murder. The film closes with Sam Spade being made chief investigator for the district attorney's office and informing the prison matron to treat Ruth well (at the expense of the DA).

As Hammett was actively involved with Warner Bros. at the time, the film is a close approximation of the novel, even incorporating many lines of dialogue. Hints of homosexuality and adultery were even translated into film, something that would not have been possible after the implementation of the Hays Code a few years later. Perhaps the film's most risqué shot depicted Bebe nude in a bathtub. Although tame by 21st century standards, the scene was unprecedented enough at the time to elicit a complete explanation in the papers. In addition to painting a picture of Bebe's life on set, it also demonstrates changing mores in Hollywood over the decades:

> When a feminine film star takes a bath for the benefit of the all-seeing camera, it is quite an event on any motion picture lot.
> Bebe Daniels did such a scene for *The Maltese Falcon*, her new Warner Brothers picture.... The usual procedure on these interesting occasions was followed. First, the especially built bathroom set was carefully boxed off so that prying eyes could not see. The "monitor room," the glass cage occupied by the sound expert, was moved back about fifty feet from the set. Before the scene was taken, an extra girl sat in the empty bathtub, fully clothed, while electricians adjusted the lights and cameramen adjusted their cameras.
> When all was ready the property man filled the bathtub with water—and it had to be just the right temperature. Soap for suds, a body brush, a fancy washcloth and all the other trimmings were put within reach. Then Miss Daniels came out of her nearby dressing room, clad in a bathrobe, and entered behind the walled-in set with her maid.
> There was the sound of splashing water, the maid came out with the bathrobe, the star said, "All ready to shoot," and they turned over the cameras, which means that the motors were started on them.
> Director Roy Del Ruth, out of sight around a corner of the set, clicked a little tin gadget in his hand as the signal for the action, and the bath was under way.
> "You have a hard time with your women," the leading lady called to the leading man, Ricardo Cortez, who was sitting in a chair out of view of the cameras—and the bathtub. (This was a line of dialogue.)
> "Everything's all right now, baby," the leading man replied, then got up and walked quietly back to his newspaper at the side of the stage.
> More sounds of splashing.

"Do it again," said the director, without stopping the camera.

The leading man hurried back; the action was repeated.

"That's good," the director called, and the cameras stopped running.

"Alice!" called Miss Daniels. The maid, bathrobe in hand, heavy Turkish towels over her arm, hurried behind the barricade.

And thus the bath scene made by Bebe Daniels for *The Maltese Falcon* was completed.

When thrown upon the screen only the head and shoulders of Miss Daniels will be seen, and theater patrons, as did the studio employees on the set, may speculate:

"I wonder if she wore a bathing suit!"[2]

As Hammett's work was a massive success the year before, anticipation for the film adaptation was high. By many accounts, it did justice to the novel. Premiering at the end of May and getting a wide release in June, the film was massively successful. All of its elements—the script, Del Ruth's direction, Daniels and Cortez's acting, the supporting cast—were praised, contributing to one of the studio's biggest successes of 1931.

Five years after its release, Warner Bros. attempted to rerelease the picture, only to find out that it would have to be heavily cut. This led to the production of *Satan Met a Lady*, a much more liberal adaptation starring Bette Davis and Warren William. Both of these earlier adaptations would be eclipsed by the blockbuster 1941 version, leaving Bebe's version in unfortunate obscurity.

Recent reappraisal has been kind to Bebe Daniels' performance, and some critics consider the earliest adaptation superior to the latest.[3] Certainly the tone of the film is truer to the original novel, and the film holds up as one of Daniels' most enjoyable talkie performances. The film is widely available, but it remains in the shadow of Bogart and Astor.

In the midst of filming *Honor of the Family*, Bebe received a phone call from Louella Parsons: "I want you to tell me truthfully: are you going to have a baby?"

Bebe Daniels in the first film adaptation of Dashiell Hammett's *The Maltese Falcon*.

Bebe had done everything she could to keep the information secret, but omnipresent Parsons noticed Bebe buying baby clothes. Not wanting to start a false rumor, she felt it best to confront Daniels directly.

Parsons was one of the most feared names in Hollywood, and Bebe was smart enough to know that a lie would undoubtedly come back to harm her. But Bebe also knew that Louella had enough integrity to hold off on a scoop if asked. She was cutthroat, but she wasn't immoral. Bebe came clean: "Yes Louella, I'm going to have a baby. But I want to finish the film I'm doing and it wouldn't do to let the news out at the moment."

"Well, that's great news. I won't say a word until you tell me I may."[4]

The Hollywood rumor mill never rests, though, and quickly news of Bebe's pregnancy made its way into the papers. "It was admitted yesterday [May 25, 1931] that the stork is expected to visit the home of Mr. and Mrs. Ben Lyon in September,"[5] the *Los Angeles Times* revealed. Bebe completed *Honor of the Family* by the beginning of June, at which point she retired from the public spotlight for several months.[6] Less than a year after her highly publicized wedding, Bebe was about to become a mother.

Bebe and Ben took advantage of her forced hiatus from the movie industry and hopped a steamer for a month-long vacation in Honolulu to celebrate their first wedding anniversary. Such a trip was a rare luxury for a couple as busy as the Lyons, and the lack of media attention was welcomed by the mother-to-be. As they left for Hawaii, Bebe granted the *Los Angeles Times* her last interview before becoming a mother.

> LAT: Aren't you afraid to go sailing the ocean with a little Lyon expected?
> BEBE: Of course not. The baby won't be here until September and I'm going right ahead with everything, just as usual. I cannot act any more, but I can keep busy.
> LAT: Do you want a boy or girl?
> BEBE: I don't care. Either one would be lovely. And what can be done about it, anyway? Ben doesn't say. All men, I suppose, like the idea of having the first-born a son, but he's sweet. He says whatever I decide will be all right with him.

Upon their return to the mainland, whispers arose that the birth of Bebe's child might mark the end of her film career. Whether by contractual mandate or personal choice, those close to the couple were telling the press that Bebe would never return to movies. Even the reassurance of Bebe and Ben themselves did nothing to quell these rumors, and for moviegoers across the nation, the uncertainty of Bebe's future added a new level of interest to her pregnancy. Terminated contracts, countless injuries and even marriage had not stopped Bebe from gracing the screen; would a child prove the final nail in her career's coffin?

A week and a half before her due date, Bebe was the recipient of what some called the most lavish baby shower Hollywood had ever seen. Hosted by Mrs. George Fitzmaurice, wife of the director, and Louella Parsons, the event was attended by Bebe's friends past and present. Norma Talmadge, May Allison, Sally Eilers, Betty Compson and Billie Dove were amongst the guests who presented the expectant mother with extravagant gifts.[7] Everything was embroidered "B.L." as the child's name was to be either Barbara or Ben, depending on gender. The world awaited news about the new addition to the Lyon family.

"Bebe Daniels Presents Lyon With 'Lyoness,'" read the headlines.

At 3 p.m., September 9, 1931, Barbara Bebe Lyon, five pounds, 14 ounces, was born. "We are very happy and proud," Ben reported to the press the following day. "Both Bebe and Barbara are getting along fine."[8] This last statement was only partially true; the birth was taxing on Bebe, and complications kept her in the hospital until the beginning of October. Once home, she quickly had a full recovery.

In addition to Ben, there was one other person with Bebe at the hospital on the afternoon that Barbara was born: Harold Lloyd.[9] His presence demonstrates the intimacy he and Bebe kept throughout their later lives.

Mother and child recuperated at the Lyons' Santa Monica home, where a special nursery had been designed. Amongst the furniture was a cradle that had been used by Ben's mother, his siblings and himself. The newborn received a flood of telegrams from her parents' friends, many remarking on the show business career she was certain to have, given her pedigree.

In the midst of the news coverage surrounding Barbara's birth, *Honor of the Family* was released on October 17. In the last movie she made before her hiatus from the screen, Bebe played heroine Laura in a liberal retelling of Honoré de Balzac's *La Rabouilleuse* (and Émile Fabre's subsequent play of the same name). Lloyd Bacon, who would later find success in musicals, directed, while Warren William made his talkie debut opposite Bebe.

Media response was tepid, and the film proved to be one of Bebe's more forgettable efforts. Critics were quick to comment on its dissimilarity to Balzac's original work, and considered Daniels' performance "satisfactory" in an "average film."[10] The inadvertent exposure given by Barbara's birth the previous month meant that people flocked to the theater simply to see Bebe.

In the weeks following Barbara's birth, Bebe occupied herself with her favorite pastime—bridge. Rather than leave her baby in the care of a nurse, she always brought Barbara along with her, keeping her carriage by her side as she played cards. When Barbara developed her own skill for card games later in life she often joked, "Can you wonder, when my mother weaned me on cards?"[11]

For the time being, all was quiet and peaceful in the Lyon household. Perhaps the biggest news came when, one November day, Ben left his blonde wife at home to attend a football game. Upon returning home, he was greeted by a brunette. "I never had a blonde personality and always felt a bit uneasy with the gay and golden topknot,"[12] she gleefully explained to him.

But even the birth of Barbara could not keep Bebe sedentary for long, and by the end of November the Lyon trio was in San Francisco for a revival of Frederick Lonsdale's 1925 play *The Last of Mrs. Cheyney*. After an extremely successful initial run in London and a popular picture starring Norma Shearer in 1929, Bebe was pegged to play Mrs. Cheyney. Playing to sell-out crowds at the Alcazar Theatre, the show became something of a sensation. Immediately there was talk about bringing the production to Hollywood to play the El Capitan. Before Barbara was three months old, it was announced that Bebe would be making her thrilling return to Los Angeles.

"That's the last of Mrs. Cheyney and the first of Lady Dilling."

With those words, the curtain fell on what was hyperbolically called "the most brilliant premiere in the history of the theater."[13] Not only did it mark Bebe's return to the limelight after the birth of Barbara, it was also Bebe's first stage performance since she was 14. The opportunity to see Daniels in-person onstage made *Mrs. Cheyney* one of the hottest tickets in Hollywood. Performances were added during the show's first week to meet the demand.

Opening night featured a full house, carefully orchestrated by Ben to include many of Bebe's closest friends. In the audience that night were Betty Compson, Marilyn Miller, David O. Selznick, Constance Bennett, Sid Grauman, Mary Pickford, Constance Talmadge, Thomas Meighan, Billie Dove, Irving Thalberg, Norma Shearer, Lionel Barrymore, Hal Roach, Eddie Sutherland, George Fitzmaurice, Jack Warner, William LeBaron, Sally Eilers, Hoot Gibson and—of course—Mr. and Mrs. Harold Lloyd.

Bebe's performance lived up to the public's high expectations. "What Miss Daniels accomplishes in this first stage adventure can only be reckoned as exceptional," the *Los Angeles Times* reported after opening night.[14] Another reviewer remarked that Bebe "simply oozed poise."[15] All the compliments in the world could not shake Bebe's characteristic humility, and she provided her own self-deprecating review of her first performance:

> It was much harder opening in Hollywood, with the house packed with friends, than up in San Francisco. Oh, but I was nervous! And you see, when a strange audience applauds, you sort of know everything is all right, but one's friends would applaud anyway. Fancy me tripping over that rug on my very first entrance! And oh, dear, so many little things went wrong. They gave me a cup and saucer without any tea in it and I had to stir an empty cup and just pretend to drink. Then, I had had my dress cleaned and it shrunk a little on the left side....[16]

*The Last of Mrs. Cheyney* played to enthusiastic audiences for three and a half weeks. One night Bebe looked out into the audience and was greeted by the men of her honorary Army Air Corps unit, the 322nd Pursuit Squadron. As the play wrapped up, it was announced that Colleen Moore would be starring in her own production at the El Capitan, trying to capitalize on the immense success Daniels had had. Bebe, it seemed, was more beloved that ever before.

During Bebe's period of relative inactivity, an uncharacteristic suit was filed against Ben Lyon. Allegedly, on December 23, 1931, Bebe had paid Ben a visit at Columbia, where he was filming *The Big Timer* with Thelma Todd and Constance Cummings. Clerk Cedric LaMar asked Bebe to wait, which allegedly enraged Lyon and sparked a physical attack on LaMar.[17] He sought $35,000 from the star for injuries sustained. The case elicited only limited media attention, and ultimately was settled out of court for $450. There is little reason to believe that the claims leveled by LaMar had much validity, as Lyon was known throughout the movie industry for his civil temperament.

In April, Bebe and Ben joined some of Hollywood's biggest names to support Colleen Moore, who was appearing in *A Church Mouse* at the El Capitan.[18] The affection Moore received from both silent and talkie stars rivaled the reception that Bebe herself had garnered for *Mrs. Cheyney*. The solidarity demonstrated amongst silent film actors and actresses would prove to be a constant in Hollywood for decades; for Bebe, supporting her peers like Colleen Moore seemed natural.

As 1932 rolled on, there was still little word about Bebe's return to films. Already it had been eight months since *Honor of the Family*, and there was still no word of her next project. The press was grasping at straws for stories to print about Bebe; it was uncharacteristic for her to be so far removed from the public eye.

The *Hartford Courant* asked Bebe point-blank about her impending comeback, to which she replied with characteristic honesty. "Good artists get bad pictures and give good performances in them, but it is not regarded that way by the public,"[19] she began. "Then the artist, sick of being baited with careless material, takes a stand and gets a good picture once again. The artist gives the same type of performances he's always been giving but the result is a 'comeback.'"

As Bebe prepared for her return to moving pictures, rumors began to circulate about her contract with Warners. On June 6, 1932, the studio owed her $100,000 as part of a two-film deal.[20] As none of the films offered to her were deemed suitable (Bebe was looking to star rather than play supporting roles), the dispute nearly marked the end of her association with the studio. Legal action was ultimately averted when the two parties settled on a lesser sum, allowing Bebe to remain with Warner Bros. for several more features.

At the end of July, the public was greeted with the news that Bebe would finally return to the screen. The source material was *Silver Dollar*, a biography of Colorado silver tycoon Horace Tabor by socialist author and journalist David Karsner. Starring in the role of Tabor (renamed Yates Martin in the film) would be Edward G. Robinson, one of Hollywood's biggest stars following the release of *Little Caesar* one year earlier.

Filming of Bebe's scenes commenced during the last week of August. The production proved fairly elaborate; it was reported that actual items from Tabor's collection were purchased at an estate sale to add authenticity.[21]

Bebe's role in the film was a much smaller part than the star was used to. In *The Maltese Falcon* and *Honor of the Family* she had received top billing over Ricardo Cortez and Warren William, respectively. In *Silver Dollar*, Daniels was clearly secondary to Robinson. "After a dazzling career embracing slapstick, drama, and musical comedy," one publication wrote, Bebe "is now content to be overshadowed by that dynamic little man, Edward Robinson."[22] Bebe does not appear onscreen until more than half an hour into the film.

While Bebe's talkies were generally successful, she had failed to recapture the success of *Rio Rita*. *Love Comes Along* had lacked the spectacle of her first musical, while *Dixiana* suffered from a weak plot, cast and production. As musicals were quickly falling out of fashion in Hollywood, Bebe stayed away from the genre for her next several productions. It seemed as if the strong singing voice she had carefully developed would do her no further good.

It seemed that Bebe's return to musicals would be a picture titled *Radio Girl*, which Warner Bros. began advertising as early as June 1932. Bebe was to be paired with Dick Powell in the picture, which would feature music by Harry Warren and Al Dubin, the team responsible for nearly all of Warner Bros.'s hit musicals.[23] A letter from Bebe to Darryl Zanuck describes her excitement about the project:

> Dear Darryl—
>
> You do not know how very happy your letter has made me and you may be assured that I will cooperate with you in a sincere effort to make the production of *Radio Girl* an outstanding one.
>
> Harry Warren and Al Dubin are too well-known to require comment. I am looking forward to their new numbers with the keen enjoyment their past successes have afforded us all.

With the marvelous spirit you are showing, Darryl, *Radio Girl* is bound to be a winner and I am prepared to do my utmost to help make it one.

Ben joins me in kindest regards and all good wishes.

Sincerely,
Bebe

For months there was little news about the production—in large part because the studio had another project they were working on.

At the end of August 1932, Warner Bros. announced their adaptation of Bradford Ropes' novel *42nd Street*. A backstage story about the passing of the torch from one actress to another, the cast was set to feature Kay Francis, Joan Blondell, Warren William, George Brent, Ruby Keeler and Dick Powell. Reporters declared it the greatest collection of actors since *Grand Hotel*.

Media speculation was particularly high surrounding the film, as it seemed like a serious financial risk for Warner Bros. The directorial addition of Mervyn LeRoy, fresh off the success of *Little Caesar* and *Five Star Final*, fueled interest in the movie. Fortunately, Warner Bros. had a wild card that no one could have seen coming: the choreography of a young man named Busby Berkeley.

A month after the film was announced, Kay Francis' role was given to Bebe. (Also, Ginger Rogers replaced Joan Blondell.) Francis was one of the studio's biggest stars, and Bebe had not had a major commercial success in several years. *Radio Girl* was promptly put on indefinite hold while the studio focused all of their attention on *42nd Street*.

The part of Dorothy Brock—a jaded Broadway actress, past her prime but making her return to the stage—was perhaps better suited for Bebe than Kay. Bebe had been making pictures for over two decades, and few people expected that she had a blockbuster performance left in her.

During the filming of *42nd Street*, which began the first week of October, Bebe maintained a very public persona. In the middle of October she appeared at Long Beach Airport for an air show overseen by Hap Arnold; while there, she directed a bomb squadron by radio.[24] Later that same month, she appeared at the Shrine Auditorium alongside Buster Keaton, Colleen Moore and others at a Republican Party fundraiser. Pictures of Bebe, Ben and Barbara were frequently in papers around the country. Excitement was swelling for *Silver Dollar*; it was even higher for *42nd Street*.

Posters for *42nd Street* show how much Hollywood relied on top stars in advertising their productions. The film's most notable plot line revolves around the trials and tribulations of young Peggy Sawyer (Keeler), an aspiring chorus girl who must rise to the occasion of a starring role in the film's climactic scene. Along the way she is assisted by Billy Lawler (Dick Powell), the play's male lead. Keeler and Powell are arguably the film's protagonists and receive the most screen time of anyone.

However, in promotional material for the film it is not Powell but Warner Baxter who receives top billing. Baxter had won the Academy Award for Best Actor several years prior and was a much bigger draw than Powell, who was making his debut in a starring role. Both George Brent and Guy Kibbee are also billed above Powell, despite the fact that both have roles that are much less consequential.

Bebe's residual appeal is demonstrated by the fact that she was billed above Keeler,

Bebe Daniels meets with famed aviator Lieutenant Colonel Henry "Hap" Arnold in Long Beach, California (November 30, 1932) (U.S. Air Force).

the film's heroine. Keeler was making her film debut, while Bebe was a star; anticipation was particularly great for this film because it marked her long-awaited return to musicals. As late as the release of *42nd Street*, Bebe was still one of the most popular and respected names in Hollywood; the film would mark the last truly great success of her cinema career.

Both commercial and critical reception were overwhelming, with *42nd Street* running for weeks on end across the country. The *New York Times* called it "invariably entertaining" and "one of the most tuneful screen musical comedies that has come out of Hollywood."[25] *42nd Street* established the musical comedy as one of *the* most successful genres and helped to make household names of Ruby Keeler and Dick Powell, who would go on to star in *Gold Diggers of 1933*, *Footlight Parade*, *Dames* and *Flirtation Walk*.

Today, *42nd Street* is still celebrated as one of the greatest movie musicals of all time. In 1980 it was adapted into a Tony-winning Broadway musical of the same name; more recently, the American Film Institute placed it 13th on their list of classic movie musicals. Songs from the movie—"Shuffle Off to Buffalo," Bebe's own "You're Getting to Be a Habit with Me" and the title number—all have remained pop standards to this day. While similar Busby Berkeley-Warner Bros. musicals such as *Footlight Parade* and *Gold Diggers of 1933* have remained popular, *42nd Street* has remained legendary.

# 19

# To England

*Right now, you are liable to bump into a dozen Americans on any English set. Mr. Fairbanks and his son are playing there; Laura LaPlante, Thelma Todd and Elizabeth Allan are there. Not long ago Bebe Daniels and Ben Lyon were making pictures near London.*
—Anna May Wong, *New York Herald Tribune*, June 22, 1934[1]

Through the early 1930s, Bebe's real estate prowess was well documented by the press, and the fortune she had acquired in property ensured that she never had to act another day in her life if she so chose. However, Daniels was always looking for new ways to spend her free time, whether through aviation, bridge or building new homes. When the opportunity presented itself for Bebe to start a new line of clothing and retail outlets, she naturally said yes.

A large part of Bebe's decision to undertake such an endeavor can be attributed to the fact that one of her closest friends, Pauline Gallagher (*née* Mason), was the driving force behind the business. The wife of screen comedian "Skeets" Gallagher, Pauline had known Bebe for a number of years and was one of her bridesmaids. A Ziegfeld Girl before retiring from the public eye, Pauline served as the business manager for the new shop—she "put the hard work into the day-to-day running of the business," Ben would remark[2]—while Bebe spent the majority of her time purchasing the clothes they would sell.

Reporters were quick to praise Bebe's fashion sense. Even more than her acting ability, Bebe's choice of dress at red carpet events was lauded by the press. Bebe was also careful to shy away from the shock value of revealing outfits—something that cannot be said of many 1920s stars. It made perfect sense for Bebe and Pauline to go into business to create a line of sportswear and other women's clothing.

Their shop, called "American Maid," would sell only clothing made in the United States—an idea well ahead of its time in the 1930s. The patriotic basis for the brand was not lost on a nation at the height of the Great Depression. "They Run a Red, White, and Blue Shop,"[3] read one headline about American Maid's opening, which went on to state that "the young women—both of them pretty and intelligent—have undertaken to help out President Roosevelt" with their new venture.

American Maid's first retail outlet was located at the corner of Glendon Avenue and Lindbrook Drive in Westwood Village.[4] It was a good location; adjacent were Phyllis Daniels' French lingerie shop and Mary Pickford's millinery shop.

American Maid proved so successful that by winter of 1934 they were opening a second shop, this one in Palm Springs. S.S. American Maid featured much of the same merchandise but was distinct in its nautical theme. An article celebrating the opening of the shop describes the meticulous detail the two women put into the design:

> The S.S. American Maid is the latest addition to this city's resort shops—a veritable ship in the desert. Opened recently by "Captain" Bebe Daniels and "Skipper" Pauline Gallagher, proprietors of the American Maid Shop in Westwood Village, the S.S. American Maid lives up to its name to the fullest extent....
> 
> The interior is the masterpiece—a lovely, refreshing replica of a ship's deck. On one side is the rail, set into a wall that blends the glorious blues of ocean and sky, filled in below with canvas, lashed to the rail and broken by lifesavers bearing the name of the S.S. American Maid....
> 
> The floor is covered with woven rope matting, and display cases on the side opposed the rail are in white, roped in canvas. Stock cases are reproductions of ship's cabins, with little metal steering wheels for knobs and handles and portholes for display niches. A ship's clock strikes the bells....
> 
> The S.S. American Maid carries a "cargo" of women's resort wear, including play togs, sports dresses, and evening frocks, as well as lingerie, hosiery, handbags, handkerchiefs, Drumstick cosmetics and infants' to 6-year-olds' apparel....
> 
> [Daniels and Gallagher] will continue the Westwood shop, dividing their time between the two places.[5]

An additional American Maid shop was opened in Avalon on Catalina Island, and very quickly the Lyons and Gallaghers had a factory in downtown Los Angeles producing clothing for their stores. Bebe and Ben discussed the company's history in great detail in *Life with the Lyons*, with Lyon joking about how much money was poured into the brand with very little tangible result. Indeed, the entire history of American Maid seems to have been more of a labor of love than anything else; Bebe's impeccable business sense in terms of real estate did not carry over to her clothing line.

While media attention was heavy due to the cachet of Bebe's name, American Maid failed to become a sustainable business venture. By the time the Lyons had relocated to London in the mid–1930s, the brand's stores had been shuttered and the factory closed. Although the couple chalked their losses up to other manufacturers copying their designs and sabotaging their endeavor, the truth was probably much more simple: founding a clothing business during the Great Depression was nearly impossible, especially for a group of people acquainted solely with show business.

At the beginning of April, it was announced that Bebe would be loaned to Columbia for her next starring picture. Based on James Kevin McGuinness' story "Pearls and Emeralds," *Cocktail Hour* revolved around Cynthia Warren (Bebe), "a genius in business but a novice at love" (per the film's poster). Cynthia was rumored to have been inspired by "a famous American woman illustrator,"[6] although the prototype was never revealed. Prolific director Victor Schertzinger helmed the production and composed several original songs for Daniels to perform.

Cynthia, a wealthy poster artist, refuses to conform to the institution of marriage. Sexually liberated, she leaves Randolph Morgan (Randolph Scott) behind in New York and sets sail for Paris, breaking several hearts along the way. A confrontation between two of Cynthia's suitors almost leaves one of them dead. She finally relents to Randy's advances and consents to marry him.

Although *Cocktail Hour* is practically forgotten today, at the time it was considered one of Bebe's greatest successes. "The only difference between 'Bebe Daniels' and

Bebe Daniels dons a negligee in the Columbia Pictures production *Cocktail Hour.*

*Cocktail Hour,"* one reviewer wrote, "is that the sparkle of Bebe is lasting and the sparkle of the cocktail hour is momentary.... [T]he two in combination make entertainment de luxe."[7] Daniels' performance of "Listen, Heart of Mine," written for the movie, was particularly lauded. As it was her first release following *42nd Street, Cocktail Hour* convinced audiences and critics that Bebe did not merely have to be relegated to supporting roles; she was still capable of carrying an entire picture.

*Variety* printed a particularly favorable assessment of Bebe's performance: "She has charm and a good figure; she can sing right up close to the camera without her mouth looking distorted ... and she can play a broken-hearted drunk with enough gaiety and humor to negate most of the distaste a volubly potted lady evokes. More important, she's the sort to throw her whole heart into any emotional situation at hand; her generous response and warmth assures everybody's liking her."[8]

While *Cocktail Hour* was far from the spectacle that *42nd Street* was—filming took just three weeks—it did prove that Bebe did not need elaborate production values to succeed. As long as the script was passable and her supporting cast was adequate (Randolph Scott deserves particular praise), Bebe's magnetism on the screen was still such she could score a major hit. While much of the cast of *42nd Street* went on to produce the equally extravagant *Gold Diggers of 1933* and *Footlight Parade*, Bebe's follow-up picture is almost austere by comparison.

While *42nd Street* was still setting records and *Cocktail Hour* was in post-production, Bebe and Ben left on a steamship for England. British International Pictures had engaged them to co-star in a film, which was to be their first produced outside of the U.S. Bebe and Ben's first trip to Europe would plant the seeds for their future more than either could have predicted. Joining them was their good friend Sally Eilers, who had recently completed Will Rogers' *State Fair* and Richard Barthelmess' *Central Airport*.

Eilers' inclusion in the trip was more diplomatic than anything, as she had recently separated from her husband of three years, Hoot Gibson. "Honestly, I mean it when I say Hoot is my best friend,"[9] she explained as she left on the trip; four months later, she would be remarried. The trip to England with her confidante Bebe provided her a much-needed escape as the divorce was finalized. Upon arriving overseas, she would herself find work in the British studios.

Sally's presence caused some chaos at the beginning of the voyage, as Ben would later recall. "Sally Eilers came over on the boat with us," he wrote, "and, believing firmly—as we do—that stars should be annoyed only when fans don't want their autographs, signed everything that was thrust in front of her and, in the excitement of waving goodbye to Phyllis, Sally accidentally autographed her passport and handed it to a fan."[10] Despite Ben's best efforts, he was unable to locate the missing document.

The Lyons' trip to England was given a huge amount of attention in the British media as it represented part of a greater trend of American actors making European pictures. Constance Cummings, Jeanette MacDonald, Edward Everett Horton and James Gleason were amongst the other actors taking a leave of absence from Hollywood during the Depression, bringing great prominence to British film studios.

In addition to their contracts with BIP, another reason for Bebe and Ben's extended holiday was much more practical. Hollywood was in the midst of a kidnapping panic, and getting Barbara out of town provided the couple with short-term peace of mind. Although it was an unfamiliar country, at least they did not have to worry about their daughter's wellbeing while on set.

Upon her arrival in England, it was announced that Bebe was no longer slated to appear in a picture with Ben. Instead she would make two films during her stay, while Ben would star with Sally Eilers. The first of these two films, titled *The Song You Gave Me*, was directed by the noted Paul L. Stein, who began his career in Weimar Germany. The musical comedy co-stared Victor Varconi.

The film was lacking in plot: Bebe played Mitzi Hansen, a stage star who falls in love with her newly hired secretary. But it was very well received, particularly overseas. Its success was due in no small part to top production values. According to one report, "Miss Daniels will wear no less than twenty-one frocks of the most glamorous kind," an expense "worthy of one of the most beautiful actresses on the films."[11] The costumes and dance numbers rivaled any other films being produced in England at that time.

The part of Mitzi was perfectly suited to Bebe's talents and temperament, and she played it remarkably well. Upon the film's preview release at the London Hippodrome on July 25, *Variety* wrote that Bebe "has never looked or played better. She sings with charm and the numbers fit her. Her American accent is not too marked, either.... Smartly cut, the picture should prove a draw on both sides of the Atlantic."[12] For her first production in a foreign market, *The Song You Gave Me* proved both an artistic and commercial success.

By all accounts Bebe greatly enjoyed her time filming in England. The BIP Elstree

Studio was better-equipped and more efficient than many of Hollywood's best studios, Bebe remarked with characteristic positivity.[13] Ben, too, was delighted by the country as he occupied himself with the filming of *I Spy*. A thoroughly average spy caper, it was only notable for having been directed by Allan Dwan.

British customs delighted Bebe, and her enthusiasm for the culture is evident in her interviews. "When a picture is completed there," she said upon returning to Los Angeles, "they give a big dinner at one of the leading hotels, to which actors, press and staff are invited. They did that for both my husband, Ben Lyon, and for me when we finished pictures over there. They also serve coffee every morning at ten and tea every afternoon at four. Those things buck up fagging spirits and don't stop production a bit. It goes right on and actors get their coffee or tea in their idle moments." It was these first encounters with British life that would inspire her and her husband to return several years later.

Her first trip to England marked one of the most productive times of her career, and Bebe was able to finish a second picture during her three-month stay. *Southern Maid* was yet another musical comedy, this time starring Daniels in a dual role.

Juanita (Bebe), a beauty queen in Santiago, elopes with the English Sir Jack Rawden (Clifford Mollison). Twenty years later, Dolores (also Bebe), Juanita's cousin, elopes with another Englishman under eerily similar circumstances. The screenplay was adapted from Harold Fraser-Simson's 1917 operetta of the same name.

While *The Song You Gave Me* was a success, *Southern Maid* proved to be a sensation. "The Greatest British Musical Extravaganza Ever Made!," advertisements touted. "It is the first really ambitious musical from an English studio,"[14] one reviewer wrote. When it was released in December, long after Bebe had returned to America, it quickly became one of the most popular British productions of the 1930s. The South American setting made the most of Bebe's Spanish beauty, and the musical numbers were once again the perfect complement to the actress' talents. Four years earlier, *Rio Rita* helped to popularize the musical spectacular in the U.S.; now, *Southern Maid* was serving that same purpose in England.

By the second week of August, Bebe and Ben's work was completed in England. As a trip to Europe was a rare luxury for the couple, they decided to vacation for ten days in France. Upon their arrival home, both Ben and Bebe were already engaged for their next pictures: the former at MGM for *The Women in His Life*, the latter at Universal for *Counsellor-at-Law*.

Bebe's appearance in *Counsellor-at-Law* is almost inconsequential, as the film is best remembered for its leading man John Barrymore and its director, William Wyler. Barrymore, suffering from alcoholism and waning popularity, scored one of his last critical successes, while Wyler still had his greatest heights ahead of him. If nothing else, the film brought Bebe widespread exposure in a well-respected production.

The film's rigorous production schedule did not afford Daniels any rest. She arrived in Los Angeles from New York at midnight on September 7; the next morning, she reported to the set.[15] *Counsellor-at-Law* was notoriously plagued by delays, most notably Barrymore's inability to remember any of his lines. Initially scheduled to be finished in two weeks, the movie ended up taking almost a month. As Barrymore was being paid $25,000 per week (or $500 per hour)—an unheard-of sum during the Depression—

Wyler sought to finish shooting as quickly as possible, eventually resorting to cue cards for the actor.[16]

Elmer Rice's wildly popular play of the same name, which made its debut in 1931, was the source material for Universal's film. To preserve as much as the play's integrity as possible, nine cast members were retained from the Broadway production, giving the film a very staged, theatrical feel. Supporting Barrymore from Hollywood were Doris Kenyon, Thelma Todd, Onslow Stevens and Daniels, amongst others. Kenyon acted alongside Daniels once before, in *Monsieur Beaucaire.*

The film's plot revolves around George Simon (Barrymore), a successful attorney whose career is upended by a serious legal scandal. Adding insult to his impending disbarment, his wife (Kenyon) threatens to leave for Europe with another man. In the film's climax, Simon contemplates jumping from the window of his Empire State Building office, only to be saved at the last moment by his loving secretary Regina Gordon (Daniels). As Rice himself wrote both the play and screenplay, the story was extremely faithful to its source material.

Bebe's role was more domestic than audiences had become accustomed to; a secretary is much less exotic than a former stage diva or a South American beauty. Fortunately, her low-key performance was perfectly suited for such a simple part, leaving the audience with a "much more retrained, dignified Bebe than we are accustomed to see."[17] As a testament to her talented work in the shadow of Barrymore, *The New York Times* deemed it "one of her best screen performances"[18]—high praise for someone who had been making blockbuster films for over a decade.

As 1933 came to a close, so did Bebe's contract with Warner Bros. It was announced in December that her last picture with the company was to be *Registered Nurse*, a medical drama originally set to star Barbara Stanwyck.[19] Lyle Talbot was selected as her leading man. Production proceeded very rapidly—certainly more rapidly than Warners' lavish musicals—and the film was completed by early 1934. Perhaps the most notable incident to occur on set was Bebe's misplacement of her wedding ring, which also happened during the filming of *Silver Dollar*. The papers did not report Ben's reaction to Bebe's carelessness.

After a quiet start to 1934, Bebe and Ben made the decision to go on tour as themselves. Already the couple had demonstrated their charming rapport over the radio, and Bebe's everpresent desire to return to the stage is well-documented. Rather than appearing in a scripted drama, though, a series of personal appearances with her husband afforded Bebe flexibility that was otherwise impossible. First and foremost, it would be easier to bring young Barbara on the road if both Bebe and Ben were traveling. Additionally, their pay would be significantly higher for much less work (their personal appearances averaged about 15 minutes). A brief vaudeville act seemed just the thing to quench Bebe's desire to perform.

On April 6, Bebe and Ben made their highly anticipated debut together at the Chicago Theatre. The show opened with a series of excerpts from their most popular films—Ben's *I Cover the Waterfront* and *Hell's Angels*, and Bebe's *Rio Rita* and *42nd Street*. Having whet the audience's appetite sufficiently, the Lyons then appeared in a mock radio studio onstage. What ensued was a mixture of gags and musical numbers that demonstrated both actors' talent and charm.

**Bebe Daniels and John Barrymore relaxing on the set of 1933's *Counselor at Law*.**

The response they received was overwhelming. "They are a cinch for business, as was demonstrated at the first show here,"[20] praised *Variety*. The *Chicago Daily Tribune* was equally complimentary: "It seems that the Daniels-Lyon alliance is taking the stage easily, effectively, and without too much Hollywood pomp and circumstance."[21] Bebe and Ben knew what their audience wanted to see, and they delivered exactly that. A highlight was the show's closing, which featured Bebe performing a medley of *Rio Rita* numbers while tossing flowers to audience members in the front row.

From Chicago Bebe and Ben took their show to Detroit, where it was met with equally impressive reviews (and revenue). Brooklyn, too, proved a receptive audience; people began lining up at 1 p.m. for the couple's first evening performance. With ease, the Lyons managed to sell out the 4000-seat Brooklyn Paramount Theatre several nights. Riding the wave of publicity that their performances were receiving, Bebe and Ben next crossed the East River, poised to conquer Manhattan's Paramount Theatre.

Although promoted heavily, the Lyons were ultimately forced to cancel their tour prematurely when Bebe contracted mumps (allegedly from kissing a baby brought backstage to see her[22]). The condition put a two-week halt to all public appearances, and considerably tempered the amount of attention the couple had been receiving. It was announced that Bebe and Ben would forgo Manhattan altogether and resume their tour in Washington, D.C., once Bebe had recuperated.

While Bebe was regaining her health in New York City, the *Herald Tribune* ran a short article that demonstrates just how popular the Lyons still were. Although no longer at the peak of their fame (as they had been a few years earlier), Bebe and Ben still ranked amongst the most identifiable—and beloved—actors in the nation. Upon attempting to enjoy a quiet evening together, the following ensued:

> Chinatown demonstrated effectively last night that it has a lot of Bebe Daniels admirers. The motion picture actress, who has been confined with the mumps for the last two weeks, sought a change of diet last evening and she and her husband, Ben Lyon, took a window table on the second floor of the Lum Fung Restaurant, at Canal and Baxter Streets. As she dipped into a rice cake she heard a shrill voice outside cry "Hello, Miss Bebe!"
> Miss Daniels smiled at the seven-year-old boy who was waving up at her and returned to her chop sticks. Five minutes later she heard a clamor outside and, looking down, perceived the bright-eyed lad returning at the van of fifteen more children, all calling to the actress who was so conspicuous in her big pancake hat. Uncomfortably Miss Daniels and Mr. Lyon finished their meal and watched the crowd swell in proportion.
> When they finally left the restaurant at 10:45 500 persons of all ages swarmed in the street waving photographs, pencils and papers and begging for autographs. Five policemen from the Elizabeth Street station hurried to assist the three already on duty in the vicinity, struggling to hold back the crowd. Finally the police rushed Miss Daniels and Mr. Lyon through the crowd with a flying-wedge formation to a taxi cab for their escape.[23]

*Registered Nurse* hadn't broken any box office records, and already *42nd Street* was beginning to fade from public view, but Bebe was still a force in American popular culture. Her mere presence at a Chinese restaurant could cause chaos—a testament to her nearly two decades of highly regarded work.

After a final string of successful shows in Washington and a brief detour to Baltimore to visit Ben's parents, the Lyons returned to Los Angeles as triumphant as ever. Their tour of personal appearances served as something of a victory lap.

Bebe and Ben soon fell back into everyday life. With the exception of the occasional radio broadcast (whether *Hollywood on the Air* or the short-lived *Maybelline Musical Romance*), the couple maintained a remarkably low profile. There were rumors of a visit to Japan and China, as well as public appearances in Dallas and Houston, but as the months wore on, nothing materialized. Bebe had her hands full with motherhood and her clothing line, and after some of her most productive years ever in 1932 and 1933 a brief interlude was much-needed.

Bebe was restless to a fault, however, and come October she and Ben returned to the East Coast to play the cities they had missed on their first tour. This second leg of appearances almost opened with tragedy when engine trouble forced pilot Lyon to make an emergency landing in rural eastern Pennsylvania. (Lyon, who still had his commercial pilot license, took every opportunity he could to fly himself.) Also traveling with the couple from San Francisco to New York was Hal Roach.

Walking away from the safe landing, they continued their trip to New York City via bus. While in New York, the couple's choice of hotel was always the Lombardy, built by William Randolph Heart at the height of 1920s opulence for Marion Davies. However, their stay in the city would be fleeting, as they had an engagement at Boston's Metropolitan Theatre.

Following the first run of their vaudeville act, word spread about how delightful and entertaining the couple was on stage. Anticipation was high in Boston, where the Lyons were set to appear on a bill with the William Powell film *Happiness Ahead*. Their stints a few months earlier had allowed them to conquer any nerves, and by the time they arrived in Boston their routine was even more refined than before.

"Bebe Daniels and Ben Lyon may not be the biggest names in Hollywood, but they know what to do when they land in front of a live audience,"[24] read one review of opening night in Boston. They successfully played to Buffalo and Montreal audiences in the following weeks, then returned to Los Angeles in time for the holidays.

Bebe made only one picture in 1934 (after five the previous year), marking a distinct period of transition for her. Although she was not officially retired from Hollywood, it was nevertheless becoming apparent that she was beginning to phase films out of her life. The emphasis she placed on live theatrical performances marked a trend that would continue in the future, no doubt spurred by the response she received.

# 20

# Hollywood Holiday

*Once upon a time I made $30 a week and received, if I was lucky, an average of 12 fan-mail letters for the same period. I supplied my own costumes, my own makeup and the expense of the autographed pictures I sent out to my loyal rooters. It was hard work, but it was fun. I often wonder if young and fabulously salaried film actresses today can enjoy their work as we did in primitive movie times.*
—Bebe Daniels, *Baltimore Sun,* February 17, 1935[1]

By 1935 the face of the motion picture industry had changed. The top box office draw, Shirley Temple, was born the same year Bebe made her last silent film. Jean Harlow, Bette Davis, Ginger Rogers, Miriam Hopkins and Olivia de Havilland were unheard of just a few years earlier, while Colleen Moore, Clara Bow and the Talmadge Sisters would never make another film.

Bebe had already begun to distance herself from the ruthless machine that was Hollywood, and her decreased output in 1934 was by choice rather than necessity. The movie industry of the 1930s was vastly different than the scene she had cut her teeth in, and very few familiar faces remained. As motherhood and marriage were taking up more and more of her time, the warm welcome she received on the stage satiated her desire to perform. Perhaps most importantly, her disillusionment with Hollywood quelled any desire she may have had to continue her career in American motion pictures.

In lieu of any movie contracts at the start of 1935, Bebe returned to the stage. She once again brought Ben Lyon with her, as well as their good friend "Skeets" Gallagher. Their starring vehicle was written specially for them by Kay Kenney and Douglas Gilmore: *Hollywood Holiday* (originally *No Man's a Hero*) involves a movie star couple vacationing in New York City. While indulging in the city's social scene, playboy Jeffry Crane (Lyon) finds himself embroiled in a scandal that leads to both his movie studio invoking his morality clause and his wife (Daniels) leaving him. Gallagher, serving as comic relief, played the Cranes' butler.

Opening in mid–February to a moderate audience in Ben's childhood home of Baltimore, it was performed in Princeton, Wilmington, Hartford, Boston and Philadelphia before closing in Chicago. The play was far from the critically acclaimed success that *The Last of Mrs. Cheyney* had proved to be a few years earlier. "The acting is rather better than the script, [and] Mr. Lyon and Miss Daniels are in top form,"[2] said one writer after opening night. Ben's playboy antics consistently received laughs.

Many reviews failed to mention the quality of the play, instead focusing on the novelty of Bebe, Ben and "Skeets" Gallagher appearing in person. (Bebe and Ben received the lion's share of the attention—no pun intended.) To many, it didn't matter if the play itself was any good: Audiences were simply paying for the chance to see three beloved actors in the flesh.

*Hollywood Holiday*'s three-month run was largely uneventful for Bebe. It was a minor news story when her $3000 fur coat was stolen in Boston, as well as when the American Legion sent 200 of its members to support Bebe's show. The most notable incident came in Philadelphia, where Bebe fell ill and had to have Pauline Gallagher fill in. With Gallagher in the leading role, revenue fell from $9000 the first week to $4000 the second. The public, it was obvious, wanted to see Bebe Daniels more than they wanted to see a good play.

Barbara, now almost four, seemed to enjoy herself on the road. The Gallaghers had a young son and daughter who made for perfect playmates while their parents were working, and newspapers often ran photographs of the couples' children together. Barbara was even made the star for once when she was selected to cut the ribbon for the Broadway Limited's new service from Chicago to New York. Bebe and Ben proudly watched.

While backstage in Chicago, Bebe, Ben and "Skeets" unwittingly became part of a popular culture trend. The early 1930s saw a boom in the manufacture of coin-operated amusements, which provided cheap entertainment during the Great Depression. Chief amongst these games was pinball, which was quickly becoming a cultural phenomenon. On May 25, 1935, *Billboard* ran a photo of Bebe playing a pinball machine, with her two co-stars looking on in excitement. She could hardly have imagined that such a simple picture would have the ramifications it did.

The image was reprinted in Hearst's *New York American*, sparking a massive wave of publicity for the burgeoning game. One pinball manufacturer ran a full-page advertisement in *Billboard* stressing the game's positive impact: "When large metropolitan dailies publish pictures of celebrities like Paul Whiteman, Ben Lyon, Bebe Daniels and others playing pinball, that is an admission of the games into amusement circles that will break down prejudice and create public approval in a way that could not be obtained by any other method."[3]

Following the initial run of *Hollywood Holiday*, Bebe and Ben returned to L.A., where they were both engaged to make pictures. These projects came at a volatile time in Hollywood; the Fox Film Corporation was going bankrupt, and Joseph Schenck and Darryl F. Zanuck were arranging for a merger with 20th Century Pictures. The project Ben was working on, *Navy Wife* with Claire Trevor, was one of the last films made by Fox as the company was in dire straits. Bebe's film *Music Is Magic* holds the distinction of being the first film produced by the newly minted Twentieth Century–Fox Film Corporation. *Music Is Magic* (produced under the title *Ball of Fire*) is also important for the fact that it was Bebe's last American film.

*Music is Magic* touched upon similar themes as *42nd Street* had two years before. Instead of Dorothy Brock, an over-the-hill actress coming to grips with a new generation of starlets, Bebe played Diane De Valle, another over-the-hill actress facing the same set of insecurities. The idea of permanence in the entertainment industry was more poignant than ever to Daniels, as she had a tough decision to make: try to stay young and relevant, risk obscurity with character actress roles, or simply leave the silver screen for good. A number of unexpected factors would contribute to her eventual choice.

The film itself was not a particularly high note for Bebe to go out on, although her role was cited as one of the film's saving graces by many reviewers. In one of the most positive assessments, a writer stated, "[I]t's Bebe Daniels' polished performance that raises *Music Is Magic* from the ranks of the mediocre. She has developed into SUCH a good comedienne, and, to be paradoxical, while she isn't the star—she is the star."[4]

The themes of *Music is Magic* led Bebe to muse on what it meant to be an aging star in real life. Gone were the niceties of the 1920s, as Daniels had nothing to lose. Her words—no longer as positive and complimentary as they once were—hint at her growing resentment towards the current state of Hollywood:

> Women get into an awkward age, just like children. A child actress retires in its awkward age until she becomes of ingenue or leading lady age. But the most awkward age is when she steps from leading women parts into character roles. The trouble with a majority of actresses (and women, too) is that they always want to be the leading lady or still worse, the ingenue.
>
> I don't mind telling my age and weight: I'm 34 and I weigh 118 pounds before breakfast, without clothes. A woman of my age easily could be the mother of a 16-year-old, but most of us won't admit it. On the stage, an actress can play young women until she is 48, but it can't be done on the screen.
>
> A woman still can be romantic, however, but at a different age. There is romance in every age, if you know how to live. The greatest romances in the world have been those of elderly couples. So when you're 34, it doesn't mean there is no romance. If there is anything disgusting, it's a woman trying to be a kitten. It is so pathetic.
>
> I think it is a great thing for a woman to know her limitations as well as her assets. I think one of the greatest mistakes Hollywood actresses make it when they refuse to accept roles that will make them older than they are—or even as old as they are.[5]

As 1935 came to a close, a nefarious figure reentered Bebe's life. During the last week of October, Bebe and Ben noticed a suspicious car parked outside of their Santa Monica home. Around the same time, Bebe received a series of letters that threatened both the life of Ben and the kidnapping of four-year-old Barbara. Having been the object of such behavior before, Bebe took no chances and called the Santa Monica Police Department. By the time they arrived, the car had left, but the letters themselves provided a clue to the miscreant's identity.

It was Lyon who identified the man's handwriting as that of Albert M. Holland, the disabled war veteran who had made similar threats two years earlier. Following that case, which the Lyons had taken to court, Holland was committed to the Patton State Hospital in San Bernardino. By 1935, he had been released and was once again setting his sights on Bebe. The incident had a lasting impact on her.

It would certainly have been easy to dismiss the hostile letters as the ramblings of a madman—a man who, while intimidating, would not have acted on his psychopathic threats. And perhaps the entire incident would have been written off, had not the child of Charles Lindbergh been kidnapped and murdered less than four years earlier. Called "the greatest story since the Resurrection" by H.L. Mencken, the Lindbergh baby kidnapping remains one of the most highly publicized crimes in American history to this day.

Richard Hauptmann's sensationalized trial was held in January and February of 1935, eight months before Bebe and Ben received Holland's threatening letters. Fearing copycat crimes inspired by Hauptmann, many celebrities began to worry for the safety of their children. Fortunately, this mass-paranoia would prove merely cautionary. But for Bebe and Ben, it would prove to be too much. Bebe—now a mother first and actress second—no longer felt safe in Los Angeles.

Bebe and Ben began 1936 on the road, bringing their immensely popular vaudeville routine to some of the country's biggest markets. Although the couple had recently completed a nationwide theatrical tour, demand for public appearances by the Lyons was still at a record high. Their 1936 tour, playing massive theaters in ten different cities (sometimes for up to a week), would prove to be their swan song in the United States.

Opening at Pittsburgh's Stanley Theater on January 17, the Lyons were greeted with overwhelmingly positive response. At each city they played, their act was incorporated into a program that often included a motion picture, local vaudevillians and other screen stars. Despite the economic despair of the Depression, Bebe and Ben regularly sold out multiple shows on the same day. Each week, their performances grossed between $10,000 and $20,000, an incredible sum for the time.

A *Billboard* review of opening night in Pittsburgh captures the essence of the show:

> Bebe Daniels and Ben Lyon, of Cinemaland, are making their first appearance here and scored solidly. [They] build their act around a comedy sketch that has some clever lines and permits Bebe to sing Irving Berlin's "The Little Things in Life," a sentimental tune that fits her personality like a glove.
> She exits to change into her *Rio Rita* costume while Ben is left alone to gag. Bebe registers well in the noted tune and reveals a highly pleasing and romantic voice. The couple then gag with [emcee Johnny] Perkins, and for the final number Bebe sings a Spanish song and from a platform across the pit tosses flowers to the audience. Heavy applause.[6]

For many, Bebe was still most fondly remembered for her talkie debut in *Rio Rita*; her performance of the film's title track was consistently a highlight for audiences.

From Pittsburgh, the Lyons took their act to Chicago for a week of sold-out performances at the Oriental Theater. Again reviews were glowing, with the *Tribune* remarking that the couple's "pleasant personalities and human off-screen conduct are an antidote to the satirical anti–Hollywood jokes that are current in the theater."[7] Few other movie stars were versatile enough to adapt to stage performances so seamlessly. For Bebe, who cut her teeth in theater, it seemed the most natural thing in the world.

They then traveled to Philadelphia, Washington, D.C., Detroit, Cincinnati, Cleveland, Boston, Baltimore and Indianapolis. In every city Bebe and Ben were praised by the audiences and press alike. It didn't matter that their cinematic output had declined so much; the couple's reputation was such that their appearance in each city was momentous.

Along the way, various stars joined Bebe and Ben's traveling show for an evening or two. In Boston, it was Lillian Roth; in Detroit, Wallace Beery (who demanded almost $10,000 for his appearance). While these special guests certainly helped in terms of publicity, their presence was typically overshadowed by the unmatched rapport of the Lyons. Their multitude of radio and stage appearances had allowed them to hone their comic timing and back-and-forth banter, which was never more apparent than it was during their theatrical performances.

Throughout their tour, both Bebe and Ben were regularly contracted for other personal appearances. On one occasion, it was a benefit for moving picture operators; on another, a relief show for flood victims in Cambridge, Massachusetts. The couple made numerous radio broadcasts from the road, including several performances with Ben Bernie's orchestra. They even managed to find time to attend the funeral for Marilyn Miller, Ben Lyon's ex-lover who died unexpectedly at the age of 37.

Their whirlwind tour of the Midwest and East Coast concluded in April and they returned home. It was announced with much fanfare that the Lyons would be returning to Europe and bringing their successful act to Dublin and London in the coming months. The family was the toast of Great Britain, seemingly at the peak of its popularity.

Then things took a turn. A kidnapping scare—the most serious threat yet—forced L.A. District Attorney Buron Fitts to meet with Bebe to describe the danger her family faced. A nurse employed by the Lyons had exhibited strange behavior, and it was determined that Barbara's life was very much at risk. Fitts advised the couple to take an extended vacation to Europe, at least until the kidnapping wave had subsided. The warm reception they had received made this a very appealing prospect, and the Lyons purchased a house in London.

While residing in England in the mid–1930s, the Lyons were coaxed out of semi-retirement to star in several British motion pictures. Produced on shoestring budgets and lacking any real artistic merit, they didn't achieve the level of success that marked almost all of their American productions. Their bread-and-butter was the British stage, and films would remain ancillary for the time being.

Based on the 1933 British stage play *Murder in the Stalls* by Maurice Messinger, the low-budget *Treachery on the High Seas* was the first movie produced by Dela Films. Helmed by Emil-Edwin Reinert, an obscure French director. It was shot at British Lion's Beaconsfield studio, one of England's most popular studios dating back to the silent era.

The film's plot is hackneyed and simple. Johnny Howard (Ben) teams up with Logan (Charles Farrell) and May Hardy (Bebe) to steal a ruby necklace from Edward Brailstone (Tom Helmore) while on an ocean liner from New York to London. By the time they reach their destination, everyone has double-crossed one another and what was intended to be a simple jewel heist has unexpectedly become an charade.

The few critics who bothered to review *Treachery on the High Seas* (alternately titled *Not Wanted On Voyage*) did not mince words. "On the whole, a pale counterpart of many such stories that have been made and forgotten in the U.S."[8] is how *Variety* described it. Daniels, who sang in the ship's nightclub, was said to have performed admirably in such an unremarkable film. However, spotty distribution prevented many from even being able to see her performance; initially released in December 1936, *Treachery on the High Seas* did not reach Ireland and India until 1938 (and was probably never shown outside of the British Empire). A generally poor picture that failed to garner much attention, it remains a footnote in Daniels' career—which perhaps is for the best.

*Treachery on the High Seas* was followed two years later with *The Return of Carol Deane*. Based on Joseph Santley's story *The House on 56th Street* (already made into a 1933 Warner Brothers film with Kay Francis and Ricardo Cortez), it involves a woman sentenced to 20 years in prison for a murder she didn't commit. Produced by Warners'

Teddington Studios in London and directed by Arthur B. Woods, the film showed more potential than Bebe's previous British film in terms of production value. It would, however, experience a similar fate.

Carol Deane's release from prison and acclimation to everyday life comprises the majority of the plot. As one critic noted, "it is a long and complicated story." Despite its verbose nature, *Carol Deane* was well-received and considered to be one of the better films to come out of England in the late 1930s. *Variety* mused that if 15 minutes had been cut, the movie might have been successful in the U.S. Like its predecessor, *Carol Deane* suffered from limited distribution and publicity. While it demonstrated definite potential for Bebe in more mature dramatic roles, it would prove to be her last serious picture.

Ben, too, continued to make films in Great Britain, becoming somewhat more prolific than his wife. *Stardust* (1938) with Lupe Velez, *Who Is Guilty?* (1939) and *Confidential Lady* (1940) were all moderate successes which kept Lyon in the public eye. Although neither Bebe nor Ben were making the same quality films as they had been at the beginning of the decade, it was nevertheless work that they both enjoyed.

The year 1937 began with the variety show *All Fun and Folly* which headlined Bebe and Ben alongside music hall staples Nellie Wallace and Vera Nargo. The Lyons' act remained largely unchanged since the last time they had visited England, although audiences still relished the opportunity to hear Bebe sing "Rio Rita," "You're Getting to Be a Habit With Me" and "Only a Rose," the latter a minor hit for Daniels. Ben continued his reliable comedy routine which, while not as beloved as Bebe's voice, was nevertheless a highlight for many amongst the crowded vaudeville bill.

While Bebe and Ben were by no means the only American actors to bring their talents to England in the 1930s, it became apparent that their intention to remain there might be more long-term. *Billboard* noted that the "combo has out-lasted all other flicker stars seen this side, due to the entertaining quality"[9] of their act. Their popularity amongst the British people was more than a passing fad, and the couple quickly adopted England as a surrogate home. The audiences were large and the pay was good; there was no immediate need for a return to Los Angeles.

Beginning at the Victoria Palace Theatre and continuing on the Paramount circuit of theaters, the first months of 1937 were invariably successful for the couple. They played to many smaller markets that did not typically receive entertainment of such a high caliber; the Lyons' reputation preceded them throughout the entire country. Along the way their charitable work was prolific; benefit performances at both the Princess Louise Children's Hospital and Charing Cross Hospital were just a few of the ways Bebe sought to help the British people. More than merely an American actress looking for a new audience, Daniels was immersing herself in British society.

For fans unable to see Daniels and Lyon perform in person, their regular radio appearances ensured that all were aware of their presence. BBC's *Music Hall* program featured Bebe's singing half a dozen times in 1937 and 1938, and other shows vied to have such popular stars perform for them (a surefire way to boost ratings). In July 1937, one writer remarked (somewhat incredulously) that Bebe and Ben had been performing to sold-out crowds for 15 consecutive months. This feat spoke to their newfound appreciation overseas.

Although the basic structure of their vaudeville act remained unchanged from tour to tour (after the Paramount circuit, they again traversed the country on the Empire circuit), new songs and sketches were occasionally incorporated. By the middle of 1937, they were including a gag devised for a 1934 appearance on Rudy Vallee's *Fleischmann Yeast Hour* radio show. In it, they play a couple in the year 1960—Lyon the stay-at-home father, Daniels the family breadwinner. The routine, charmingly self-deprecating towards Ben, became one of their most popular.

Given the Lyons' success in the U.S. and England, it was natural for theater promoters to try to bring them to other corners of the world. Although talk about a tour of Australia never materialized, it was announced with much fanfare that the Lyon family would be the main attraction of a vaudeville tour of South Africa.

South Africa welcomed the Lyons just as warmly as England had. Bebe and Ben recalled massive crowds wherever they performed, as well as the particularly hospitable reception they received from local tribesmen who were completely unaware of the couple's fame. Throughout the entire trip, she recalled, they were greeted with "the sort of thing you see on the newsreels—the friendly crowds, the brass bands, the gifts, the flowers—the whole works."[10] From Capetown and Johannesburg to Port Elizabeth and Kimberley, the Lyons were demonstrating that they were worldwide celebrities.

Upon their return from Capetown, Bebe and Ben picked up where they left off with a tour of Ireland and Scotland. Again reviews were glowing, as evidenced by an article in *The Scotsman*:

> Bebe Daniels and Ben Lyon are described on the programme as the famous American stars of screen and radio. Empire audiences have already found out, however, how they can also scintillate as music-hall entertainers, and their "turn" last night made a distinctive appeal to large audiences. Together they have a quick-fire style of cracking jokes that is attractively amusing, and Miss Daniels, beautifully gowned, makes several appearances in front of the microphone, where the quality of her voice, and the accomplished ease of her technique are agreeably effective. It says something for the personal touch she brings to her songs that even "Little Old Lady" seems comparatively fresh as she renders the tune made so familiar by a legion of crooners and whistling message boys.[11]

In 1938 and 1939 Bebe and Ben grew remarkably as British personalities. Their radio and stage appearances became more frequent, bringing them to the forefront of British popular culture. Humorously, it was noted that when Bebe and Ben appeared in New York in 1939 they were billed as "England's favorite duo," a curious title for two born-and-raised Americans who had only been abroad for a few years.

In May 1939 it was announced that Bebe and Ben would be return to the U.S. for their first vacation in three years. "Two old friends came sailing into port the other day," one reporter wrote poetically, "a man and woman who were movie pets of yesterday before the screen began to yell."[12] For the millions who remembered them from a decade earlier, their homecoming was a welcome occasion.

Following a five-day layover in New York City, the Lyons flew to Los Angeles. As their Santa Monica house was being leased to Madeleine Carroll, they had to rent a nearby beachfront home. Immediately upon their arrival, they were greeted by old friends. Louella Parsons and Sally Eilers joined Phyllis Daniels in welcoming the couple home. But new friends were also made on the journey; Parsons recalled Bebe's first meeting with Hedy Lamarr (who she remarked reminded her of silent film actress Barbara La Marr).[13]

## 20. Hollywood Holiday

While in L.A., the Lyons made headline news by formally adopting Richard Lyon, the four-year-old boy who had been living with them for two years. Interestingly, they waited to adopt him until returning to California because Bebe and Ben said they "still consider Los Angeles their home."[14] Bebe's rationale for the adoption was that she didn't want Barbara to be raised alone and always hoped to have a son. Richard, who had been taken by the couple from the English Adoption Society, was quickly assimilated into the family.

The Lyons' grand return to L.A. ended after only three weeks, as the couple had engagements on the London stage. Most impressive was a six-week residency at the Holborn Empire that featured Bebe and Ben as the vaudeville bill's headliners. By rehashing the same charming domestic gags that had been winning them popularity for years, the Lyons became more and more beloved amongst the British people. The stage was set for greater success than ever before.

# 21

# Loyal to England

*When we are at home, everybody comes to my house for a big breakfast and then we ride all afternoon and come back starving for a buffet supper. I always serve Southern food, for I was born and grew up in Texas, you know. And some day when peace comes back, the house in Santa Monica will see us all there again, riding and breakfasting and suppering.*

—Bebe Daniels, *Baltimore Sun*, 1941

When Bebe and Ben returned to England in August 1939, Europe was on the eve of World War II. Less than a month after they arrived aboard the SS *Normandie* (alongside Edward G. Robinson, Jack Warner and Bob Hope), England declared war on Germany. For two actors born and raised in the U.S., it would have been perfectly understandable to return home immediately. However, Bebe and Ben were amongst the highest profile stars who remained in England. They would not permanently leave for the duration of the war.

In later years, they attributed their time in England to patriotism and devotion to the people who had provided them with a prolonged career. But the real reason for their continued residence overseas may indeed be much more practical. The shortage of transportation and entertainment caused by the war effort meant that actors, musicians and other performers were "drawing proportionately higher salaries than before the hostilities."[1] Another report several months into the war found that lack of talent in Europe led to American entertainers "doubling and tripling"[2] their workloads, leading to an increase in royalties.

This should not cast doubt on their devotion to their adopted homeland. But knowing that their financial situation was better off in England than America certainly helped to make their decision to stay easier. In the U.S. there was much more competition in terms of live entertainment and radio air time; in England, their name recognition provided them with seemingly more opportunities.

On December 16, 1939, George Black's latest production opened at the Holborn Empire theater. Titled *Haw Haw*, the revue included Bebe, Ben, "The Cheeky Chappie" Max Miller, Syd Seymour, Constance Evans and Gaston Palmer. The show featured little cohesion or production value, instead choosing to individually highlight the talents of its stars. Its musical numbers included "a Havana scene with Bebe Daniels vocalizing 'I Went to Havana,' with the eight Haw-Haw girls and Darmora ballet providing a living background of color."[3] Her other musical numbers: "As Round & Round We Go,"

"Your Company's Requested" and her only duet in the show with Ben, "Start the Day Right."

The same report noted that Bebe and Ben "receive but scant opportunity" to entertain, while Max Miller and Gaston Palmer stole the show. Despite this, *Haw-Haw* had a successful run (over seven months) before closing on July 20, 1940. It was just one of Bebe and Ben's multiple wartime successes.

May 26, 1940, seemed like a typical night in wartime London. Winston Churchill had become prime minister barely two weeks earlier, and that very evening the Battle of Dunkirk had begun in Northern France. The blackout had been in effect for almost a year, and radio was more important than ever in improving morale both amongst civilians and the armed forces. That week, a radio play of Thackeray's *Vanity Fair* and recordings by Guy Lombardo entertained the masses on BBC Radio, occasionally punctuated with updates on the Nazis' seemingly unstoppable progress.

At 9:30 p.m., during a programming block aimed specifically at Britain's armed forces, a new weekly radio show debuted: *Hi, Gang!* was a comedy revolving around the lives of its principles Bebe Daniels and Ben Lyon and a third player named Vic Oliver. No one could have predicted the show's enduring legacy, but the enthusiastic response it immediately received seemed a glimmer of hope and laughter during an otherwise joyless time.

While Bebe and Ben were certainly still celebrities in 1940, they were most often referred to in the past tense. Papers tended to dwell on their former reputation as silent film legends in America. While the occasional talkie or stage play may have kept them in people's minds, the couple were still relics to many. *Hi, Gang!* would once again catapult Bebe and Ben to stardom, with their fame in England during World War II rivaling even their fame in America at the peak of the silent era.

The two were always anxious to take part in all aspects of their productions, so the show's initial script was drafted by its stars. "Bebe and I were appearing in Bristol," Ben remembered, "and during that week we began working on a sample script which we wrote mostly in the lounge of the Grand Hotel.... The essence of the idea was a three-way comedy format, for two men and a girl, and including an important guest star. It was a program, first of its kind, designed to burlesque films, stage-plays and pantomimes, and was the forerunner of many radio shows to follow."[4] While the idea seems simple today, at the time it was revolutionary.

Almost entirely forgotten today, Vic Oliver's life was fascinatingly complex; tragic at time, triumphant at others. A true Renaissance man, he incidentally found himself alongside some of the most significant figures of the 20th century on multiple occasions.

Born Viktor Oliver Samek in Vienna in 1898, he was hailed as a violin prodigy by age six. He set his sights on medicine as a career, but soon left school to pursue music full-time. As an aspiring violinist and composer, he studied at the Vienna Conservatory under Gustav Mahler.[5] His dreams of being a musician were put on hold by the outbreak of World War I. It is alleged that, as a member of the Austrian cavalry, he served alongside a young Adolf Hitler (Oliver would never confirm or deny the claim).

In America after the war, Oliver attempted to revive his musical career. He unexpectedly found his true calling in the mid–1920s: While he was at a benefit concert, his broken English evoked a roar of laughter from the audience. Very quickly he became renowned as a comedian, appearing in a variety of musical revues and vaudeville shows. In England he met a young stage actress by the name of Sarah Churchill; their romance culminated with an elopement on Christmas Eve of 1936. Sarah's father, a prominent Englishman named Winston Churchill, vehemently opposed the marriage, going as far as to call his son-in-law "common as dirt"[6] in private correspondence. Eventually his harsh feeling towards Oliver would lessen, although the perceived embarrassment the family suffered from Sarah's marriage to a commoner was evident to many.

It was while married to Sarah Churchill that Oliver was teamed with Bebe and Ben. Ben would later recall that, although they'd met before on several occasions, it became quite an ordeal to hire him for *Hi, Gang!* Ben wrote, "When [a sample script] was finished we sent it to John Watt, then head of BBC Variety.... We said we thought Vic Oliver would be just the man for the third member of our team, if he were available."[7] Watt replied by asking if Bebe and Ben had ever worked with Oliver before, to which they replied they had not. When Watt confessed that he did not think a star of Vic's caliber would commit to the show, Ben took matters into his own hands. He immediately went to the London Hippodrome where he confronted Oliver between performances.

"He read the script which Bebe and I had roughed out, grinning all over his face and occasionally bursting out into a typical Vic chuckle,"[8] Ben continued. "'Well, well—I like that!' [Vic] said at length. 'I thought you would, Vic,' I said. And that was that." Ben had convinced one of England's biggest stars to join the cast of *Hi, Gang!* With three celebrities behind the project, the show was almost guaranteed to be a success.

The radio program's perennial opening—Ben exclaiming "Hi, Gang!" and the rest of the cast responding "Hi, Ben!"—became instantly recognizable. Within four weeks of its first airing, *Hi, Gang!* had already become the most popular program on BBC Radio.

As the war raged on, many American entertainers returned home, fearful about the future of England. One by one, countries fell to the Nazis: the Netherlands, then Belgium, then Norway. With the German occupation of Paris, it seemed inevitable that the war would cross the Channel. And yet Bebe and Ben showed no signs of planning to return home.

Newspapers were quick to pick up on the devotion Bebe and Ben showed to their adopted home. "Only 14 American Performers Left as Invasion Is Expected," read one July 1940 headline.[9] Even Nazi threats to level the city of London did not stop the Lyons from standing by the British people, for better or for worse.

Despite their overwhelming desire to stay in England, the emergence of a new law almost compromised the lives of entertainers such as Ben Lyon and Vic Oliver. In May 1940, the British Home Department declared that all male "aliens"—even so-called "friendly aliens"—between the ages of 16 and 60 needed to report in person to a police station each day, weren't allowed to use private motor vehicles, and had to remain indoors during nighttime hours.[10] While the rationale behind such a law certainly makes sense in the context of war, the consequences on foreign-born entertainers choosing to remain in England were entirely unanticipated.

Fortunately Ben had a sense of humor about the law, even going as far as to print calling cards that read: "Mr. Ben Lyon/Friendly Alien/At Home from 10 p.m. to 6 a.m."[11] Bebe and Ben had committed themselves to the people of Great Britain; they weren't going to let inconveniences interfere with their larger mission. In due time, the restrictions were lifted from the Lyons. Their significance was recognized by the British government and the British people alike, and they were never again hassled for their decision to stay.

An article in *Melody Maker* epitomizes the British sentiment at the time:

### NICE PEOPLE!

Bebe Daniels and Ben Lyon came to this country from the States in June 1936. They planned to stay three weeks—and they're still here, four years later, still enthusiastic about Britain in general, and British soldiers in particular.

Since the war, they have given up every Sunday to play concerts for the troops, but they felt that they would like to entertain an even wider Services audience. That's what gave them the idea of their radio show *Hi, Gang!* which goes over to the Forces every Sunday evening.

And just to show why everybody who knows them loves them, they devote the whole of their BBC fee to comforts for the troops—equipping hospitals, destroyers, minesweepers, etc., with radio sets; sending cigarettes and sweets to the troops, and keeping nothing at all for themselves.

As American subjects, it would have been understandable if Bebe and Ben had gone back home when the war took such a serious turn.

But this is what Ben Lyon says about it: "The way you British people opened your arms to us has been so friendly that we just don't feel we can take everything in good times and duck out in bad."

We raise our hats to BEBE DANIELS & BEN LYON.[12]

Nineteen forty-one saw a nonstop continuation of their war work, with the exception of a two-month vacation to America in September and October. Waiting for them upon arrival in New York City was Phyllis Daniels, who had brought Richard and Barbara on a train from Los Angeles to see their parents. Although they embarked on a publicity tour while in America, visiting their children remained the primary purpose for Bebe and Ben's visit. "The children are out in our Santa Monica house with my mother and grandmother," Bebe told the press. "It's best for them to be over here, of course, but it is hard to leave them."[13]

The couple was quick to inform the media regarding what they had been up to. "Besides writing and acting a script for a weekly broadcast on the BBC and making two British pictures a year," Bebe explained, "we have been putting on as many as five shows a day. We dash from factories to RAF barracks, to camps, to seamen's institutes, to London halls where we play for those wonderful wartime fire fighters. The thing that's hard about it, is rushing from place to place. But we love to do it—the one thing we can do."[14]

While visiting Hollywood in late 1941, the Lyons spent a great deal of time with their old friend Louella Parsons. An article that she wrote summarizes, more than any other piece, what life was like for the Lyons in the midst of World War II:

### Bebe Daniels and Ben Lyon Are Loyal to England

Bebe Daniels and Ben Lyon return to England with hundreds of thousands of dollars in offers to make American movies and to do radio and personal appearances. But there has never been one moment of hesitation or any thought of remaining in safe territory, even though their old-time friends and their mothers have tried to persuade them to remain in America until the war is over.

"It isn't," Ben explained, "that we don't love our own country, and that we ever feel that we are anything but 100 percent Americans, but England was so good to us, and both Bebe and I feel that we couldn't be cowards now and run away when there is trouble.

"There is much more than the mere danger of living in England these days. There are many sacrifices, rations on butter, sugar, meat, tea and most of the staples are rationed. There is no cream on the market. Oranges and lemons are very scarce. There is very little candy, eggs or canned fruit, and of course, the menus served in restaurants are very restricted," Ben went on.

"We'll never want for fish," Bebe added, "even though meat is scarce, for a fisherman from Blackwell sends us 18 pounds of fish a week. He said as long as there was fish in the sea we will get it because he enjoyed us so in *Hi Gang*. We share our fish with our friends each week."

"Tell about the clothes, Bebe," Ben suggested.

"You see," said Bebe, "we are only allowed 66 coupons a year. Stockings cost two coupons, shoes five, a coat one, nightgown six, gloves four, wool dress 16, silk dress 14, hankies one-half a coupon. It is surprising how little you can do with in the way of clothes," said Bebe. "But my fans have sent me their coupons because they seemed to feel as an actress I needed to have clothes, but I refused their offer. I feel I should take my sacrifices with anyone else. Of course, when I am on the stage, and playing in movies I need costumes, and the government has taken that into consideration and made it possible for me to have some very beautiful clothes."

Bebe and Ben have all the privileges of the English-born citizen. Aliens must be off the London streets between 10:30 p.m. and 6 a.m. "But," Ben said, pulling out a special permit, "Bebe and I can be on the street any time we wish. We also have an automobile, because we do so much entertaining for the troops."

Neither Ben nor Bebe has lost their sense of humor, and Bebe tells with great glee about going to spend the weekend at the home of a millionaire friend and carrying three eggs as her contribution. No one thinks of spending a week with friends without taking their ration card, or carrying what food they have on hand.

Said Bebe, "Someone sent us six oranges and we had them on exhibition. A lemon will be cut up into tiny pieces and hoarded. And yet," she went on, "the British spirit is never down."

"But weren't you afraid of the bombing?" I asked them. I had plenty of opportunity to talk to both Bebe and Ben as they are my house guests while they are in Hollywood.

"Well, at first I'll admit we were frightened, but only once could I make Ben go into a shelter," said Bebe, "and that was the time the house across the street was hit, and our house shook, and we thought every moment was the last."

"One of our very good friends had an interesting experience," Ben said. "They came home and were hungry. The wife wanted a sandwich and the husband did his best to talk her out of it, but she insisted she was starved, so they went down to the kitchen, there was a sudden bombing, and every room except the kitchen was completely demolished. They found themselves sitting right out in the street before the world in their negligees, with their whole house gone and the kitchen intact."

The theaters, Ben and Bebe say, are doing a thriving business. There is no place else money can be spent, and the people feel they can get away from all their worries by going to see plays and movies. Both Bebe and Ben gave a command performance for the King and Queen, and Bebe says the spirit of Elizabeth and George has had a great influence on the English people. They have taken all the sacrifices along with everyone even to doing without their usual comforts such as the King's valet. They have accepted the food rationing, too.

Both Bebe and Ben said they were dazzled by the lights of New York and Hollywood after the darkness of London. As for the food at parties given for them, it was bewildering.

When someone suggested that Ben and Bebe might remain permanently in England, they were very emphatic in saying "We are Americans and we are coming home after the war. We accepted what England had to offer us in good times, and so we think we should not run out when there is trouble."[15]

# 22

# War and Peace

*A whole chapter should probably be written about Ben Lyon and Bebe Daniels, both Americans, who have been in England for the past half-dozen years or more. They rank at the absolute peak of radio entertainers with their Hi, Gang show on BBC. Lyon and Miss Daniels have been in a number of highly successful English pictures and legiters, too. They are No. 1 morale builders in the British Isles.*
—*Variety*, January 7, 1942[1]

On May 24, 1942, almost two years to the day after *Hi Gang!*'s premiere, Bebe and Ben debuted a new shortwave radio program, *Stars and Stripes in Britain*. Lyon would interview men in the armed forces while Bebe would interview nurses, surgeons and hospital attendants. Americans on the homefront, living vicariously through the radio and newsreels, would be provided with "a colorful and timely picture of the activities and daily habits of the members of our armed forces in England, Scotland and Northern Ireland."[2] The interview subjects would also provide personal messages for their families at home, assuring them of their wellbeing and strong morale.

Each edition of the program opened with a medley of "God Bless America" and "Stars and Stripes Forever," setting the stage for the patriotic messages broadcast every week. Sometimes Bebe and Ben's guests were notable; for example, on May 23, 1943, the crew of the *Memphis Belle* appeared,[3] while on June 6 the couple spoke with fellow Hollywood legend Clark Gable.[4] Gable's interview was significant because it was his first public appearance since arriving in the European Theater of Operations.

Much more common, though, was for Bebe and Ben to speak with average men and women serving in the American armed forces. *Stars and Stripes in Britain* was designed, in large part, to give a voice to those who would not typically have a chance to tell their stories. A bomber from Texas, for example, spoke after his brother was shot down by a German aircraft. The young man's parents at home, grieving over the loss of one of their sons, were certainly consoled in small part by hearing the other's voice.

*Stars and Stripes in Britain* was not a traditional radio show along the lines of *Hi Gang!*; it served as a kind of public service. One reviewer wrote, "This one from London should effectively serve its purpose [which is] to assure the parents of American servicemen in the British Isles that their boys are well taken care of and happy."[5] The program's 16-month run, which brought little fame or exposure to Bebe and Ben, demonstrates their devotion to the war effort.

In the midst of the war, it was announced that Bebe would yet again return to the

British stage. *Panama Hattie*, with music and lyrics by Cole Porter, was immensely successful on Broadway in 1940 (over 500 shows with Ethel Merman in the starring role). An MGM movie featuring Red Skelton and Ann Sothern came in 1942, and by early 1943 Lee Ephraim and Tom Arnold had optioned the rights for a West End production.

Daniels' appearance in Merman's role was surprising given her numerous wartime obligations. She had, just several months before, completed a production of *Gangway*, and her near-constant radio appearances and philanthropic efforts were consuming much of her time. But Bebe, always restless, could not keep away from the stage for long. When rehearsals began in mid–June, she committed herself to the role of Hattie Maloney completely.

Before its long-awaited premiere in London, *Panama Hattie* toured the British Isles for three months. After opening to rave reviews in Manchester on July 27, the production travelled to Liverpool, Edinburgh, Glasgow, Birmingham and Leeds, breaking records at almost every theater it played. Bebe in particular was praised, as were the largely unknown British actors comprising the rest of the cast.

Anticipation was building in London as positive reviews poured in. Finally Ephraim and Arnold were able to secure the Piccadilly Theatre, and on November 4 Bebe opened to a full house. The three months spent on the road had perfected the production: The success of *Panama Hattie* was unprecedented during the war years.

While not as blatantly philanthropic as Bebe's other endeavors, shows such as *Panama Hattie* nevertheless helped the War effort by providing civilians with an escape from the terrible reality of the conflict. The thousands of men, women and children who flocked to the Piccadilly Theatre were awarded a couple of hours of joy and laughter before returning to the darkened streets of London.

Less than a month into *Panama Hattie*'s run, Bebe received devastating news. Little Mother, 89 years old and still as vibrant as ever, had died of a heart attack.[6] She was still living at the West Adams home where Bebe had resided during the early years of her Paramount contract. Stories about Eva de la Plaza Griffin's relationships with some of the silent era's biggest stars were nostalgically printed in her obituaries. She had assumed a matronly position in Hollywood during the 1920s, and many had very fond memories of her.

Bebe was torn apart by the news, particularly because it had been several years since she had last seen Little Mother. "It was fortunate Bebe and I had so much work to do," mused Ben. "It gave us so little time to think."[7] Tragic as the loss was for Bebe and her family, she and Ben had important jobs ahead of them. Rather than dwell on her sadness, she doubled down on her commitment to *Panama Hattie*. There was no alternative for Bebe.

After 308 wildly successful performances, *Panama Hattie* came to an unexpected and almost tragic halt. During the early morning hours of July 9, 1944, Bebe had a scheduled broadcast to troops stationed in the Middle East. When she returned home she was exhausted but unwilling to forgo her evening performance. She told her secretary Joan that no one was to wake her before two p.m.

Several hours later, Joan rapped on the bedroom door. "Mr. [Val] Parnell is on the phone and absolutely insists on speaking to you," she called in to Bebe. Worried at the frantic tone of her voice, Bebe picked up the receiver.

"Sorry to wake you up," said Val, "but don't worry about being rested for your show tonight—a buzz bomb has just hit your theater—go back to sleep."[8]

The German V-1 flying bomb—colloquially known as a "buzz bomb"—had been in development for years, but wasn't used against London until June 1944. Launched from the shores of France, buzz bombs wreaked havoc on the city; between June and October, a total of 9521 were fired at England. The one that put an end to *Panama Hattie* hit the neighboring Regent Palace Hotel, damaging the theater just enough that the show had to be cancelled.

It was announced that *Panama Hattie* would again tour the British Isles—and this time for the armed forces. While Ephraim and Arnold searched for a new London venue, Bebe and company played many of the same cities they had visited on the show's first run. For the troops, such high-quality live entertainment was a rare treat. Everywhere that *Panama Hattie* played, Bebe was met with enthusiastic servicemen thanking her. It was the kind of work she cherished.

Certainly the most storied facet of Bebe's war work was her presence in France in the weeks after the American invasion in June 1944. Daniels was, by all accounts, the first female civilian to be present on the beaches of Normandy following the invasion—

**Bebe Daniels lights a solider's cigarette on the beaches of Normandy shortly after the Allied invasion.**

a risk that she took not for glory or fame, but out of devotion to the young men and women risking their lives. A simple paragraph in *Variety* is all the contemporary coverage she received: "Bebe Daniels interviewed Americans wounded in the invasion of France in a pickup from an English hospital as a new and timely feature of *The American Eagle in Britain* program, which BBC feeds to Mutual. Miss Daniels, a favorite on the British radio, had the boys and the nurses very much at ease before the mike."[9]

Most proud of Bebe's selfless work on the front lines of battle was Ben Lyon, who wrote a letter to *Variety* several months later:

U.S.A.A.F., Europe, Oct. 5. '44.
*Editor, Variety*:

In a recent issue of *Variety* you ran an ad in which an actor stated he was the first entertainer to set foot on French soil. He was probably unaware of the fact that my wife, Bebe Daniels, was the very first entertainer to go to France. She arrived in Normandy early in July [actually late June]. The purpose of her trip was to entertain our boys and also make recordings of the evacuation of our wounded. These recordings have been used in the *American Eagle in Britain* program on Mutual network every Saturday night.

Probably this letter may seem out of order, but I can't help being very proud of Bebe for the wonderful job she has done throughout this entire war. As for the families of our wounded, she has been as close as 600 yards from the front lines to obtain interviews with stretcher-bearers and the wounded being carried off the battlefield, so that the folks in the U.S. would know what wonderful care our boys are receiving. At present, Bebe is in Italy carrying on this work and has been there for eight weeks.

I sound like a press agent, don't I? Really I'm not. I'm just proud of my wife.

Lt. Col. Ben Lyon, A. C.[10]

Fortunately, as the war came to a close in Europe, the burden placed on Bebe began to ease. The long hours she was working were taking a toll on her physically (Ben attributed her later health problems to them), and her selflessness continually seemed to border on self-destructiveness. But for both Bebe and the allied troops—it would all come to a close within the year.

Bebe began 1945 by bringing *Panama Hattie* to the troops in Scotland, in anticipation of the show's long-awaited return to London. At the Adelphi Theatre, much of the cast remained the same—Bebe assumed the title role ("a part that might have been made for her"[11]), while Claude Hulbert, Max Wall and Jack Stamford returned to their respective parts. On opening night, January 25, Colonel Ben Lyon was in the front row.

*Panama Hattie*'s revival was as successful as the play's first runs had been, and by late March Bebe was giving her 555th performance. (Someone calculated that more than two-thirds of a million people had seen Bebe as Hattie.) Although Bebe is most often remembered for her wartime radio broadcasts, the immense impact *Panama Hattie* had on boosting morale in London should not be overlooked. A high-quality production of an acclaimed Cole Porter musical during such a bleak time in England's history not only helped to distract the populace from the horrors of war, but also provided a source of civic pride and joy. If her radio efforts made Bebe a war hero, then her continued appearances in *Panama Hattie* worked to make that doubly true.

A little more than a month after V-E Day, Bebe and Ben returned to the United States. After a brief stop in Washington, D.C., they continued on to California. The flight coincided with their 15th wedding anniversary. Bebe would be seeing her children for the first time in four years.

**Bebe Daniels and a priest stand amidst the ruins of a bombed-out church during World War II.**

While she toured Europe during the war, Richard carved out his own Hollywood career. He began with uncredited parts not long after Bebe and Ben had adopted him, and first achieved recognition for his performance in *The Unseen*, a 1945 film that, while critically panned, nonetheless solicited praise for the ten-year-old. His film career would last only a few more years before petering out.

On June 15, 1945, Bebe Daniels and Lieutenant Colonel Ben Lyon touched down in a C-54 Skymaster in Long Beach and were reunited with family and friends.[12] Richard, then attending a military academy, saluted his father before embracing him. Barbara was now 13. Also present that day was Bebe's mother Phyllis, with whom the children lived in San Diego during the war years.

Upon their return, Bebe and Ben were treated like royalty. Although Hollywood had changed drastically in the years since they had left, there were still some familiar faces anxious to greet them. On one of their first nights back, a celebratory dinner party was given by Eddie Sutherland, who had introduced them over 20 years earlier.[13]

Almost immediately, the Lyons returned to their normal family life. Richard soon got a part in another film, *The Green Years* (1946), while Bebe toyed with the idea of putting her experiences as a war correspondent down on paper. (This idea would never

**Barbara Lyon, Ben Lyon, Bebe Daniels, and Richard Lyon (left to right) pose arm-in-arm shortly after the end of World War II.**

materialize.) For a short time at least, everything seemed quiet and peaceful: the Lyons were a normal American family.

When it was announced that the Lyons were to return to America, gossip columnist Hedda Hopper ran with a rumor that Bebe and Ben were filing for divorce after sending several months apart from one another.[14] The news spread like wildfire. Few readers suspected, however, that the real fighting going on was not between Bebe and Ben but between Hopper and rival columnist Louella Parsons. The two were notoriously hostile towards one another, always vying for the title of "Queen of Hollywood Gossip." Parsons, extremely close friends with both Bebe and Ben, often had the scoop on their personal lives; it comes as no surprise, therefore, that Hopper was so quick to spread anti–Lyons rumors in her widely read column.

Ben denied the allegation. "We've never had a cross word ... these divorce rumors were terribly embarrassing to the kids,"[15] he told one reporter. "Louella Parsons, a lifelong friend of mine and Bebe's, printed a story that we were coming back to the United States and along came another columnist who blasted the divorce rumor in her column." His thinly veiled reference to Hedda Hopper was not lost on anyone.

Although Bebe had all but retired from acting by the 1940s, it would prove impossible for her to entirely escape the pull of Hollywood. Towards the end of 1945 her return to the movie industry was announced, this time as a producer. And not only did it mark the end of a creative drought in America for Bebe, but it also reunited Bebe with the first man to give her acting career a break: Hal Roach.

The news did not elicit as much excitement as it would have had it come a couple of years earlier. The movie industry was changing at a startling pace. Pickford, Swanson and Gish would still make occasional pictures, but were largely forgotten by the public. Even Ginger Rogers, whose career began when she starred alongside Bebe in *42nd Street*, had already peaked in popularity. Now a new crop of actresses including Greer Garson and Ingrid Bergman were on the minds of moviegoers. Hollywood was cutthroat; after a self-imposed exile of nearly a decade, Bebe had little chance of making a big mark again.

While Bebe and Ben were supporting the war effort overseas, Roach had been contributing in a very different way back home. The Hal Roach Studios in Culver City—where Bebe and Harold had made a comedy a week decades earlier—affectionately became known as "Fort Roach" when the First Motion Picture Unit began producing training film and propaganda films for the U.S. Army Air Forces. Roach, drafted and in uniform, worked alongside Clark Gable, William Holden and Ronald Reagan on the production of over 400 films, many of which were released to theaters.

By early 1946 Roach was able to resume normal operations at his studios, using methods he had learned during the war to optimize his output. He invented what he called the "streamliner," a comedy film that ran approximately 50 minutes and did not exceed $110,000 in production costs (a quarter of the budget of a typical feature). By producing a larger number of these short, low-budget films, Roach would (in theory) make more money than a typical studio.

Bebe's setup on the Roach Studios consisted simply of an office, a secretary, a typewriter and "a bookshelf almost filled with bound volumes containing thousands of gags, alphabetically listed."[16] Undoubtedly many of these gags were familiar to Bebe from her one-reelers with Harold. Friends from those early days of Hollywood often stopped by the Roach Studios to reminisce.

Newspapers jubilantly announced that Bebe had been hired to produce four of the 12 streamliners Roach had in the works. The first, *The Fabulous Joe*, was an original script about a talking dog. Before filming began, it was announced that Bebe's second production would be an adaptation of Robert Lawson's *Mr. Wilmer* (also known as *The Man Who Talks with Animals*). The latter would never be made.

Written by Hal Roach, Jr., *The Fabulous Joe* is a somewhat inane screwball comedy about a man who inherits a talking dog named Fabulous Joe. Down on his luck and constantly pestered by his family, he is urged by Joe to stop letting his family walk all over him. This eventually leads to the man's divorce. One of the film's stars, Margot Grahame, recounted that Bebe was "very excited"[17] about producing her first film for Roach. "When I asked her what the film was about," Grahame said, "she laughed and said, 'About a talking dog.' It was the kind of story Bebe loved ... a dog getting a girl in and out of scrapes."

Production delays plagued *The Fabulous Joe*, which was supposed to begin filming in March 1946. It was released on August 29, 1947, almost a year and a half later. Many critics ignored the low-budget streamliner; the reviews it did get were tepid at best. "[It] recalls the style of comedy popular in the 1920s, although it has the modern addition of color,"[18] said one critic. Others were more blunt with their dismissal.

The thousands of gags Bebe had at her disposal may have helped spell the film's downfall. By the 1940s, the style of comedy that she had cut her teeth on was nonexistent. While adults may have supported a film simply because of Roach's name, once synonymous with brilliant comedy, the younger generation simply would not go for such a silly production.

Further compounding *The Fabulous Joe*'s troubles was the fact that many theaters would not screen a double feature of two 50-minute streamliners. As an answer to this, Roach combined *The Fabulous Joe* with the unrelated *Curley* to create the *Hal Roach Comedy Carnival*. *Curley*, a reinterpretation of Roach's famous Our Gang comedies, had been released only a week before *The Fabulous Joe*. But even the two films combined into one could not attract audiences. Despite announcements that Bebe was to produce four streamliners, her stint as a producer for Roach was over after only one.

Bebe decided to enter a market that was wholly new for her: children's records. In the postwar years the novelty record industry (affectionately called "kidisks") was booming and many Hollywood stars decided to enter the market. Effort was minimal, and name recognition alone would often make a record a success. The Little Folks Favorites label, for example, was releasing songs and stories by Gene Raymond and William Boyd (better known to many youngsters as Hopalong Cassidy).

Bebe's first foray into children's records came in November 1946, when she recorded half-talking, half-singing versions of *Aladdin and His Wonderful Lamp* and an original story called *The Doll Who Ran Away*. The albums were released just in time for Christmas. *Billboard* noted that they would "hit the kids right in their parents' pocketbooks, while the Bebe Daniels tag should attract the adults."[19]

It was soon announced that Bebe would be heading her own department at Enterprise Records, Bebe Daniels Production. Like her movie producer tenure with Hal

Roach, her time as a record producer would prove fleeting. After producing 18 records, including *The Tales of Uncle Remus* by radio star Jimmy Scribner,[20] Enterprise Records was absorbed by United Artists Records. United Artists Records likewise folded, and after a prolonged legal battle Bebe's masters were left unreleased.

Down but not out, Bebe tried one more time to enter the music industry: She founded her own label, Castle Records. Focusing on adults instead of the children's market, Castle's first and only release featured David X. Miller performing "Linger Awhile" and Romo Vincent performing "It All Depends on You." Ultimately the market was too saturated to allow for an independent label to succeed, especially one founded by someone with so little knowledge of the music industry.

# 23

# After the War

> *There is hereby established a medal to be known as the Medal of Freedom with accompanying ribbons and appurtenances for award to any person, not hereinafter specifically excluded, who, on or after December 7, 1941, has performed a meritorious act or service which has aided the United States in the prosecution of a war against an enemy or enemies and for which an award of another United States medal or decoration is considered inappropriate.*
> —Harry S. Truman, Executive Order 9586

December 7, 1946, was a warm day in Southern California. Scattered clouds cleared in the afternoon as a group of military personnel gathered at March Army Airfield in Riverside, 60 miles east of Los Angeles. Many events like this one, intended to decorate those who had distinguished themselves overseas, were held in the years after World War II. Lieutenant General Ira C. Eaker of the Army Air Forces, who had risen to prominence in the Mediterranean Theater, conducted the ceremony.

There was one thing that made this ceremony different from all of the others held in the aftermath of the war. For perhaps the first time in American history, a husband and wife were to be decorated at the same time. Lieutenant Colonel Ben Lyon and Bebe Daniels stood side by side as General Eaker recognized their unfailing service to the Allied Nations from the onset of the war until its end. While many celebrities had served in the armed forces, most notably Henry Fonda and James Stewart, few dedicated as much of their lives to the war effort as Bebe and Ben did.

Lyon was awarded the prestigious Legion of Merit for "exceptionally meritorious conduct in the performance of outstanding services to the Government of the United States from September 1942 to August 1945." His service in the Army Air Forces was remarkable by any standard; the fact that he had once been a beloved matinee idol made his sacrifice and commitment to his country even more admirable. Hollywood celebrities at this time were used to making contributions to the homefront; enlisting for overseas duty was a true anomaly at this time.

Bebe was presented with the Presidential Medal of Freedom, the highest possible decoration for a civilian. Authorized by President Harry Truman, Bebe's full citation read:

> Bebe Daniels Lyon, American civilian, for exceptionally meritorious achievement which aided the United States of America in prosecution of a war against the enemy in continental Europe from 16 December 1941, to 26 May 1945. During this period she distinguished herself by her initiative and unfailing interest in the welfare of the American soldier.

With outstanding ability she organized, produced and acted in theatrical productions presented to civilians and troops and was the first woman civilian to follow the troops in the Normandy landing in order to entertain wounded American soldiers 600 yards behind the front line.

Her unselfish services and willing sacrifice under the most dangerous conditions contributed immeasurably to the maintenance of a high state of morale among the troops, thus materially contributing to the success of the war effort.

Bebe Daniels—the "Good Little Bad Girl," an icon of the Roaring Twenties who had miraculously conquered talkies, was now a war hero. To those who knew her at the height of her acting career, it simultaneously seemed unexpected and perfectly natural. Her nerve and confidence, instilled in her by her mother, made her the perfect candidate to contribute the war effort. In her younger years, she had channeled this determination into her career. Now, having retired from Hollywood, she was able to focus this energy on something important not only to her, but to millions across the globe.

American audiences were largely unfamiliar with Bebe and Ben's work as radio stars. Although *Hi Gang!* was an immediate hit in the U.K., it was never broadcast in the U.S., so most of the country was oblivious to Bebe's continued success following her retirement from cinema in the 1930s. Many of the silent star's former fans were also unaware of Bebe and Ben's two children. Richard and Barbara had been kept out of the American limelight almost entirely, apart from a handful of movie roles for the former.

Therefore it was an occasion when the four Lyons appeared on *Skippy Hollywood Theater* on October 24, 1947. An extremely popular syndicated show that was little more than a carbon copy of *Lux Radio Theatre*, the program ran from 1941 to 1949 and featured such stars as Joan Bennett and Vincent Price in pre-recorded, scripted scenarios.

The October 24 episode featured all four Lyons in a Halloween-themed story called "Pranks for Parents." Les Mitchell, the show's host, opened the program with the following monologue:

> This is a red letter day for our program. Instead of one star, we have four stars. And when I say star, I do so advisedly. We have with us two of the most idolized figures of the motion picture world. Two people who went to England on a tour and stayed to help fight a war. Who have not only proven that fine acting has nothing to do with temperament, but also that a happy family life is possible when there is more than one career in the family. Now in just a moment we want you to meet the famous Lyon family: Bebe Daniels, Ben Lyon, and their two children Barbara and Richard.

Those who had grown up with Bebe's motion pictures were presumably surprised to hear her first radio broadcast following the war. After falling out of the public's consciousness, she was back: still married to Ben, still performing, still maintaining the unblemished reputation she had created for herself decades earlier. Following a brief but obligatory advertisement for Skippy Peanut Butter, the broadcast continued:

> LES MITCHELL: First, everyone will remember the beautiful and glamorous star of many motion pictures, Miss Bebe Daniels.
> BEBE DANIELS: Thank you, Les, and hello everybody.
> LES: Bebe, you know, you certainly confound the average opinion of Hollywood. You've had the same house, the same husband and the same children for quite a few years now.
> BEBE: Yes, I haven't made much progress, have I?
> LES: Well, I'd say that such progress makes for very fine living as well as artistry. Now next, we want

you to meet the star of many great motion pictures. A gentleman who did not quibble about giving his wife first billing, Mr. Ben Lyon.

BEN LYON: Well, Les, Bebe will always have top billing with me. I think she's a great actress, a great mother and a very great wife.

LES: You know, that's the kind of billing anyone could be proud of, Ben. And now we come to the beautiful and talented young lady who is making her professional debut, Miss Barbara Lyon.

BARBARA LYON: Thank you Mr. Mitchell. I suppose I should feel a little nervous right about now. But I can't help but feel at home in this company.

LES: Well, I'm certain that you'll come through with flying colors, Barbara. You know, you may even rival your brother for the acting honors in the younger generation. We want you to meet the young man they call the ham of the house. Richard Lyon, whose reputation as an actor has already been established in numerous motion pictures and particularly by his performance as Anna's son in *Anna and the King of Siam*.

RICHARD LYON: Thank you, Mr. Mitchell. It won't take very much acting to play this part. I guess it's a real example of typecasting.

BARBARA: Oh, stop being a ham, Richard.

This performance foreshadows the Lyons' later success on radio and television, and serves as a segue between *Hi Gang!*—with only Bebe and Ben—and *Life with the Lyons*, starring all four family members. The roles assumed by each—the ever-graceful Bebe, gentlemanly Ben, reserved Barbara and precocious Richard—are suggestive of the characters the family would expand upon several years later. Ultimately, the actual skit the family performs is somewhat silly and ultimately forgettable. What is much more interesting is the fleeting glimpse given of Bebe's domestic life.

Eagle-Lion Films, a low-budget studio located on Santa Monica Boulevard, was to be Bebe's new home beginning May 1, 1947.[1] Bryan Foy, its vice-president in charge of production, thrilled to have a former star as part of his fledgling enterprise, told Louella Parsons, "I gave [Bebe] carte blanche to do things her way. Of course, with an okay from me."[2]

This creative freedom was something Bebe did not have with Roach, where she was more or less confined to his vision for his films. It seemed promising, then, for someone as independent as Bebe to have full control over her productions. However, it quickly became apparent that her time with Eagle-Lion would not be fruitful. Their extremely small budget, combined with her impending return to England, meant that the partnership would never even get off the ground.

Bebe was not assigned her first feature until the April after her hiring, when Eagle-Lion announced the sequel to 1947's *The Red Stallion*. Titled *Red Stallion in the Rockies*, the film was eventually released in 1949—with Aubrey Schenck producing instead of Daniels. After several more months of inactivity, Eagle-Lion divulged that Bebe's first work as a producer for the company would actually be *Police File*, "a juvenile delinquency story to be done in a semi-documentary style."[3] Production was scheduled to begin in mid–1948.

Ultimately, *Police File* was never produced; two years later, Eagle-Lion merged with Film Classics. Both Roach Studios and Eagle-Lion suffered from severe budget restrictions at a time when Hollywood was still dominated by the major studios. Bebe's producing career was all but fated to fail from the start; but as always, new and unexpected plans lay in her future.

It was while working as casting director for 20th Century-Fox in the summer of 1947 that Ben Lyon made what was perhaps his greatest contribution to Hollywood.

**Bebe Daniels and Brian Aherne help Richard Lyon study his lines for the 1948 film *Smart Woman*, which starred Aherne and Constance Bennett.**

The story of the naming of Marilyn Monroe (*née* Norma Jeane Baker Dougherty) has been retold countless times, and is only included here in brief form for the sake of completeness. The *Atlanta Journal and Constitution* provided the best summary of the now-legendary tale:

> Ben Lyon first met Norma Jean Baker Dougherty in the summer of 1947. He was head of casting at 20th Century-Fox Studios—and she walked into his office unheralded. But he knew immediately that she was a potential star.

The beauty and vitality of the whispery-voiced hopeful—then a 20-year-old Los Angeles model who had divorced the policeman she had married at 16—immediately reminded him of another blonde. Lyon thought she resembled the famed Jean Harlow. In 1929, he helped Jean Harlow land the lead opposite him in the aviation drama, *Hell's Angels*—the picture that sent her a long way on the road to stardom. She won such fame that she probably was known even to little Norma Jean Baker, who was a scrawny waif making the rounds of foundling homes at that time.

"From the moment that Norma Jean [sic] Daugherty walked into my office," Lyon recalled recently, "I was certain she had star qualities. She came in at 11 a.m.—and within one hour I signed her to a seven-year optional contract, starting at $125 a week. At 6 p.m. that day, we tested her in color, and within a week exercised our option on her services.

"She was the most conscientious youngster signed by the company. She devoted all her time to study, training and exercise so that when an opportunity came she would be prepared. I have the greatest admiration for her."

Lyon created one of the world's most-talked-about names by adding Monroe, the maiden name of Norma Jean's mother (who was born Gladys Monroe), to Marilyn, a name for which he had a sentimental attachment. It seems that Norma Jean reminded him of the late Marilyn Miller, the Broadway musical comedy star of the 1920s, in addition to Jean Harlow. Marilyn Miller once co-starred with Lyon in a movie and was a favorite of his.[4]

Marilyn Miller was rumored to be engaged to Ben at the same time that Bebe was rumored to be engaged to Jack Pickford—an arrangement made more scandalous by the fact that Miller and Pickford were at the time married.

Seven years after he first signed Marilyn Monroe, Ben visited her on a set. She autographed a photograph to him that he kept for the rest of his life. It read: "You found me, named me and believed in me when no one else did. My love and thanks forever."

Monroe was far from his only discovery at 20th Century–Fox; he was also credited with signing Richard Widmark for *Kiss of Death* and casting an eight-year-old Natalie Wood in *Miracle on 34th Street*. Regarding the latter, he joked, "She used to sit on my lap and call me Uncle Ben. I wish she'd do it now!"[5]

Bebe was renowned for her dinner parties at the height of Hollywood's opulence during the 1920s. It is therefore fitting that upon her return to Los Angeles in 1946 she remained something of a *maître d'* to the city's elite. Frequent cocktail parties and dinners were held at Daniels' Santa Monica beach house, each attracting a mix of silent era standbys and Hollywood's new class of elites. Chief amongst her friends remained Louella Parsons, for whom Bebe substituted on the radio when Parsons was unable to broadcast. Although Hollywood had continued to grow and develop without the Lyons, there were still many familiar faces left for Bebe and Ben to reminisce with.

On September 25, 1948, Bebe and Ben were honored at a ceremony at New York's Madison Square Garden recognizing the contributions of entertainment personalities to the war effort. Sponsored by the Air Force Association, the highly publicized event also featured Bob Hope, Jack Warner, Hal Roach, Adolphe Menjou, Eddie Albert, Merian C. Cooper, James Stewart *et al*.[6] After more than a decade abroad, Bebe was still beloved, and her selfless work overseas was constantly being recognized.

On October 22, 1948, Darryl F. Zanuck made the announcement that Ben Lyon had been promoted from casting director at 20th Century–Fox.[7] His new position would be executive assistant to Lyman Munson, head of 20th Century–Fox in Great Britain. Beginning his new job almost immediately, Ben began making plans to move from Hollywood to London—much to the surprise of everyone who expected the Lyons to remain permanent residents of California now that the war was over. Bebe, experiencing little success with Eagle-Lion, announced that she would follow him in December in order for the family to spend Christmas together.

When Bebe left Eagle-Lion, she had yet to produce a film for the studio. *Catch Me Before I Kill*, a tale of juvenile delinquency, had been in the works for months but never made any headway. Despite a renewed career as a Hollywood producer that lasted two years, her only credit during this time was her one Hal Roach picture. Whether or not this was due to Daniels' incompetence as a producer is difficult to ascertain, but it seems more likely that her failures were due to the fact that she was working at small, low-budget studios. Whatever the case, her producing career was cut short by Lyon's reassignment.

Ben and Barbara left for London aboard the *Queen Elizabeth* on December 7. Bebe followed two weeks later, while Richard remained in America to attend St. John's Military Academy. The family's next chapter of life in Britain was set to begin.

Following the end of *Hi Gang!*'s revival run in 1949, Bebe developed the idea for another radio comedy. Although scripted, the show would be based on the Lyons' real family life—and this time, Barbara and Richard would be part of the cast. A pioneer of domestic comedy (earning Ben and Bebe many comparisons to Ozzie and Harriet), the show was groundbreaking in its depiction of everyday life. Ben worked at a film studio, Bebe had to cope with all the trials and tribulations of mothers across England, Richard was a lesson in neurotic frugality, and Barbara became known for her maudlin catch-phrase when relationships didn't go her way: "I'll die, I'll just die."

Premiering on November 5, 1950, *Life with the Lyons* was an instantaneous success. Gracing the Sunday three p.m. slot, the show ran for 11 seasons. Over the course of more than a decade, the British people were able to follow every (fictitious) move of the Lyon family. Amongst the show's countless fans were Al Stewart and John Lennon, both of whom reference the show's title in their music.

The show was very much the brainchild of Daniels, who drafted the scripts for nearly every episode. A recurring cast of characters supported the four Lyons, each integral to the production. Most notably, Molly Weir appeared as their housekeeper Aggie, Horace Percival as their neighbor Mr. Wimple, and Doris Rogers as Bebe's friend Florrie Wainwright. Other characters came and went over the show's 12-year run (from 1950 to 1961), including a younger son introduced when Richard was sent to America to enlist in the Army.

*Life with the Lyons* only ran for about half the year, affording the Lyon family much free time. During a 1954 return to Los Angeles, they were greeted with a luncheon at the Brown Derby. But the trip had a more specific purpose: an appearance by Bebe on an episode of *This Is Your Life*. Of course, Bebe didn't know this.

"I've been away so long, they won't remember me."

These were the first words out of Bebe Daniels' mouth during the September 29, 1954, episode of *This Is Your Life*. The roaring applause from the audience that evening proved that her fear was not warranted.

Amongst the episode's guests were four men who defined her life. There were Hal Roach, the producer of short comedies, who gave Bebe her first big break in Hollywood long before his success with Laurel & Hardy and Our Gang. Then there was Roach's

**A promotional photograph autographed by all four family members during the highly-successful run of** *Life with the Lyons.*

leading man Harold Lloyd. "The Boy" in the horn-rimmed glasses not only co-starred Bebe in well over 100 films, he was also her first true romance.

Sending his regards remotely from Egypt where he was filming *The Ten Commandments* was Cecil B. DeMille. DeMille was the first to see Bebe's dramatic talent and her potential for stardom when he signed her to Famous Players–Lasky. And there was the man who unfailingly stood by Bebe's side for more than four decades: her husband, her co-star, the love of her life, Ben Lyon.

Bebe, despite the well-deserved praise being heaped on her, remained as humble and gracious as she had been since the day she first set foot on a stage. She returned to London still embarrassed about the attention that had been given to her.

Despite the continuous success of *Life with the Lyons*, it had been more than a decade since Bebe's last screen appearance in *Hi Gang!* and audiences clamored for a chance to see the Lyons' antics rather than simply hearing them. By 1954 *I Love Lucy* was already in its third season, so there was reason to believe that Bebe and Ben—considered by many to be the British analogue to Lucy and Desi—would be successful if they attempted to conquer a different medium. The stage was set for the Lyons to grow their unique brand of domestic comedy.

The family decided to begin with a film rather than a television show. Ben and Bebe had both been actively involved in the production of their own films decades earlier, and their familiarity with the format made a movie the perfect option for reintroducing their aged selves to the British public. And so it was announced that the movie *Life with the Lyons* would be released on May 24, 1954. Almost 20 years after Bebe had retired in Hollywood, she would be making a return to the silver screen.

The Lyons worked with Exclusive Films, a small-budget production company, to bring their concept to life. Although Exclusive could not provide much financial backing (the movie cost less that $80,000), they gave Bebe and Ben creative control—which, in the long run, was more important. Val Guest, a prolific figure in British cinema, was selected to direct while Michael Carreras, head of Exclusive Films, was slated to produce.

The film's plot, in keeping with the radio show's domestic theme, features the Lyons returning home from a holiday and moving into a new home. To win the landlord's favor, the family tries such humorous schemes as throwing a "jive party" and installing an alpine garden. With the assistance of the landlord's daughter, they are able to sign the lease. Molly Weir, Horace Percival and Doris Rogers reprised their Aggie, Mr. Wimple and Florrie Wainwright radio show roles.

*Life with the Lyons* represented a major risk for the Lyon family. Producing such an inexpensive, unrefined project had potential to backfire, especially since some of Bebe and Ben's best-known films (*Rio Rita* and *Hell's Angels*) were renowned for their production values. *Life with the Lyons* was unlike anything they had ever done before; inspired by the organic, all-hands-on-deck approach they took to their radio show, it would be completely up to the Lyons whether the movie succeeded or failed. Although outside writers were brought in, the film scenario came from the minds of its two stars.

In the end, it was this very unorthodox means of production that accounted for much of the film's success. "It isn't slick, it isn't fancy, at times it isn't even very coherent ... but it's *alive*,"[8] wrote one critic at the film's premiere. Another astutely observed, "[W]ith no Oscar-winning illusions, [the film] sets its sights no higher than that of entertaining people."[9] By crafting a product that their radio audience would enjoy rather than aiming for high art, the Lyons created a sleeper hit that received unanimous praise from the press. Against all odds, it grossed over $200,000.

## 24

# The Lyons Take Television

> *If you're too young to recall, ask your parents about Ben Lyon and his wife, Bebe Daniels. They'll tell you that Ben and Bebe were just about America's most popular movie stars in the early thirties, as "hot" as Rock Hudson and Marilyn Monroe today.*
> —*New York Herald Tribune*, June 24, 1956[1]

The success of the *Life with the Lyons* film seemed to necessitate a sequel. The first film was still in theaters when Exclusive began filming *The Lyons in Paris*. Filmed at Southall Studios and directed by Val Guest, this film deviated little from the formula of the first. Some scenes were shot on location in Paris, providing a change of scenery, but *The Lyons in Paris* was in no sense groundbreaking. For fans, it was an appealing yet unchallenging offering.

This time, the brunt of the family's ire falls on Ben: Bebe worries that he has forgotten their anniversary while Richard and Barbara suspect he's having an affair with a French cabaret dancer. All of their fears are allayed when he announces a family vacation to Paris to celebrate their anniversary (he had merely purchased a car ferry ticket from Fifi the dancer). In Paris, typical Lyon family antics ensue: Barbara develops a crush on an existentialist painter, Richard becomes enraptured with Fifi, and the family car constantly threatens to break down. It was by no means a highbrow plot, but immensely entertaining to the target audience.

Both of the Lyons films were at their best when they relied on fast-paced slapstick. The same frenetic energy that powered Bebe's earliest films with Harold Lloyd was also responsible for the warm response her family received four decades later. The two Lyon family films tapped into the essence of early Hollywood, when films such as these weren't intent on providing anything more than good-humored entertainment. They were simple, formulaic and inexpensive, but audiences were willing to overlook these facts if the movies could make them laugh—and on this last point they delivered.

The success of their two films again raised questions about the potential for a television program. Ben shot these inquiries down immediately. "You've got to be loyal to radio—it gave us the breaks," he explained, before explaining, "[Bebe and I] regard our film as a kind of personal appearance."[2] It appeared that, despite the almost guaranteed success of such a show, audience would be limited to experiencing the Lyons on the big screen and on their radios.

In early 1955, Barbara followed in her mother's footsteps and made her vocal debut.

## 24. The Lyons Take Television

Her first solo record, consisting of "Stowaway" and "The Pendulum Song," was recorded on April 14 for Columbia Records with accompaniment from Ray Martin and his Orchestra. Regarding her time in the studio Martin said, "Barbara is a 'natural.' She has a great vocal style, with a fine sense of rhythm and phrasing and excellent diction.... I feel we have discovered a new singing star."[3] As a tie-in, Barbara performed "Stowaway" on *Life with the Lyons* shortly after the record was released.

Her foray into recorded music, it was explained, was a direct result of her parents' successful careers as singers (Bebe more so than Ben). Once she overcame her stage fright and was able to enter the studio, the 23-year-old's career took off almost immediately. While certainly her success had some basis in the fame of her parents, Barbara's voice *was* praised by several music critics. Her radio appearances led to legitimate stage offers, as well as more records under her year-long Columbia contract.

At the same time Barbara's music career was beginning to take off, the elder Lyons were making preparations to celebrate their silver wedding anniversary. The novelty of a Hollywood couple remaining married for 25 years was not lost on anyone, and the media celebrated the achievement. For the occasion, the couple threw a party for all of their closest friends in Dorchester, while the BBC ran a special radio program paying tribute to the longevity of their devotion to one another.

In November 1955, it came as a surprise when Richard's impending engagement to rising starlet Jill Ireland was announced. The two were frequently seen together around London, and at 20 years old the youngest Lyon was certainly an eligible bachelor. However, nothing further was ever reported about their relationship; two years later, Ireland married actor David McCallum before going on to have a successful career in film.

Barbara, following the positive response to her records and radio performances, decided to take her singing career one step further with the creation of her own television program. *Dreamtime with Barbara* was a 15-minute BBC "late night singing show"[4] produced by Russell Turner. The simple premise was that Barbara, now a rising talent in the British music scene, would perform songs with various bandleaders.

Not everything the Lyons touched turned to gold: Barbara's show fell flat. With a generic premise that couldn't distinguish itself amongst a crowded BBC television lineup, the program was cancelled after its initial six-week run. The show barely even registered in the British press and was never syndicated abroad. With the exception of several Columbia singles and a four-song extended play released as tie-ins to the show, *Dreamtime with Barbara* was forgotten almost as soon as it debuted.

Richard wasn't the only Lyon toying with the idea of matrimony: On April 4, 1956, five days after *Dreamtime* premiered, Barbara announced her engagement to her producer Russell Turner. Turner, 28, was very successful with the BBC, having produced shows with Petula Clark and Richard Attenborough. "I met Russell for the first time when we started working together on the TV show," she said in an interview. "We shall be married in July—the date is not set yet—and I will continue with my radio and recording career."[5]

Barbara's engagement to Turner the week of her TV show's debut certainly calls to mind her mother's "engagement" to Charley Paddock in the weeks leading up to the release of *The Campus Flirt* 30 years earlier. But while it would be easy to dismiss the timing of Barbara's announcement as a publicity stunt (granted, an unsuccessful one), the public was pleased to find out that Barbara Lyon was married to Russell Turner on July 21 at St James' Church in London.

The wedding was attended by many of the top entertainers living in Britain at the time: The crowd of 400 guests included Tyrone Power, Douglas Fairbanks Jr., Barbara Kelly, and Bernard Braden. Newswire photographs showed Barbara and Russell joyously cutting the cake as Bebe and Ben proudly looked on. Although her professional career was turning out to be something of a bust, at least Barbara Lyon, beloved by millions of listeners across Great Britain, had found success in her private life.

Hardly a year after Ben's proclamation that the Lyons would "be loyal" to radio, a *Life with the Lyons* TV show was announced. The public was thrilled at the prospect of new adventures from one of Britain's favorite families. The first episode aired on June 29, 1955.

Bebe and Bob Block, writers of the radio show, also wrote the TV program, which helped to create continuity. Broadcast on Associated-Rediffusion from London, the 30-minute show was initially slated for a four-episode, bi-weekly run. Again focusing on the "zany antics of the family,"[6] it offered little in the way of innovation. But by bringing to the small screen Ben, Bebe, Barbara and Richard (not to mention Aggie, Florrie, and Mr. Wimple), the show was almost guaranteed success from the start.

Almost as soon as *Life with the Lyons* aired it was renewed for additional episodes, as everything that audiences had loved about the radio show and movies had translated remarkably well to television. As *Spectator* wrote:

> *Life with the Lyons* has something engaging about it. For all its platitudes of calf-love, brother-and-sister rows, male vanity, Mom's niceness, burnt food and parental meanness, it still manages, by its sheer self-confidence and professional slickness, to amuse and amaze. The transition from sound to sight has been accomplished with no basic change at all in the structure of the programme. The same jokes, the same situations are used; all that's happened is that the family's had to learn its lines, and act a little—just a little.[7]

The TV *Life with the Lyons* ran until 1960, staying popular for its entire run. It was also syndicated in the U.S. for a short time. The show's scenarios across the six years it aired varied very little, but its formulaic nature was beloved by audiences and there seemed little reason to deviate from such a successful model. It kept the Lyons in the forefront of British popular culture, and kept the Lyon family busy.

In a 1958 interview, Ben described the Lyon family's typical annual schedule:

> We do 26 radio programs per year, which originate on Sunday and are repeated on Friday evenings. Our TV schedule consists of ten shows per year. These are networked throughout the British Isles. I am referring, of course, to our eight-year-old family show, *Life with the Lyons*, in which our daughter Barbara (age 25) and our son Richard (age 22) appear with us.
> 
> In addition to the family show, Barbara appears individually on a lot of TV shows as a singer, and she makes records for Columbia. I do a lot of emceeing for various shows. Bebe, unfortunately, cannot appear individually on TV as her entire time is taken up writing the scripts of *Life with the Lyons*.[8]

On July 27, 1959, after only three years of marriage, Barbara announced her divorce from Russell Turner. When her divorce was finalized in March 1960 it came out that Turner had committed adultery within a year of their wedding. As their marriage seemed to have a distinctly practical component (Barbara's brief career on television was directly linked to his production), it is unfortunately unsurprising that Turner was not romantically invested in the relationship.

## 24. The Lyons Take Television

The year after Barbara's divorce, Richard married Angela Andree, a stage dancer. Their wedding was held on July 1, 1961, in Sheerness, Kent. "When Richard and I became engaged," Angela recalled, "Bebe paid me the biggest compliment anyone could pay. She said, 'If Richard had asked me to go out and find him a wife, I would have picked you.' I always thought that was a lovely thing to say."[9]

As *Life with the Lyons* came to the end of its TV run, the Lyons moved to a new "den" (a pun courtesy contemporary tabloids). When their home at 18 Southwick Street was slated to be demolished, the family took up residence at 67 Abbotsbury Road, a three-story brick structure overlooking the picturesque Holland Park. After 21 years at their previous home the move was a big deal for Bebe and Ben, although the new dwelling quickly became as beloved as the old. Daniels spent her final 12 years in London at the new address.

On February 20, 1959, Phyllis Daniels died at the age of 73. She had been living in London with her daughter for a short time following a period of particularly poor health (her fatal condition was pneumonia developed from influenza). Her obituaries recounted the critical role she played on introducing Bebe to the stage and to motion pictures. It is not an overstatement to say that Bebe's early career was entirely due to the support of her mother. Their bond ranks amongst the closest of any mother and daughter in the history of Hollywood.

In the wake of her mother's passing, Bebe wrote the following tribute:

As twilight drew a soft curtain over the sky and stopped to wait for night—God reached down and gently gathered our Bunny to His arms like a sleeping child. For one brief moment she opened her eyes and saw what we could not see—a glimpse of where God had taken her. For Bunny was truly a child of God and she died as beautifully as she had lived.

Bunny was a rare person who never said an unkind word about anyone in her life. She bore no malice nor hated any man.

She was natural.... She was friendly.... She had profound wisdom and great charm.... She was fun.... She was gay.... She was the kind of person you met for the first time and yet felt you had known all your life. She was intelligent and interesting and comfortable to be with, to talk to and listen to—whether you were young or old, godly or worldly—because Bunny loved people and understood them and saw goodness in the worst.

When you were in trouble, hers was the voice you wanted to hear. You were never afraid to tell her your innermost thoughts, and she never betrayed a confidence. She was always there when you needed her. Her love for others was her purpose in life. She helped to keep your vision clear and gave you strength and moral courage. Somehow Bunny could always find sunshine in the darkness.

Bunny was a rare person. She walked through life with a firm step. Her road was broad and sunlit and she feared no winds that blew.

She loved God and all things of beauty and Nature. She was never in too much of a hurry to stop and admire a lovely blossom ... a tree ... or a blue sky.

When I was a child she taught me how to find pictures in the clouds and to see beauty in a weed. She pointed out the colours in the rainbow and drew enchanting pictures in the sand. She taught me to fear no man as much as myself. She showed me how to make friends with small wild creatures. Once she picked up a small wounded bird from the road and took it home and nursed it until was well enough to fly away.

I remember how she could never rest if she thought an animal was hungry or a flower was out of water.

Her heart was always doing beautiful things and she gave freely of all she had.

Bunny was a rare person. Her friends were legion and she was greatly loved. The twilight of her passing lies heavy in our hearts ... for we will never see her face again or hear her voice on Earth. But she has left us rich in all things that matter ... and one thing is certain—as long as someone can see goodness in the worst, find sunshine in the darkness, comfort a friend.... As long as someone stops to admire a lovely blossom, a tree, or a blue sky.... As long as someone cannot rest while a flower is out of water or a tiny bird needs help—Bunny will live. Please God keep her vision clear.

Her daughter,
Bebe

By the late 1950s, the Lyon family was beginning to fade from the public eye. As Richard and Barbara grew up, they lost interest in the brand their parents had built and pursued solo endeavors. The decade had been incredibly kind to all four members of the Lyon family, but Bebe and Ben's age made it difficult to continue their prolific output. But as the generation that had grown up to their voices during the war aged, the family—graceful as ever—bowed from the spotlight.

# 25

# Still Only the Honeymoon

*She has a form of stroke and investigations are under way.*—a spokesman for the National Hospital for Nervous Diseases, May 21, 1963[1]

These words were printed in newspapers around the world. Bebe Daniels had unexpectedly fallen seriously ill—that much was certain. Whether she would ever walk or speak again was unknown. The irrepressible "Good-Little-Bad-Girl" of decades past, seemingly invincible through illness and injury, was looking death in the face.

The afternoon of Monday, May 20, seemed just like any other. It was cool and cloudy, typical for a London spring. Bebe was working at the antique shop with Ben and Barbara when she suddenly collapsed. Her husband and daughter were at her side within seconds; neither of them were able to revive her. They called an ambulance.

She was transported to the nearby St. Mary Abbot's Hospital. The cause of her stroke was quickly determined to be cerebral hemorrhage, and at the request of her doctor, she was transferred to the National Hospital for Nervous Diseases Bebe remained in a coma through the night.

Tuesday morning reports from the hospital seemed positive. A spokesman said, "She is a little better than she was Monday night, but she is still gravely ill."[2] In a statement to the press, Ben confirmed that she had come to; "She recognized us, the family, smiled and has also spoken a few words."[3] Hour by hour, her prognosis improved ever so slightly.

News continued to trickle out of the National Hospital throughout Tuesday. "This afternoon she is to be seen by Dr. Wylie McKissock, the brain surgeon who attended [racing driver] Stirling Moss when he was injured,"[4] the next bulletin announced. The surgery was as successful as it could have been. Although her condition remained critical, the slight improvements in her health continued.

The next few days were torturously long for Ben and the children. Bebe's condition seemed to change by the minute. On Wednesday, the hospital announced that she showed no further sign of improvement; on Thursday, Ben assured fans that she was certainly doing better. "We are thrilled and delighted with the improvement she seems to be showing," he said, "but she is still gravely ill."[5] Newspapers on both sides of the Atlantic carried daily updates that, more often than not, seemed to contradict themselves. Nobody, not even the doctors who provided her around-the-clock care, knew what would become of Bebe Daniels.

As the weeks wore on, updates on Bebe's health became less frequent. "We are all very hopeful she will pull through,"[6] Ben was quoted as saying at the end of June. It was hardly a month since the tragedy had struck, and already more pressing news stories had pushed Bebe to the back pages of the papers (if they chose to cover her at all). Bebe's condition was stable, and in the absence of real news she slowly faded from the public eye.

Three months after her stroke, a reporter checked in on Bebe and Ben. What he found was a selfless display of devotion that exemplified the couple's love.

Lyon, it was reported, remained at Bebe's bedside 16 hours a day. She was still partially paralyzed, but her condition continued to progress in the right direction. Putting her wellbeing above his own, Ben had lost 16 pounds from taking care of her.

"I've had plenty of time to think about how wonderful Bebe has been to me, and I'm more in love than ever,"[7] he proudly said. "The World War drew us closer together, and gave us a purpose and an appreciation for life." Asked about what allowed their love to remain so strong, he replied, "Couples should change their lives intelligently from time to time. If they merely try to float through life as comfortably as possible, they are likely to float right out of each other's affections."

Ben concluded the interview by saying that after 33 years, "It's still only the honeymoon."

Ben's devotion to Bebe stayed true—not only in the immediate aftermath of her stroke, but also through the multi-year recovery process. This is best-evidenced by a 1967 *Los Angeles Times* article, which summarizes the last years of Bebe's life poignantly and powerfully:

Bebe Daniels and Ben Lyon's Fabled Love Story Goes On

LONDON—Ben Lyon was one of the handsomest movie stars of his time and Bebe Daniels was one of the most beautiful. [...] The love story of Bebe and Ben, the stuff of which true romance is made, still goes on. [...][8]

During her last years, Daniels was so private that her story can only be told as a series of fleeting public appearances picked up by the press. As compared to the 1920s, when the minutiae of her life was captured by reporters, the 1960s saw stretches of several months without so much as a mention of her name in the papers. The eight years after her stroke afforded Bebe a chance to spend time with her family and, for once in her life, relax.

On a 1966 episode of *The Today Show*, Bebe and Ben were interviewed along with a slew of other British actors, including Anna Neagle and Laurence Olivier. The Lyons' appearance, their last on American television, stood out as a highlight of the episode for many who remembered the couple from their Hollywood days.

As Bebe continued to recuperate, Ben explored new business ventures. In the mid–1960s he partnered with David Oxley to found a talent management company specializing in booking American stars overseas. "Having been an actor, and a producer, I know the importance of this individual attention,"[9] he told a reporter regarding his new endeavor. After a lifetime in show business, Lyon was able to adapt and stay relevant in the field even in his old age.

In 1968, a humorous incident was recounted by *Variety*: "At one of the early evening performances of the Buster Keaton retrospective, being held at the British Film Institute's

## 25. Still Only the Honeymoon

**Ben Lyon in the hospital in February of 1965 after suffering acute appendicitis. Bebe Daniels was still recovering from the stroke she suffered two years prior.**

National Film Theatre in London, a young photographer hired by film curator Raymond Rohauer ... pointed to a still from Warners' *42nd Street* in front of the theatre and said, 'My mother was a star in that film.' He turned out to be Richard Lyon, commercial photographer son of Bebe Daniels and Ben Lyon."[10]

On December 14, 1968, Barbara Lyon was wed again, this time to Bebe's accountant Colin Birkett. Like her first marriage, this one too would be short-lived, although on May 13, 1971, Barbara would give birth to a son named Bruce. Unfortunately, his birth came just three months after Bebe's death, and newspapers lamented the fact that Daniels was never able to meet her grandson.

On September 22, 1970, Cinema City opened at the Roundhouse in North London. A 26-day long celebration of the first 75 years of the movie industry, the event was a joint venture by the *Sunday Times* and the National Film Archive. The special guest on opening night of the festival was someone very familiar with Bebe Daniels: Harold Lloyd.

"'Mr. Lloyd will be along any minute,' was the insistent buzz at the Cinema City preview early yesterday,"[11] wrote the *Irish Times*. "'I think he'll be wearing spectacles,' said someone else, clearly well clued up for Harold Lloyd's appearance." Despite the fact that he had not made a film in 23 years, the anticipation to see Lloyd in person was immeasurable. The first film shown at Cinema City was *The Kid Brother*.

While in London in October 1970, Harold Lloyd saw Bebe for the last time. Neither was in particularly good health, but their time together—joined by Ben Lyon and fellow silent star Colleen Moore—allowed the foursome to reminisce about old times. There were countless memories to share. Within six months, both Harold and Bebe would be dead.

The spark once ignited between Lloyd and Daniels had not been extinguished in the 55 years since they first met. Harold, the first man that Bebe had ever loved, was still wearing the cufflinks she had given him upon their breakup. "It was evident," biographer Annette D'Agostino Lloyd writes, "that the feelings the two once shared had not totally disappeared: their affection was quite strong."[12]

Bebe would, in an ethereal sense at least, always be "the girl" to Harold Lloyd's All-American "boy." The bond of 144 films together and years of a passionate romance could not be broken, no matter how happy the two were with their respective spouses.

Bebe's condition took a turn for the worse in November 1970: a bout with pneumonia that confined her to a hospital for several months. On February 6, 1971, Ben's 70th birthday, she was allowed to return home. Ben was heard saying that it was "the best and only birthday present I want."[13] Her final days were spent in the comfort of her Abbotsbury Road apartment. She was able to receive visitors, reminisce about days gone by, and partake in life's simple pleasures like backgammon and caramel custards.[14]

Jill Allgood was perhaps Bebe's closest friend in her later years and occasional collaborator on writing projects. When Bebe and Ben had both passed away, Allgood took it upon herself to write a biography of the couple. She remembered Bebe's last days well, writing that Ben "did everything humanly possible for her, installing a special bed and equipment in the flat. 'I don't care if I spend every penny I have,' he said." A day and night nurse were employed, and her hairdresser and masseuse (more like adopted family than employees) were frequent guests. Her children and their spouses spent much of their time with her, and Ben never left her side.

Although she continued to fight her illness, Bebe knew the end was near. She was growing weaker by the day, and her thoughts began to grow more philosophical. "She would say things like, 'As we grow older and come nearer to death, time becomes more precious,'" wrote Allgood. Resolute in her Catholic faith, Bebe braced for the end.

The news that broke on the morning of March 9 certainly did not help Bebe's frail condition. Harold Lloyd, who had been battling cancer for 18 months, died in Beverly Hills. Daniels' response to the news is unknown, although given the depth and longevity of their friendship it is a safe assumption that she was heartbroken. Although their love affair had ended more than 50 years earlier, their continued emotional attraction was undeniable. Bebe had found Ben and Harold had found Mildred—but the specter of lost love had never left either Daniels or Lloyd.

Of course any impact of Lloyd's death on Daniels' condition remains only pure speculation, but the timing of the two events certainly seems more than coincidental. Did the shocking news of his passing take a toll on her physical health? Or did the sadness caused by his death cause Bebe to simply quit fighting, unable to live in a world without her first true love? The answer will obviously never be known.

## 26

# "She Was My Life"

> *Bebe Daniels, one of Hollywood's brightest stars in silent films and the early talkies, died early today at her home in London. She was 70. Miss Daniels has lived in seclusion with her husband, actor Ben Lyon, since suffering a stroke in 1963.*
> —*Los Angeles Times*, March 16, 1971[1]

At five a.m. on March 16, 1971, Bebe Daniels died of a cerebral hemorrhage. At her bedside were Ben and her two children. Richard informed the press that his mother's death was peaceful. Ben, inconsolable, was only able to say, "I am completely shattered. She was more than my wife, she was my life."[2]

Of the countless obituaries written, perhaps the most interesting came from the Associated Press. Just a week before her death, it came out, Bebe had welcomed an interviewer into her home—her first interview in years. The content of their exchange, which did not become public until after her passing, sheds light on her final days:

> The gray-haired little lady looked up from her hospital-type cot and said impishly: "I'll get out of here real soon."
> Her husband smiled and said: "Of course, you will."
> She didn't.
> Bebe Daniels, star of *Rio Rita*, and of countless films with Rudolph Valentino, Harold Lloyd and her own husband, Ben Lyon, died in that cot in her London apartment at 5 o'clock yesterday morning. She was 70.[3]

Tributes poured in from around the globe. One poignant note was sent from Mary Pickford to Ben Lyon:

> Dear Ben,
> Only time can softer the ache in your heart, but may you find comfort in the thought that you and Bebe had so many happy years together.
> Some of my most cherished memories are those Bebe gave our family and most especially my mother, whose favorite she was.
> She was full of a contagious "joy in living" which brightened the lives of those around her.
> She will be greatly missed but she will live in our hearts always a symbol of not only great physical beauty, but a beauty of soul that she so generously shared.
> Buddy [Rogers] joins me in sending our sincerest sympathy to you, Barbara and Richard.
> Affectionately yours,
> Mary Pickford

On March 20, a ceremony attended by 300 mourners was held at St. Edward the Confessor Church. The requiem mass was said by the Reverend C. de Felice, who

**The final resting place of Bebe Daniels in Hollywood Forever Cemetery's Chapel Columbarium.**

honored Bebe by saying, "There is a broadcaster who ends his program, 'Thank you for allowing me into your home.' I would say on behalf of countless millions of the Lyons, thank you for allowing us into your home."[4] The lessons at the mass were read by Richard Attenborough and Dame Anna Neagle, both friends of the family. At Ben's request, Daniels' coffin was decorated in red roses.

Ben lived for another seven years after Bebe's death. In April 1972, Lyon wed Marian Nixon, a silent film star whom he had known since the 1920s. Nixon herself was a widow (she had been married to William A. Seiter until his 1964 death; Lyon was her fourth husband). The couple moved back to the United States; Lyon explained in interviews that following Bebe's death, he felt that his time in London had come to a close. He was awarded an Honorary Order of the British Empire in 1977 for his service to Great Britain. Nixon and Lyon maintained a quiet apartment in Westwood, a stone's throw from where he and Bebe had once been "the happiest couple in Hollywood."

Today, Bebe Daniels is interred in the Chapel Columbarium at Hollywood Forever Cemetery. Ben Lyon remains by her side in death as he unfailingly did in life.

# Epilogue

Bebe Daniels' legacy has suffered due to apathy from her family. Barbara Lyon passed away on July 10, 1995; Richard died on October 16, 2013. Both were reluctant to dwell on their youth. Attempts to reach Bruce Birkett, Barbara's son, initially seemed promising; however, after a number of phone calls to his office, it became apparent that he had no interest in speaking about his grandmother (who died shortly before he was born). Bebe and Ben's scrapbooks were donated to the British Film Institute; at the time of writing, these materials were not accessible to the public because of a construction project. The living members of the Lyon family do not appear to have any memorabilia or artifacts passed down from Bebe and Ben.

# Filmography

This is the most complete filmography of Bebe Daniels' American films to date. Included is every American film she is known to have acted in, based on an exhaustive survey of contemporary publications, advertisements, photographic archives and Bebe's own writings. *Not* included are cameo appearances, newsreel footage and promotional shorts. Bebe acted in a number of such films, but compiling a complete and accurate list of them needs to be the subject of further research.

## Early Films (1910–1915)

The early filmography of Bebe Daniels is incomplete. Only films for which there is primary evidence of Bebe's involvement (advertisements, reviews, photographs) are included here. This excludes several titles that have historically been linked to Daniels, most notably the 1910 Selig version of *The Wizard of Oz*.

One can hope this filmography can be updated as further evidence comes to light.

*The Common Enemy*
Selig Polyscope Company
Released: April 4, 1910
Length: One reel
Note: Bebe Daniels' first film.

*Dr. Skinnem's Wonderful Invention*
Kalem Company
Released: September 11, 1912
Length: One reel

*Anne of the Golden Heart*
Vitagraph Company
Released: January 22, 1914
Length: One reel
Note: Bebe Daniels' first on-screen credit.

*Aunt Matilda Outwitted*
Albuquerque Company
Released: August 1915
Length: Unknown

*Crazy with the Heat*
Albuquerque Company
Released: circa June 1915
Length: Unknown

*The Savage*
Director: James Youngdeer
Released: Unknown
Length: Five reels

## Rolin Films (1915–1919)

Bebe Daniels starred in 144 films with Harold Lloyd, as well as two Rolin Films productions without him. Bebe was, by far, Lloyd's most frequent leading lady. Unless otherwise noted, all of the pictures listed featured Harold Lloyd and Harry "Snub" Pollard. Other frequent cast members included Gene Marsh, Margaret Joslin, Bud Jamison, Fred C. Newmeyer, Harry Todd, Charles Stevenson and Margaret Joslin.

Note: Synopses for the 144 Harold Lloyd films can be found elsewhere, particularly Annette D'Agostino Lloyd's *Harold Lloyd Encyclopedia*.

*Giving Them Fits*
Released: November 1, 1915
Length: One reel
Note: Bebe's first film released for Rolin, but the third produced.

*Bughouse Bellhops*
Released: November 8, 1915
Length: One reel

*Tinkering with Trouble*
Released: November 17, 1915
Length: One reel

*Great While It Lasted*
Released: November 24, 1915
Length: One reel

*Ragtime Snap Shots*
Released: December 1, 1915
Length: One reel

*A Foozle at the Tee Party*
Released: December 8, 1915
Length: One reel
Note: Bebe's first film produced for Rolin, but the sixth released.

*Peculiar Patients' Pranks*
Released: December 22, 1915
Length: One reel

*Lonesome Luke, Social Gangster*
Released: December 29, 1915
Length: One reel

*Lonesome Luke Leans to the Literary*
Released: January 5, 1916
Length: One reel

*Luke Lugs Luggage*
Released: January 12, 1916
Length: One reel

*Lonesome Luke Lolls in Luxury*
Released: January 19, 1916
Length: One reel

*Luke, the Candy Cut-Up*
Released: January 31, 1916
Length: One reel

*Luke Foils the Villain*
Released: February 14, 1916
Length: One reel

*Luke and the Rural Roughnecks*
Released: March 1, 1916
Length: One reel

*Luke Pipes the Pippins*
Released: March 15, 1916
Length: One reel

*Lonesome Luke, Circus King*
Released: March 29, 1916
Length: One reel

*Luke's Double*
Released: April 12, 1916
Length: One reel

*Them Was the Happy Days!*
Released: April 26, 1916
Length: One reel

*Luke and the Bomb Throwers*
Released: May 8, 1916
Length: One reel

*Luke's Late Lunchers*
Released: May 22, 1916
Length: One reel

*Luke Laughs Last*
Released: June 5, 1916
Length: One reel

*Luke's Fatal Flivver*
Released: June 19, 1916
Length: One reel

*Luke's Society Mixup*
Released: June 26, 1916
Length: One reel

*Luke's Washful Waiting*
Released: July 3, 1916
Length: One reel

*Luke Rides Roughshod*
Released: July 10, 1916
Length: One reel

*Luke—Crystal Gazer*
Released: July 24, 1916
Length: One reel

*Luke's Lost Lamb*
Released: August 7, 1916
Length: One reel

*Luke Does the Midway*
Released: August 21, 1916
Length: One reel

*Luke Joins the Navy*
Released: September 4, 1916
Length: One reel

*Luke and the Mermaids*
Released: September 18, 1916
Length: One reel

*Luke's Speedy Club Life*
Released: October 1, 1916
Length: One reel

*Luke and the Bang-Tails*
Released: October 15, 1916
Length: One reel

*Luke the Chauffeur*
Released: October 29, 1916
Length: One reel

*Luke's Preparedness Preparations*
Released: November 5, 1916
Length: One reel

*Luke, the Gladiator*
Released: November 12, 1916
Length: One reel

*Luke, Patient Provider*
Released: November 19, 1916
Length: One reel

*Luke's Newsie Knockout*
Released: November 26, 1916
Length: One reel

*Luke's Movie Muddle*
Released: December 3, 1916
Length: One reel

*Luke, Rank Impersonator*
Released: December 10, 1916
Length: One reel

*Luke's Fireworks Fizzle*
Released: December 17, 1916
Length: One reel

*Luke Locates the Loot*
Released: December 24, 1916
Length: One reel

*Luke's Shattered Sleep*
Released: December 31, 1916
Length: One reel

*Luke's Lost Liberty*
Released: January 7, 1917
Length: One reel

*Luke's Busy Day*
Released: January 21, 1917
Length: One reel

*Luke's Trolley Trouble*
Released: February 4, 1917
Length: One reel

*Lonesome Luke, Lawyer*
Released: February 18, 1917
Length: One reel

*Luke Wins Ye Ladye Faire*
Released: February 25, 1917
Length: One reel

*Lonesome Luke's Lively Life*
Released: March 18, 1917
Length: Two reels
Note: The first "Lonesome Luke" two-reeler.

*Lonesome Luke on Tin Can Alley*
Released: April 15, 1917
Length: Two reels

*Lonesome Luke's Honeymoon*
Released: May 20, 1917
Length: Two reels

*Lonesome Luke, Plumber*
Released: June 17, 1917
Length: Two reels

*Stop! Luke! Listen!*
Released: July 15, 1917
Length: Two reels

*Lonesome Luke, Messenger*
Released: August 5, 1917
Length: Two reels

*Lonesome Luke, Mechanic*
Released: August 19, 1917
Length: Two reels

*Lonesome Luke's Wild Women*
Released: September 2, 1917
Length: Two reels

*Over the Fence*
Released: September 9, 1917
Length: One reel
Note: The first of Lloyd's "Glasses Character" shorts.

*Lonesome Luke Loses Patients*
Released: September 16, 1917
Length: Two reels

*Pinched*
Released: September 23, 1917
Length: One reel

*By the Sad Sea Waves*
Released: September 30, 1917
Length: One reel

*Birds of a Feather*
Released: October 7, 1917
Length: Two reels

*Bliss*
Released: October 14, 1917
Length: One reel

*From London to Laramie*
Released: October 21, 1917
Length: Two reels

*Rainbow Island*
Released: October 28, 1917
Length: One reel

*Love, Laughs and Lather*
Released: November 4, 1917
Length: Two reels

*The Flirt*
Released: November 11, 1917
Length: One reel

*Clubs Are Trumps*
Released: November 18, 1917
Length: Two reels

*All Aboard*
Released: November 25, 1917
Length: One reel

*We Never Sleep*
Released: December 2, 1917
Length: Two reels
Note: The last of Lloyd's "Lonesome Luke" shorts.

*Move On*
Released: December 9, 1917
Length: One reel

*Bashful*
Released: December 23, 1917
Length: One reel

*Step Lively*
Released: December 30, 1917
Length: One reel

*The Tip*
Released: January 6, 1918
Length: One reel

*The Big Idea*
Released: January 20, 1918
Length: One reel

*The Lamb*
Released: February 3, 1918
Length: One reel

*Hello Teacher*
Released: February 10, 1918
Length: One reel
Note: One of Bebe's two Rolin films without Harold Lloyd. Instead "Snub" Pollard plays the leading role. The film was intended as a pilot for a series of Pollard shorts. Lloyd was not featured because of a contract dispute with Rolin; he would soon return to the studio, however. Also in the cast were William Blaisdell, James Parrott, Fred C. Newmeyer, Sammy Brooks and Billy Fay.
   Synopsis from *Moving Picture World*: A knockabout number, featuring Harry Pollard and Bebe Daniels. The former plays the part of a hobo who is mistaken for the teacher of a country school. The scenes in the school house, where the unruly pupils play all sorts of tricks on the visiting

trustees, are laughable. The number is a successful one of the type.

*Hit Him Again*
Released: February 17, 1918
Length: One reel

*Beat It*
Released: February 24, 1918
Length: One reel

*A Gasoline Wedding*
Released: March 3, 1918
Length: One reel

*Look Pleasant, Please*
Released: March 10, 1918
Length: One reel

*Here Come the Girls*
Released: March 17, 1918
Length: One reel

*Let's Go*
Released: March 24, 1918
Length: One reel

*On the Jump*
Released: March 31, 1918
Length: One reel

*Follow the Crowd*
Released: April 7, 1918
Length: One reel

*Pipe the Whiskers*
Released: April 14, 1918
Length: One reel

*It's a Wild Life*
Released: April 21, 1918
Length: One reel

*Hey There!*
Released: April 28, 1918
Length: One reel

*Kicked Out*
Released: May 5, 1918
Length: One reel

*The Non-Stop Kid*
Released: May 12, 1918
Length: One reel

*Two Gun Gussie*
Released: May 19, 1918
Length: One reel

*Fireman, Save My Child*
Released: May 26, 1918
Length: One reel

*The City Slicker*
Released: June 2, 1918
Length: One reel

*Sic 'Em Towser*
Released: June 9, 1918
Length: One reel

*Somewhere in Turkey*
Released: June 16, 1918
Length: One reel

*Are Crooks Dishonest?*
Released: June 23, 1918
Length: One reel

*An Ozark Romance*
Released: July 7, 1918
Length: One reel

*Kicking the Germ Out of Germany*
Released: July 21, 1918
Length: One reel

*That's Him*
Released: August 4, 1918
Length: One reel

*Bride and Gloom*
Released: August 18, 1918
Length: One reel

*Two Scrambled*
Released: September 1, 1918
Length: One reel

*Bees in His Bonnet*
Released: September 15, 1918
Length: One reel

*Swing Your Partners*
Released: September 29, 1918
Length: One reel

*Why Pick on Me?*
Released: October 13, 1918
Length: One reel

*Nothing But Trouble*
Released: October 27, 1918
Length: One reel

*Hear 'Em Rave*
Released: December 1, 1918
Length: One reel

*Take a Chance*
Released: December 15, 1918
Length: One reel

*She Loves Me Not*
Released: December 29, 1918
Length: One reel

*Wanted $5000*
Released: January 12, 1919
Length: One reel

*Love's Young Scream*
Released: January 19, 1919
Length: One reel
Note: The second of Bebe's two Rolin films without Harold Lloyd. Instead, Alf Goulding plays a spectacled character of the same type. Goulding directed dozens of Lloyd one-reelers but only appeared in a handful of films in his lifetime. Also in the cast were "Snub" Pollard, William Blaisdell, Sammy Brooks and Lige Conley.
 Synopsis from *Moving Picture World*: Rivalry over a closely guarded girl leads to trouble of various sorts. The "cow itch" feature is quite amusing, and there are some fairly good knockabout scenes.

*Going! Going! Gone!*
Released: January 26, 1919
Length: One reel

*Ask Father*
Released: February 9, 1919
Length: One reel

*On the Fire*
Released: February 23, 1919
Length: One reel

*I'm On My Way*
Released: March 9, 1919
Length: One reel

*Look Out Below*
Released: March 16, 1919
Length: One reel

*The Dutiful Dub*
Released: March 23, 1919
Length: One reel

*Next Aisle Over*
Released: March 30, 1919
Length: One reel

*A Sammy in Siberia*
Released: April 6, 1919
Length: One reel

*Just Dropped In*
Released: April 13, 1919
Length: One reel

*Crack Your Heels*
Released: April 20, 1919
Length: One reel

*Ring Up the Curtain*
Released: April 27, 1919
Length: One reel

*Young Mr. Jazz*
Released: May 4, 1919
Length: One reel

*Si Senor*
Released: May 11, 1919
Length: One reel

*Before Breakfast*
Released: May 18, 1919
Length: One reel

*The Marathon*
Released: May 25, 1919
Length: One reel

*Back to the Woods*
Released: June 1, 1919
Length: One reel

*Pistols for Breakfast*
Released: June 8, 1919
Length: One reel

*Swat the Crook*
June 15, 1919
Length: One reel

*Off the Trolley*
Released: June 22, 1919
Length: One reel

*Spring Fever*
Released: June 29, 1919
Length: One reel

*Billy Blazes, Esq.*
Released: July 6, 1919
Length: One reel

*Just Neighbors*
Released: July 13, 1919
Length: One reel

*At the Old Stage Door*
Released: July 20, 1919
Length: One reel

*Never Touched Me*
Released: July 27, 1919
Length: One reel

*A Jazzed Honeymoon*
Released: August 3, 1919
Length: One reel

*Count Your Change*
Released: August 10, 1919
Length: One reel

*Chop Suey & Company*
Released: August 17, 1919
Length: One reel

*Heap Big Chief*
Released: August 24, 1919
Length: One reel

*Don't Shove*
Released: August 31, 1919
Length: One reel

*Be My Wife*
Released: September 7, 1919
Length: One reel

*The Rajah*
Released: September 14, 1919
Length: One reel

*He Leads, Others Follow*
Released: September 21, 1919
Length: One reel

*Soft Money*
Released: September 28, 1919
Length: One reel

*Count the Votes*
Released: October 5, 1919
Length: One reel

*Pay Your Dues*
Released: October 12, 1919
Length: One reel

*His Only Father*
Released: October 19, 1919
Length: One reel

*Bumping Into Broadway*
Released: November 2, 1919
Length: Two reels
Note: Lloyd's first "Glasses Character" two-reeler.

*Captain Kidd's Kids*
Released: November 30, 1919
Length: Two reels
Note: Bebe's last film with Harold Lloyd.

## Famous Players–Lasky/Paramount Part I (1919–1921)

Bebe acted in these seven Paramount features in roles of varying degrees of prominence. They are grouped together as they were made before she signed a starring contract with Paramount in 1922. Some were made before Realart came into existence, while others were made concurrently with her Realart contract.

*Male and Female*
Cast: Bebe Daniels as the King's Favorite, with Thomas Meighan, Theodore Roberts, Raymond Hatton, Robert Cain, Gloria Swanson, Lila Lee
Director: Cecil B. DeMille

Released: November 16, 1919
Length: 9 reels
Note: Released as a "Paramount-Artcraft Superspecial."

*Everywoman*
Cast: Bebe Daniels as Vice, with Theodore Roberts, Violet Heming, Clara Horton, Wanda Hawley, Margaret Loomis, Mildred Reardon, Edythe Chapman
Director: George H. Melford
Released: December 14, 1919
Length: 7 reels
Note: Released as a "Paramount-Artcraft Superspecial."

*Why Change Your Wife?*
Cast: Bebe Daniels as Sally Clark, with Thomas Meighan, Gloria Swanson, Theodore Kosloff
Director: Cecil B. DeMille
Released: May 2, 1920
Length: 8 reels
Note: Released as a "Famous Players–Lasky Super-Production."

*The Dancin' Fool*
Cast: Bebe Daniels as Junie Budd, with Wallace Reid, Raymond Hatton, Willis Marks, George B. Williams, Lillian Leighton
Director: Sam Wood
Released: May 23, 1920
Length: 5 reels
Note: Released as a "Paramount-Artcraft Picture."

*Sick Abed*
Cast: Bebe Daniels as Nurse Durant, with Wallace Reid, John Steppling, Winifred Greenwood, Tully Marshall
Director: Sam Wood
Released: June 27, 1920
Length: 5 reels
Note: Released as a "Paramount-Artcraft Picture."

*The Fourteenth Man*
Cast: Bebe Daniels as Marjory Seaton, with Robert Warwick, Walter Hiers, Robert Milash, Norman Selby
Director: Joseph Henabery
Released: July 19, 1920
Length: 5 reels
Note: Titled *The Romantic Meddler* during production.

*The Affairs of Anatol*
Cast: Bebe Daniels as Satan Synne, with Wallace Reid, Gloria Swanson, Elliott Dexter, Monte Blue, Wanda Hawley, Theodore Roberts, Agnes Ayres
Director: Cecil B. DeMille
Released: September 25, 1921
Length: 9 reels
Note: Titled *Anatol* and *Five Kisses* during production.

## Realart Pictures (1920–1922)

Bebe starred in ten films for the Realart Production Company, all of which were distributed by Paramount. These films were the first to star Bebe by herself. Of the ten films listed here, only two, *You Never Can Tell* and *Ducks and Drakes*, are known to survive.

*You Never Can Tell*
Cast: Bebe Daniels as Rowena Patricia Jones, with Jack Mulhall, Edward Martindel, Helen Dunbar, Harold Goodwin, Neely Edwards, Leo White, Milla Davenport, Graham Pettie, Gertrude Short
Director: Chester M. Franklin
Released: September 22, 1920
Length: 5 reels
Note: Known as *The Good Little Bad Girl* during production.

*Oh Lady, Lady*
Cast: Bebe Daniels as May Barber, with Harrison Ford, Walter Hiers, Charlotte Woods, Lillian Langdon, Jack Doud
Director: Major Maurice Campbell
Released: November 21, 1920
Length: 5 reels

*She Couldn't Help It*
Cast: Bebe Daniels as Nance Olden, with Emory Johnson, Wade Boteler, Vera Lewis,

Herbert Standing, Z. Wall Covington, Helen Raymond, Ruth Renick, Gertrude Short, Milla Davenport
Director: Maurice Campbell
Released: January 9, 1921
Length: 5 reels

*Ducks and Drakes*

Cast: Bebe Daniels as Teddy Simpson, with Jack Holt, Mayme Kelso, Edward Martindel, William E. Lawrence, Wade Boteler, Maurie Newell, Elsie Andrean
Director: Maurice Campbell
Released: February 28, 1921
Length: 5 reels

*Two Weeks with Pay*

Cast: Bebe Daniels as Pansy O'Donnell and Marie La Tour, with Jack Mulhall, James Mason, George Periolat, Frances Raymond, Polly Moran, Walter Hiers
Director: Maurice Campbell
Released: May 15, 1921
Length: 5 reels

*The March Hare*

Cast: Bebe Daniels as Lizbeth Ann Palmer, with Grace Morse, Herbert Sherwood, Mayme Kelso, Helen Jerome Eddy, Sidney Bracey, Frances Raymond, Melbourne MacDowell, Harry Myers
Director: Maurice Campbell
Released: July 10, 1921
Length: 5 reels

*One Wild Week*

Cast: Bebe Daniels as Pauline Hathaway, with Frank Kingsley, Mayme Kelso, Frances Raymond, Herbert Standing, Edwin Stevens, Edythe Chapman, Carrie Clark Ward, Bull Montana
Director: Maurice Campbell
Released: August 21, 1921
Length: 5 reels

*The Speed Girl*

Cast: Bebe Daniels as Betty Lee, with Theodore von Eltz, Frank Elliott, Walter Hiers, Norris Johnson, Truly Shattuck, William Courtright, Barbara Maier
Director: Maurice Campbell
Released: October 16, 1921
Length: 5 reels

*Nancy from Nowhere*

Cast: Bebe Daniels as Nancy, with Edward Sutherland, Vera Lewis, James Gordon, Myrtle Stedman, Alberta Lee, Helen Holly, Dorothy Hagan
Director: Chester M. Franklin
Released: January 22, 1922
Length: 5 reels

*A Game Chicken*

Cast: Bebe Daniels as Inez Hastings, with Pat O'Malley, James Gordon, Martha Mattox, Gertrude Norman, Hugh Thompson, Max Weatherwax, Mattie Peters, Charles Force, Edwin Stevens
Director: Chester M. Franklin
Released: February 26, 1922
Length: 5 reels

## Famous Players–Lasky/Paramount Part II (1922–1928)

Following the dissolution of Realart Pictures, Bebe was promoted to making films exclusively with Famous Players–Lasky. It proved to be her longest tenure with any one production company; this is where she made many of her definitive films. Remarkably few survive today.

*North of the Rio Grande*

Cast: Bebe Daniels as Val Hannon, with Jack Holt, Charles Ogle, Alec B. Francis, Will R. Walling
Director: Rollin Sturgeon
Released: May 14, 1922
Length: 5 reels

*Nice People*

Cast: Bebe Daniels as Teddy Gloucester, with Wallace Reid, Conrad Nagel, Julia Faye, Claire McDowell, Edward Martindel
Director: William C. DeMille
Released: September 4, 1922
Length: 7 reels

*Pink Gods*
Cast: Bebe Daniels as Lorraine Temple, with James Kirkwood, Anna Q. Nilsson, Raymond Hatton, Adolphe Menjou
Director: Penrhyn Stanlaws
Released: October 1, 1922
Length: 8 reels

*Singed Wings*
Cast: Bebe Daniels as Bonita della Guerda, with Conrad Nagel, Adolphe Menjou, Robert Brower, Ernest Torrence
Director: Penrhyn Stanlaws
Released: December 18, 1922
Length: 8 reels

*The World's Applause*
Cast: Bebe Daniels as Corinne d'Alys, with Lewis Stone, Kathlyn Williams, Adolphe Menjou, Brandon Hurst, Bernice Frank
Director: William C. DeMille
Released: January 29, 1923
Length: 8 reels

*The Glimpses of the Moon*
Cast: Bebe Daniels as Susan Branch, with Nita Naldi, David Powell, Maurice Costello, Rubye De Remer
Director: Allan Dwan
Released: March 25, 1923
Length: 7 reels

*The Exciters*
Cast: Bebe Daniels as Ronnie Rand, with Antonio Moreno, Burr McIntosh, Diana Allen, Cyril Ring, Bigelow Cooper
Director: Maurice Campbell
Released: June 3, 1923
Length: 6 reels

*His Children's Children*
Cast: Bebe Daniels as Diane, with Dorothy Mackaill, James Rennie, George Fawcett, Hale Hamilton, Katheryn Lean
Director: Sam Wood
Released: November 18, 1923
Length: 8 reels

*Heritage of the Desert*
Cast: Bebe Daniels as Mescal, with Ernest Torrence, Noah Beery, Lloyd Hughes, Ann Schaeffer, James Mason
Director: Irvin Willat
Released: January 23, 1924
Length: 6 reels

*Daring Youth*
Cast: Bebe Daniels as Alita Allen, with Norman Kerry, Lee Moran, Arthur Hoyt, Lillian Langdon, George Pearce
Director: William Beaudine
Released: February 1, 1924
Length: 6 reels

*Unguarded Women*
Cast: Bebe Daniels as Breta Banning, with Richard Dix, Mary Astor, Walter McGrail, Frank Losee, Helen Lindroth
Director: Alan Crosland
Released: August 17, 1924
Length: 6 reels

*Monsieur Beaucaire*
Cast: Bebe Daniels as Princess Henriette, with Rudolph Valentino, Lois Wilson, Doris Kenyon, Lowell Sherman, Paulette Duval
Director: Sidney Olcott
Released: August 18, 1924
Length: 10 reels

*Sinners in Heaven*
Cast: Bebe Daniels as Barbara Stockley, with Richard Dix, Holmes Herbert, Florence Billings
Director: Alan Crosland
Released: September 15, 1924
Length: 7 reels

*Dangerous Money*
Cast: Bebe Daniels as Adele Clark, with Tom Moore, William Powell, Dolores Cassinelli, Mary Foy, Edward O'Connor
Director: Frank Tuttle
Released: October 20, 1924
Length: 6 reels

*Argentine Love*
Cast: Bebe Daniels as Consuelo Garcia, with Ricardo Cortez, James Rennie, Mario Majeroni
Director: Allan Dwan
Released: December 29, 1924
Length: 6 reels

*Miss Bluebeard*
Cast: Bebe Daniels as Colette Girard, with Robert Frazer, Kenneth MacKenna, Ray-

mond Griffith, Martha Madison, Diana Kane, Lawrence D'Orsay
Director: Frank Tuttle
Released: January 26, 1925
Length: 7 reels

*The Crowded Hour*
Cast: Bebe Daniels as Peggy Laurence, with Kenneth Harlan, T. Roy Barnes, Frank Morgan, Helen Lee Worthing
Director: E. Mason Hopper
Released: April 20, 1925
Length: 7 reels

*The Manicure Girl*
Cast: Bebe Daniels as Maria Maretti, with Edmund Burns, Dorothy Cumming, Hale Hamilton, Charlotte Walker
Director: Frank Tuttle
Released: July 6, 1925
Length: 6 reels

*Wild, Wild Susan*
Cast: Bebe Daniels as Susan Van Dusen, with Rod La Rocque, Henry Stephenson, Jack Kane, Helen Holcombe, Osgood Perkins
Director: Edward Sutherland
Released: September 7, 1925
Length: 6 reels

*Lovers in Quarantine*
Cast: Bebe Daniels as Diana, with Harrison Ford, Alfred Lunt, Eden Gray, Edna May Oliver
Director: Frank Tuttle
Released: October 12, 1925
Length: 7 reels

*The Splendid Crime*
Cast: Bebe Daniels as Jenny, with Neil Hamilton, Anne Cornwall, Anthony Jowitt, Fred Walton, Lloyd Corrigan
Director: William C. DeMille
Released: January 4, 1926
Length: 6 reels

*Miss Brewster's Millions*
Cast: Bebe Daniels as Polly Brewster, with Warner Baxter, Ford Sterling, André de Beranger
Director: Clarence Badger
Released: March 22, 1926
Length: 7 reels

*The Palm Beach Girl*
Cast: Bebe Daniels as Emily Bennett, with Lawrence Gray, Josephine Drake, Marguerite Clayton, John G. Patrick
Director: Erle C. Kenton
Released: May 17, 1926
Length: 7 reels

*Volcano!*
Cast: Bebe Daniels as Zabette de Chavalons, with Ricardo Cortez, Wallace Beery, Arthur Edmund Carew, Dale Fuller
Director: William K. Howard
Released: June 12, 1926
Length: 6 reels

*The Campus Flirt*
Cast: Bebe Daniels as Patricia Mansfield, with James Hall, El Brendel, Charles Paddock, Joan Standing, Gilbert Roland
Director: Clarence Badger
Released: October 4, 1926
Length: 7 reels

*Stranded in Paris*
Cast: Bebe Daniels as Julie McFadden, with James Hall, Ford Sterling, Iris Stuart, Mabel Julienne Scott
Director: Arthur Rosson
Released: December 13, 1926
Length: 7 reels

*A Kiss in a Taxi*
Cast: Bebe Daniels as Ginette, with Chester Conklin, Douglas Gilmore, Henry Kolker, Richard Tucker
Director: Clarence Badger
Released: February 22, 1927
Length: 7 reels

*Señorita*
Cast: Bebe Daniels as Señorita Francesca Hernandez, with James Hall, William Powell, Josef Swickard
Director: Clarence Badger
Released: April 30, 1927
Length: 7 reels

*Swim Girl, Swim*
Cast: Bebe Daniels as Alice Smith, with James Hall, Gertrude Ederle, Josephine Dunn, William Austin, James Mack
Director: Clarence Badger

Released: September 17, 1927
Length: 7 reels

*She's a Sheik*

Cast: Bebe Daniels as Zaida, with Richard Arlen, William Powell, Josephine Dunn, James Bradbury, Jr.
Director: Clarence Badger
Released: November 12, 1927
Length: 6 reels

*Feel My Pulse*

Cast: Bebe Daniels as Barbara Manning, with Richard Arlen, William Powell, Melbourne MacDowell, George Irving, Charles Sellon, Heinie Conklin
Director: Gregory La Cava
Released: February 25, 1928
Length: 6 reels

*The Fifty-Fifty Girl*

Cast: Bebe Daniels as Kathleen O'Hara, with James Hall, William Austin, George Kotsonaros, Johnnie Morris
Director: Clarence Badger
Released: May 12, 1928
Length: 7 reels

*Hot News*

Cast: Bebe Daniels as Pat Clancy, with Neil Hamilton, Paul Lukas, Alfred Allen
Director: Clarence Badger
Released: July 14, 1928
Length: 7 reels

*Take Me Home*

Cast: Bebe Daniels as Peggy Lane, with Neil Hamilton, Lilyan Tashman, Doris Hill, Joe E. Brown
Director: Marshall Neilan
Released: October 13, 1928
Length: 6 reels

*What a Night!*

Cast: Bebe Daniels as Dorothy Winston, with Neil Hamilton, William Austin, Wheeler Oakman
Director: Edward Sutherland
Released: December 22, 1928
Length: 6 reels

## RKO Pictures (1929–1930)

Bebe Daniels made her first five talking pictures for RKO in 1929 and 1930. All five survive today. Although her contract called for several more films for the company, the changing nature of the movie industry all but put an end to Daniels' musicals for the time being.

*Rio Rita*

Cast: Bebe Daniels as Rita Ferguson, with John Boles, Bert Wheeler, Robert Woolsey, Dorothy Lee, Don Alvarado, Georges Renavent
Director: Luther Reed
Released: September 15, 1929
Length: 15 reels

*Love Comes Along*

Cast: Bebe Daniels as Peggy, with Lloyd Hughes, Montagu Love, Ned Sparks, Lionel Belmore, Alma Tell
Director: Rupert Julian
Released: January 5, 1930
Length: 8 reels

*Alias French Gertie*

Cast: Bebe Daniels as Marie, with Ben Lyon, Robert Emmett O'Connor, John Ince, Daisy Belmore, Betty Pierce
Director: George Archainbaud
Released: April 20, 1930
Length: 7 reels

*Dixiana*

Cast: Bebe Daniels as Dixiana Caldwell, with Everett Marshall, Bert Wheeler, Robert Woolsey, Joseph Cawthorn, Jobyna Howland, Dorothy Lee
Director: Luther Reed
Released: August 1, 1930
Length: 12 reels

*Lawful Larceny*

Cast: Bebe Daniels as Marion Corsey, with Kenneth Thomson, Lowell Sherman, Olive Tell, Purnell B. Pratt
Director: Lowell Sherman
Released: August 17, 1930
Length: 7 reels

## United Artists (1931)

Bebe Daniels was never contracted with United Artists, and was only hired for one film between her stints at RKO and Warner Bros.

*Reaching for the Moon*
Cast: Bebe Daniels as Vivian Benton, with Douglas Fairbanks, Edward Everett Horton, Claud Allister, Jack Mulhall, Walter Walker, June MacCloy
Director: Edmund Goulding
Released: February 21, 1931
Length: 9 reels

## Warner Bros. (1931–1933)

Between 1931 and 1934, Bebe made six films at Warner Bros. and its subsidiary First National. Her last major American film contract, her years at Warners would represent the last prolific period of her film career. All these films except for *Honor of the Family* still exist.

*My Past*
Cast: Bebe Daniels as Miss Doree Macy, with Lewis Stone, Ben Lyon, Joan Blondell, Natalie Moorhead
Director: Roy Del Ruth
Released: May 14, 1931
Length: 8 reels
Note: Known as The *Ex-Mistress* during production.

*The Maltese Falcon*
Cast: Bebe Daniels as Ruth Wonderly, with Ricardo Cortez, Dudley Digges, Una Merkel, Robert Elliott, Thelma Todd
Director: Roy Del Ruth
Released: June 13, 1931
Length: 9 reels
Note: Known as *All Women* during production.

*42nd Street*
Cast: Bebe Daniels as Dorothy Brock, with Warner Baxter, George Brent, Ruby Keeler, Guy Kibbee, Una Merkel, Ginger Rogers, Ned Sparks, Dick Powell
Director: Lloyd Bacon
Released: March 11, 1933
Length: 9 reels

## First National Pictures (1931–1934)

Part of the way through her Warner Bros. contract, Bebe began made three films with the studio's subsidiary, First National. Although not blockbusters by any means, they were successful commercially.

*Honor of the Family*
Cast: Bebe Daniels as Laura, with Warren William, Alan Mowbray, Blanche Frederic, Frederick Kerr
Director: Lloyd Bacon
Released: October 17, 1931
Length: 7 reels

*Silver Dollar*
Cast: Bebe Daniels as Lily Owens Martin, with Edward G. Robinson, Aline MacMahon, DeWitt Jennings, Robert Warwick
Director: Alfred E. Green
Released: December 24, 1932
Length: 9 reels

*Registered Nurse*
Cast: Bebe Daniels as Sylvia Benton, with Lyle Talbot, John Halliday, Irene Franklin, Sidney Toler
Director: Robert Florey
Released: April 7, 1934
Length: 7 reels

## Columbia Pictures (1933)

Towards the end of her Hollywood career, Bebe made one film for Columbia.

*Cocktail Hour*
Cast: Bebe Daniels as Cynthia Warren, with Randolph Scott, Sidney Blackmer, Muriel Kirkland, Jessie Ralph, Barry Norton

Director: Victor Scherzinger
Released: June 5, 1933
Length: 8 reels

## Universal Pictures (1933)

Bebe supported John Barrymore in her one Universal Pictures production.

*Counsellor-at-Law*
Cast: Bebe Daniels as Regina Gordon, with John Barrymore, Doris Kenyon, Isabel Jewell, Onslow Stevens, Thelma Todd

Director: William Wyler
Released: December 11, 1933
Length: 8 reels

## Fox Pictures (1935)

Bebe's last American film was a Fox musical in which she played a role in support of Alice Faye, one of the studio's biggest stars.

*Music Is Magic*
Cast: Bebe Daniels as Diane De Valle, with Alice Faye, Ray Walker, Frank Mitchell, Rosina Lawrence, Hattie McDaniel
Director: George Marshall
Released: November 1, 1935
Length: 7 reels

# Chapter Notes

## Chapter 1

1. Bebe Daniels and Ben Lyon. *Life with the Lyons*. London: Odhams Limited, 1953. 21.
2. *Ibid.*
3. Bebe Daniels and Ben Lyon. *Life with the Lyons*. London: Odhams Limited, 1953. 22.
4. "Col. George Butler Griffin." *Los Angeles Herald*, June 4, 1893.
5. "Interest Notes from Movieland for Our Readers." *Indiana Evening Gazette*, December 4, 1920.
6. "Society." *San Francisco Call*, October 5, 1899.
7. "Town Talk." *Austin Statesman*, October 27, 1933.
8. Bebe Daniels and Ben Lyon. *Life with the Lyons*. London: Odhams Limited, 1953. 13.
9. Dorothy Herzog. "Gay Grandmothers." *New Movie Magazine*, September 1930. 40.
10. "Hall Caine's 'Deemster.'" *Mount Carmel Daily News*, September 12, 1901.
11. Bebe Daniels and Ben Lyon. *Life with the Lyons*. London: Odhams Limited, 1953. 33.
12. "Classifieds." *Richmond Daily News*, May 18, 1904.
13. "Physical Culture Cured." *Baltimore Sun*, March 6, 1906.
14. Edwin Slipek, Jr. "Hollywood Dreams." *Style Weekly*, January 9, 2008.
15. "Turned on Its Mistress." *Richmond Daily News*, September 19, 1902.
16. "Classifieds." *Richmond Daily News*, September 28, 1902.
17. Bebe Daniels and Ben Lyon. *Life with the Lyons*. London: Odhams Limited, 1953. 33.
18. *Ibid.*
19. *Ibid.*
20. "Daniels Neuropathic Institute." *Grand Rapids Press*, September 28, 1912.
21. "Melville E. Daniels." *New York Herald Tribune*, August 19, 1930.

## Chapter 2

1. "Greenleaf in His Local Debut." *San Francisco Chronicle*, February 9, 1909.
2. Jill Allgood. *Bebe and Ben*. London: Robert Hale, 1975. 28
3. Grace Kingsley. "Their First Fans." *New Movie Magazine*, February, 1930. 25–26.
4. "Infant Actress Makes Big Hit." *Los Angeles Herald*, July 2, 1906.
5. "Trials of a Doll Cause Weeping." *Los Angeles Herald*, July 20, 1906.
6. "'Zaza' Appears in New Guise." *Los Angeles Herald*, August 7, 1906.
7. "Pleasing Romance Is 'A Royal Family,' Belasco's Production." *Los Angeles Herald*, May 21, 1907.
8. "New Player Makes Hit." *Los Angeles Herald*, August 13, 1907.
9. Edward Peple. *The Prince Chap: A Comedy in Three Acts*. New York: Samuel French, 1904.
10. "Prince Chap at the Valencia Theater." *San Francisco Call*, February 7, 1909.
11. "Midweek Gossip of the Theaters." *San Francisco Chronicle*, February 11, 1909.
12. "Greenleaf in His Local Debut." *San Francisco Chronicle*, February 9, 1909.
13. "At the Theaters This Week." *San Francisco Chronicle*, February 14, 1909.
14. Andrew A. Erish. *Col. William N. Selig: The Man Who Invented Hollywood*. Austin: University of Texas Press, 2012. 80.
15. *Ibid.* 88
16. Jill Allgood. *Bebe and Ben*. London: Robert Hale, 1975. 33.

## Chapter 3

1. "Selig Polyscope Co." *Moving Picture World*, April 9, 1910. 571.
2. Mark Evan Swartz. *Oz Before the Rainbow: L. Frank Baum's 'The Wonderful Wizard of Oz' on Stage and Screen to 1939*. Baltimore: Johns Hopkins University Press, 2000. 174
3. "Selig Activities." *Moving Picture World*, January 8, 1910. 18.
4. Andrew A. Erish. *Col. William N. Selig: The Man Who Invented Hollywood*. Austin: University of Texas Press, 2012. 90.
5. Still operating as the Sacred Heart Elementary School in Los Feliz, Los Angeles.
6. Richard V. Spencer. "Los Angeles Letter." *Moving Picture World*, February 4, 1911. 253.
7. "Your Own Page.[qm] *Screenland*, December, 1920. 35.
8. "Kalem." *Moving Picture World*, September 7, 1912. 996.
9. "Anne of the Golden Heart." *Vitagraph Life Portrayals*, January 1914. 41.

10. "Anne of the Golden Heart." *Moving Picture World*, January 17, 1914. 272.
11. "Albuquerque Moves to the Norbig Establishment." *The Movie Magazine*, June 1915. 28.
12. "Mutual Film Corporation." *Moving Picture World*, August 14, 1915. 1161.
13. "Return from Mojave Desert." *Motion Picture News*, June 26, 1915. 52.
14. "Doings in Los Angeles." *Moving Picture World*, July 10, 1915. 294.
15. "At the Norbig Studios." *The Movie Magazine*, August 1915. 24.
16. Mack Sennett. *King of Comedy*. Bloomington, IN: iUniverse, 2000. 174.
17. Bebe Daniels and Ben Lyon. *Life with the Lyons*. London: Odhams Limited, 1953. 90.

## Chapter 4

1. Harold Lloyd. "Autobiography of Harold Lloyd." *Photoplay*, June 1924. 109–10.
2. Norbig Studio was located at 1745 Allesandro, now Glendale Boulevard.
3. Jill Allgood. *Bebe and Ben*. London: Robert Hale & Co., 1975. 42.
4. Bebe Daniels and Ben Lyon. *Life with the Lyons*. London: Odhams Limited, 1953. 81.
5. Harold Lloyd. "Autobiography of Harold Lloyd." *Photoplay*, June 1924. 109–10.
6. "Pathé." *Moving Picture World*, February 24, 1917. 1117.
7. "'Lonesome Luke' Two-Reel Comedies." *Moving Picture World*, March 17, 1917. 1756.
8. "Pathé." *Moving Picture World*, March 24, 1917. 1875.
9. "Pathé." *Moving Picture World*, March 31, 1917. 2039.
10. Annette D'Agostino Lloyd. *Harold Lloyd: Magic in a Pair of Horn-Rimmed Glasses*. Albany, GA: BearManor Media, 2009. 84.
11. *Ibid*.
12. Annette D'Agostino Lloyd. *Harold Lloyd: Magic in a Pair of Horn-Rimmed Glasses*. Albany, GA: BearManor Media, 2009. 88.
13. Bebe Daniels and Ben Lyon. *Life with the Lyons*. London: Odhams Limited, 1953. 87.
14. "Coast Picture News." *Variety*, March 1, 1918. 46.
15. "O'connell Vs. Miller a Balanced Match." *Los Angeles Times*, June 20, 1918.
16. Beatrice Blair. "Our Own Letter from Filmtown." *Times of India*, November 22, 1918.
17. Beatrice Blair. "Our Own Letter from Filmtown." *Times of India*, December 5, 1918.
18. Bebe Daniels and Ben Lyon. *Life with the Lyons*. London: Odhams Limited, 1953. 93.
19. Jill Allgood. *Bebe and Ben*. London: Robert Hale & Co., 1975. 46.
20. Original telegrams in the USC Cinematic Arts Library's Hal Roach Collection.

## Chapter 5

1. "News of the Film World." *Variety*, July 4, 1919. 41.
2. "Bebe Daniels." *Lima News*, April 22, 1918.
3. Actually her 19th, as she was born in 1900 and not 1901.
4. "Pretty Summer Styles for Movie Actors." *Wichita Daily Eagle*, June 9, 1918.
5. Edwin M. LaRoche. "When the Movies Salute the Flag." *Motion Picture*, June 1918. 61.
6. "Studio Shorts." *Moving Picture World*, October 12, 1918. 208.
7. "Bebe Daniels Drives Four Nails." *Moving Picture World*, December 7, 1918. 1091.
8. "Studio Shorts." *Moving Picture World*, October 12, 1918. 208.
9. Guy Price. "Coast Picture News." *Variety*, December 1918. 184.
10. "Bebe Daniels Fights the Huns." *Pittsburgh Daily Post*, May 19, 1918.
11. Annette D'Agostino Lloyd. *Harold Lloyd: Magic in a Pair of Horn-Rimmed Glasses*. Albany, GA: BearManor Media, 2009. 99.
12. Annette D'Agostino Lloyd. *Harold Lloyd: Magic in a Pair of Horn-Rimmed Glasses*. Albany, GA: BearManor Media, 2009. 100.
13. These four telegrams are held in the University of Southern California Cinematic Arts Library's Hal Roach Collection.
14. Tom Dardis. *Harold Lloyd: The Man on the Clock*. New York: Penguin, 1984. 66.
15. Tom Dardis. *Harold Lloyd: The Man on the Clock*. New York: Penguin, 1984. 73.
16. Marguerite Sheridan. "Mam'selle Bebe Bonbon." *Photo-Play Journal*, December 1917. 29, 49.

## Chapter 6

1. Gabe Essoe and Raymond Lee. *Demille: The Man and His Pictures*. New York: Castle Books, 1970. 71.
2. Gloria Swanson. *Swanson on Swanson*. New York: Random House, 1980. 120.
3. Jill Allgood. *Bebe and Ben*. London: Robert Hale & Co., 1975. 48.
4. Jill Allgood. *Bebe and Ben*. London: Robert Hale & Co., 1975. 49.
5. "The Dancin' Fool." *Variety*, May 7, 1920. 34.
6. "'The Dancin' Fool' Glides as Smoothly on Screen as in Story." *Chicago Daily Tribune*, May 31, 1920.
7. "On the Screen." *New York Tribune*, May 3, 1920.
8. "The Billboard Reviewing Service." *The Billboard*, May 1, 1920. 84.
9. Bebe Daniels and Ben Lyon. *Life with the Lyons*. London: Odhams Limited, 1953. 101.
10. Hazel Simpson Naylor. "Sunlight on Black Lacquer." *Motion Picture Magazine*, November 1921. 28–29, 82.

## Chapter 7

1. "Flashes." *Los Angeles Times*, June 2, 1920.
2. "Realart Exchanges to Fight for Market with Select." *Variety*, June 27, 1919. 49.
3. "Zukor Gets Mary Miles Minter by Million Dollar Contract." *Variety*, June 20, 1919. 58.
4. "Bebe Daniels New Realart Star." June 5, 1920. 4645.

5. "'Good Little Bad Girl' Starting." *Variety*, June 25, 1920. 37.
6. "Good Little Bad Girl." *Los Angeles Times*, June 13, 1920.
7. *Motion Picture*, September 1920. 121.
8. *Saturday Evening Post.* November 29, 1919.
9. "You Never Can Tell." *Variety*, October 8, 1920. 41.
10. "Robert Warwick Plans in Portola's Picture." *San Francisco Chronicle*, July 19, 1920.
11. "Bebe Daniels Good in 'Oh, Lady, Lady.'" *Nashville Tennessean*, December 5, 1920.
12. "Offerings on Screen and Stage." *Nashville Tennessean*, December 6, 1920.
13. "Bebe Daniels Takes Trip." *Los Angeles*, December 16, 1920.
14. "Dallas Film Star Visits Old Home." *Dallas Morning News*, December 30, 1920.
15. "Bebe Daniels in Texas." *Film Daily*, January 3, 1921. 2.
16. "At the Picture Houses." *Washington Post*, February 6, 1921.
17. "Bebe Daniels Comes to Rialto Theater." *Atlanta Constitution*, January 30, 1921.
18. "Bebe's an Ambitious Girl." *Washington Post*, December 19, 1920.
19. Truman B. Handy. "Bebe's Behavior." *Motion Picture Magazine*, September 1920. 36–37, 103.
20. Hazel Simpson Naylor. "Sunlight on Black Lacquer." *Motion Picture Magazine*, November 1921. 28–29, 82.

## Chapter 8

1. In *Bebe & Ben*, Bebe would exaggerate this figure to 72 miles per hour; all contemporary sources state 56½ miles per hour, however.
2. "Car Broken, Speeded." *Los Angeles Times*, January 13, 1921.
3. Jill Allgood. *Bebe and Ben*. London: Robert Hale, 1975. 51.
4. "Bebe Daniels' New Picture to Be Shown." *Santa Ana Register*, January 17, 1921.
5. "Will Bebe Vamp Justice Cox?" *Los Angeles Times*, January 14, 1921.
6. "Star Seeks Less Stern Judge; Vail." *Los Angeles Times*, January 20, 1921.
7. "Ducks and Drakes." *The Billboard*, April 9, 1921. 98.
8. "Bebe Daniels' Latest Is Thoroughly Amusing." *Film Daily*, April 3, 1921. 4.
9. "Ducks and Drakes." *Variety*, April 1, 1921. 42.
10. Truman B. Handy. "Bebe's Behavior." *Motion Picture Magazine*, September 1920. 36–37, 103.
11. "Mixed Jury in Daniels Case." *Los Angeles Times*, January 22, 1921.
12. "Jail Term for Bebe Daniels." *Los Angeles Times*, March 29, 1921.
13. "Bebe Daniels Goes to Jail." *Los Angeles Times*, April 16, 1921.
14. "Jail Horrors for Fair Bebe." *Los Angeles Times*, April 17, 1921.
15. "Bebe Daniels Has Busy Day." *Los Angeles Times*, April 18, 1921.
16. Jill Allgood. *Bebe and Ben*. London: Robert Hale, 1975. 55.
17. Jill Allgood. *Bebe and Ben*. London: Robert Hale, 1975. 56.
18. Bebe Daniels. "56 1/2 Miles Per Hour." *Photoplay*, July 1921. 52–54, 109–111.
19. "Two Weeks with Pay." *Billboard*, June 4, 1921. 107.
20. "Lights and Shades of Shadow Land." *Nashville Tennessean*, June 10, 1921.
21. "The March Hare." *Los Angeles Times*, July 10, 1921.
22. "Reviews." *Los Angeles Times*, July 11, 1921.
23. "A Tribute to a Star." *Washington Post*, July 17, 1921.

## Chapter 9

1. "Realart Absorbed as Economy Move by Famous." *Variety*, December 16, 1921. 39.
2. "Photoplay Reviews." *Cincinnati Enquirer*, August 15, 1921.
3. "Wild? We'll Say She's Wild! Good Reason, Too!" *Chicago Daily Tribune*, September 8, 1921.
4. "Bebe Daniels." *Louisville Courier Journal*, October 16, 1921.
5. "Speed! Speed! Is the Cry." *Washington Post*, October 23, 1921.
6. "O, You Honors! Whadda You Know About This." *Chicago Daily Tribune*, November 13, 1921.
7. "The Speed Girl." *Variety*, November 18, 1921. 44.
8. *Ibid.*
9. "Bebe Daniels Lure at Clune's Broadway." *Los Angeles Times*, January 30, 1922.
10. "On the Screen." *New York Tribune*, January 31, 1922.
11. "Closeups." *Chicago Daily Tribune*, January 14, 1922.
12. "Gossip of the Movies and Close-Ups of the Screen." *Nashville Tennessean*, January 22, 1922.
13. "The Ups and Downs of Stardom." *Picture-Play Magazine*, February 1923. 43, 96.
14. "Movie Facts and Fancies." *Boston Daily Globe*, April 22, 1922.
15. "Movie Facts and Fancies." *Boston Daily Globe*, August 21, 1921.
16. "Engagement." *Cincinnati Enquirer*, February 11, 1922.
17. "Jack Dempsey Said to Be Engaged to Miss Bebe Daniels." *St. Louis Post-Dispatch*, February 12, 1922.
18. *Ibid.*
19. "Engagement." *Cincinnati Enquirer*, February 11, 1922.
20. "Jack Dempsey Denies That He Is to Marry." *Baltimore Sun*, February 15, 1922.
21. "Dempsey Ready to Meet French Idol in London." *Arizona Republican*, February 15, 1922.
22. "Bebe Daniels Finds Thrill in Camp Life." *Arizona Republican*, March 1, 1922.
23. "You Met Nice People in Jail Says Bebe Daniels." *Boston Daily Globe*, June 3, 1923.
24. Roger Kahn. *A Flame of Pure Fire: Jack Dempsey and the Roaring '20s*. New York: Harcourt Brace & Co. 117
25. "Bebe Daniels Talks of Her Six Big Romances." *Milwaukee Journal*, January 19, 1929.
26. "Jack Dempsey Very Busy as Movie Escort." *Chicago Daily Tribune*, May 21, 1932.

27. "What Are They Doing in the Movie Studios." *St. Louis Post-Dispatch*, January 8, 1922.
28. "Flashes." *Los Angeles Times*, January 21, 1922.
29. "The Ups and Downs of Stardom." *Picture-Play Magazine*, February 1923. 43.
30. Cal York. "The Girl on the Cover." *Photoplay Magazine*, February 1926. 92.

## Chapter 10

1. "Bebe Daniels Is Bright Figure." *Los Angeles Times*, February 5, 1923.
2. Bebe Daniels and Ben Lyon. *Life with the Lyons*. London: Odhams Limited, 1953. 73.
3. "Bebe Daniels Finds Thrill in Camp Life." *Arizona Republican*, March 1, 1922.
4. *Ibid.*
5. "Intruder, Threatening Life of Bebe Daniels, Arrested." *St. Louis Post-Dispatch*, May 19, 1922.
6. "Police Save Bebe Daniels's Life; Seize Intruder in Her Home Who Calls Self Hired Slayer." *Cincinnati Enquirer*, May 20, 1922.
7. "Prowler Menaces Bebe Daniels' Life." *San Francisco Chronicle*. May 20, 1922.
8. "Attempt on Life of Bebe Daniels Laid to Dope Ring." *Atlanta Constitution*, May 20, 1922.
9. "Attack on Bebe Daniels Due to 'Movie Mania.'" *Nashville Tennessean*, May 29, 1922.
10. Although *Nice People* is a lost film, several seconds (including a fleeting shot of Bebe Daniels) can be found in the Paramount compilation film, *The House That Shadows Built*, released in 1931.
11. "'Nice People' Movie to Enjoy If One Has Not Seen Stage Play." *Chicago Daily Tribune*, August 22, 1922.
12. "The Shadow Stage." *Photoplay*, September, 1922. 58.
13. Bebe Daniels and Ben Lyon. *Life with the Lyons*. London: Odhams Limited, 1953. 104.
14. *Ibid.*
15. "Closeups." *Chicago Daily Tribune*, May 6, 1922.
16. "Colors to Feature New Photoplay." *Detroit Free Press*, August 20, 1922.
17. "Glimpses of the Moon." *New York Tribune*, October 29, 1922.
18. "The Ups and Downs of Stardom." *Picture-Play Magazine*, February 1923. 43.
19. Shari Benstock. *No Gifts from Chance: A Biography of Edith Wharton*. New York: Scribner's, 1994. 272.
20. "Bebe Daniels Undergoes Operation." *Washington Post*, January 30, 1923.
21. "What Are Glimpses of the Moon?" *The Los Angeles Times*, April 1, 1923.
22. Richard Koszarski. *Hollywood on the Hudson: Film and Television in New York from Griffith to Sarnoff*. New Brunswick, NJ: Rutgers University Press, 2008. 34.
23. "Flashes." *Los Angeles Times*, December 13, 1922.
24. "Shadows on the Screen." *New York Tribune*, January 28, 1923.
25. "The Exciters." *Motion Picture News*, June 16, 1923. 2881.
26. "His Children's Children." *Variety*, November 8, 1923. 26.
27. "Flashes: Star Heads West." *Los Angeles Times*, August 30, 1923.
28. "Zane Grey's Latest Stars Bebe Daniels." *Atlanta Constitution*, January 27, 1924.
29. "Practices Her Precept." *Los Angeles Times*, July 6, 1924.
30. "Movie Facts and Fancies." *Boston Daily Globe*, May 10, 1924.
31. "*Unguarded Women* at the Rialto." *New York Herald-Tribune*, June 24, 1924.
32. "Attempt Novelty." *Los Angeles Times*, July 7, 1924.

## Chapter 11

1. Jack Holt. "Favorite Sweethearts of the Screen." *Photoplay*, July 1924. 100.
2. Bebe Daniels and Ben Lyon. *Life with the Lyons*. London: Odhams Limited, 1953. 107.
3. For the best summary, see *Dark Lover: The Life and Death of Rudolph Valentino* by Emily Wortis Leider.
4. "Valentino Coming Back." *Los Angeles Times*, December 26, 1923.
5. S. George Ullman. *Valentino As I Knew Him*. New York: Macy-Masius, 1926. 78–79.
6. Bebe Daniels and Ben Lyon. *Life with the Lyons*. London: Odhams Limited, 1953. 108.
7. *Ibid.*
8. Ted Okuda and James L. Neibaur. *Stan Without Ollie: The Stan Laurel Solo Films, 1917–1927*. Jefferson, NC: McFarland, 2012. 138.
9. Grace Kingsley. "Flashes." *Los Angeles Times*, May 28, 1924.
10. Bebe Daniels and Ben Lyon. *Life with the Lyons*. London: Odhams Limited, 1953. 113.
11. "The Screen." *New York Times*, September 10, 1924.
12. "Brief Reviews of Current Pictures." *Photoplay*, January 1925. 8.
13. "Brief Reviews of Current Pictures." *Photoplay*, March 1925. 8.
14. "The Ups and Downs of Stardom." *Picture-Play Magazine*, February 1923. 43.
15. Harold Lloyd. "Autobiography of Harold Lloyd." *Photoplay*, June 1924. 109–110.
16. Jill Allgood. *Bebe and Ben*. London: Robert Hale, 1975. 58.
17. "The Ups and Downs of Stardom." *Picture-Play Magazine*, February 1923. 43.
18. Presumably 1923, although he is not entirely clear. The narrative in *Bebe & Ben* takes some liberties with regards to timing.
19. Jill Allgood. *Bebe and Ben*. London: Robert Hale, 1975. 58.
20. Eve Golden. *John Gilbert: The Last of the Silent Film Stars*. Lexington: University Press of Kentucky, 2013. 57.
21. Marion Davies. *The Times We Had*. New York: Ballantine, 1975. 150.

## Chapter 12

1. Cal York. "Studio News." *Photoplay*, March 1925. 54.
2. "Reviews." *Billboard*, May 9, 1925. 53.
3. "The Shadow Stage." *Photoplay*, June 1925. 52.

4. Grace Kingsley. "Bebe Daniels Great in 'Crowded Hour.'" *Los Angeles Times*, May 11, 1925.
5. Cal York. "Studio News and Gossip East & West." *Photoplay*, October 1925. 41.
6. "Wild, Wild Susan." *Motion Picture News*, August 15, 1925. 848.
7. "Bebe Daniels in Hospital Denies Plastic Operation." *Chicago Daily Tribune*, May 16, 1925.
8. "Operation on Nose of Movie Actress." *Pittston Gazette*, January 7, 1927.
9. "Bebe Not So Good." *Baltimore Sun*, June 21, 1925.
10. Robert Graves and Alan Hodge. *The Long Week-End: A Social History of Great Britain, 1918–1939, Volume 1*. New York: W.W. Norton & Company, 1940. 130.
11. Grace Kingsley. "Plans to Make More Comedies." *Los Angeles Times*, December 6, 1925.
12. "The Shadow Stage." *Photoplay*, December 1925. 48.
13. "Lovers in Quarantine." *Motion Picture News*, October 24, 1925. 1947.
14. "Demille Comes into His Own." *The Los Angeles Times*, November 1, 1925.
15. "Little to Recommend." *New York Herald-Tribune*, December 14, 1925.
16. "Bebe Daniels to Head Own Unit." *Motion Picture News*, December 26, 1925. 3156.

# Chapter 13

1. "Society of Cinemaland." *Los Angeles Times*, November 8, 1925.
2. "Glimpses of Hollywood." *Atlanta Constitution*, November 22, 1925.
3. "Oh, the Tales They Tell, Do the Movie Folk!" *Los Angeles Times*, November 22, 1925.
4. "Michael and Bebe to Wed, Rumors Say." *Los Angeles Times*, November 1, 1925.
5. "Bebe Daniels Talks of Her Six Big Romances." *Milwaukee Journal*, January 19, 1929.
6. "The Picture Parade." *Motion Picture Magazine*, June 1926. 80.
7. "The Shadow Stage." *Photoplay*, May 1926. 51.
8. "Studio News and Gossip East and West." *Photoplay*, April 1926. 86.
9. "Studio News and Gossip East and West." *Photoplay*, April 1926. 94.
10. "Flashes." *Los Angeles Times*, February 10, 1926.
11. "The Picture Parade." *Motion Picture Magazine*, September 1926. 63.
12. Mae Tinee. "Bebe May Have Had Better Roles but She's Quite a Palm Beach Girl." *Chicago Daily Tribune*, May 18, 1926.
13. "Film Reviews." *Variety*, May 26, 1926. 19.
14. Laurence Reid. "The Campus Flirt." *Motion Picture News*, October 9, 1926. 1394.
15. "Bebe and Her Modern Sir Walter Raleigh." *Motion Picture Magazine*, September 1926. 54.
16. "Charles Paddock to Wed Bebe Daniels." *New York Times*, July 19, 1926.
17. "Paramount Star Repeats." *Los Angeles Times*, October 9, 1926.
18. "'Stranded in Paris' Halts Bebe's Vacation." *Los Angeles Times*, August 31, 1926.
19. Laurence Reid. "Stranded in Paris." *Motion Picture News*, December 25, 1926. 2434.
20. "Paddock Admits He's Engaged to Bebe Daniels." *Chicago Daily Tribune*, November 10, 1926.
21. Donnell, Dorothy. "Bebe's Mother Tells All." *Motion Picture Magazine*, May 1926. 37, 98–99.
22. "Bebe Daniels Talks of Her Six Big Romances." *Milwaukee Journal*, January 19, 1929.
23. "Jack Pickford Named as Bebe's Choice." *Los Angeles Times*, January 2, 1927.
24. "Bebe Ends Troth to Paddock as Pickford Affair Is Hinted." *Los Angeles Times*, June 13, 1927.
25. "Bebe Daniels Talks of Her Six Big Romances." *Milwaukee Journal*, January 19, 1929.
26. Dorothy Donnell, "Bebe's Mother Tells All." *Motion Picture Magazine*, May 1926. 37, 98–99.
27. "Studio News and Gossip East and West." *Photoplay*, January 1926. 104.
28. Dorothy Donnell, "Bebe's Mother Tells All." *Motion Picture Magazine*, May 1926. 37, 98–99.
29. Maude S. "Cheatham, Bebe, the Oriental." *Motion Picture Magazine*, November 1919. 32–33, 123.
30. Myrtle Vest, "The Court of Daniels." *Motion Picture Magazine*, August 1926. 54.

# Chapter 14

1. "'Kiss in a Taxi' at Metropolitan." *Boston Daily Globe*, March 8, 1927.
2. "Writer Busy on New Play for Comedian." *Los Angeles Times*, April 17, 1927.
3. "Bebe Daniels' Next Paramount." *Los Angeles Times*, September 23, 1927.
4. "Paramount: The Greatest Word in Show Business." *Variety*, December 1, 1926. 163.
5. "Advertisements." *New York Herald Tribune*, September 2, 1927.
6. "'Swim, Girl, Swim' at Metropolitan." *Boston Daily Globe*, September 13, 1927.
7. "'Swim, Girl, Swim' Features Program at Morning Matinee." *Atlanta Constitution*, July 5, 1928.
8. Grace Kingsley. "Bebe Daniels a Sheikess." *Los Angeles Times*, July 13, 1927.
9. "Odd Hobbies Come to Light." *Baltimore Sun*, October 9, 1927.
10. "'Feel My Pulse' Is Exhibited." *Los Angeles Times*, February 27, 1928.
11. Mordaunt Hall. "The Screen." *New York Times*, February 27, 1928.
12. The accident took place at Arroyo Boulevard and California Avenue.
13. "Actress in Fall from Film Truck." *Los Angeles Times*, February 12, 1928.
14. *Ibid.*
15. *Ibid.*
16. "Bebe Daniels Back at Studio Vows to Shake Accident Jinx." *Los Angeles Times*, February 24.
17. "Bits Aboutem." *Chicago Daily Tribune*, March 25, 1928.
18. "Bebe Daniels Hunts Good Luck Charm." *Los Angeles Times*, May 6, 1928.
19. *Ibid.*
20. "Bebe Picks a Talisman from 4,000." *Washington Post*, June 24, 1928.
21. *Ibid.*
22. "Bebe Daniels Film Amuses." *New York Times*, May 14, 1928.
23. "Bebe Tells What to Do for Health." *Washington Post*, May 12, 1928.

24. "Hard Tasks for a Girl." *Washington Post*, August 4, 1928.
25. "Bebe Finds Fingerfuls of Thrills." *Washington Post*, August 5, 1928.
26. "'Hot News' Is Lively Film Play." *Los Angeles Times*, July 3, 1928.
27. "On the Screen." *New York Herald Tribune*, July 23, 1928.

## Chapter 15

1. "Paramount Has Been Offered $150,000 to Release Bebe Daniels." *Billboard*, December 1, 1928. 21.
2. "The Shadow Stage." *Photoplay*, November, 1928. 56.
3. Cal York. "Gossip of All the Studios." *Photoplay*, October, 1928. 18.
4. "She'll Star in Polo Romance." *Harrisburg Evening News*, September 12, 1928.
5. "Bebe Daniels Not Engaged." *Los Angeles Times*, September 20, 1928.
6. Will Rogers. "Will Rogers Adds a Whisper to the Campaign Debate." *New York Times*, September 14, 1928.
7. Harry Long. "The Microphone: The Terror of the Studios." *Photoplay*, December 1929. 30.
8. Jamie Brotherton and Ted Okuda. *Dorothy Lee: The Life and Films of the Wheeler and Woolsey Girl*. Jefferson, NC: McFarland, 2013. 24.
9. Bebe Daniels and Ben Lyon. *Life with the Lyons*. London: Odhams Limited, 1953. 143.
10. Bebe Daniels and Ben Lyon. *Life with the Lyons*. London: Odhams Limited, 1953. 112.

## Chapter 16

1. "Bebe Daniels, Star, to Become Bride." *Washington Post*, January 16, 1929.
2. "Gossip of All the Studios." *Photoplay*, April 1929. 48–49.
3. "Gossip of All the Studios." *Photoplay*, May 1929. 80.
4. "Plane Service Opens." *Los Angeles Times*, May 16, 1929.
5. "Women Fliers Balk at Easy $10,000 Race." *New York Times*, June 12, 1929.
6. "In Lending Boles U. Demands Billing." *Billboard*, May 18, 1929. 22.
7. Bebe Daniels and Ben Lyon. *Life with the Lyons*. London: Odhams Limited, 1953. 146.
8. Richard Jewell. "Rko Film Grosses: 1931–1951." *Historical Journal of Film Radio and Television*. 14 (1994).
9. "*Rio Rita* Success." *Los Angeles Times*, October 10, 1929.
10. "Bebe Rediscovered." *Los Angeles Times*, October 13, 1929.
11. Louella O. Parsons. "Bebe Upsets Gossipers, Makes Talkie Grade." *Austin American*, November 17, 1929.
12. "Bebe Daniels (vocalist)." Discography of American Historical Recordings. UC Santa Barbara Library.
13. "Gossip of All the Studios." *Photoplay*, December 1929. 92.
14. Richard Jewel. "RKO Film Grosses: 1931–1951." *Historical Journal of Film Radio and Television*, Vol. 14 No. 1, 1994. 56.
15. "Bebe Daniels Does Her Best by This Talkie." *Chicago Daily Tribune*, January 8, 1930.
16. "Pictures in New York." *Billboard*, February 8, 1930. 23.
17. "On the Screen." *New York Herald Tribune*, April 14, 1930.
18. "At the Movies This Week." *Baltimore Sun*, June 10, 1930.
19. George Shaffer. "Ben Lyon Weds Bebe Daniels in Filmland Aura." *Chicago Daily Tribune*. June 15, 1930.
20. Bebe Daniels and Ben Lyon. *Life with the Lyons*. London: Odhams Limited, 1953. 166.
21. *Ibid.*

## Chapter 17

1. "Hero Spoiled for Bebe Daniels If Perfect in Role or Real Life." *New York Herald Tribune*, March 15, 1931.
2. Edwin M. Bradley. *The First Hollywood Musicals: A Critical Filmography of 171 Features, 1927 Through 1932*. Jefferson, NC: McFarland, 2004. 194.
3. "Advertisement." *Photoplay*, October 1930. 121.
4. "Advertisement." *Photoplay*, September 1930. 2.
5. Richard Barrios. *A Song in the Dark*, 298.
6. "Actress in New Role." *Los Angeles Times*, June 10, 1930.
7. "Rko-Keith's." *Washington Post*, July 20, 1930.
8. Richard Barrios. *A Song in the Dark: The Birth of the Musical Film*. Oxford: Oxford University Press, 2009. 308
9. "Advertisement." *Variety*, June 18, 1930. 26.
10. "Banff." *Variety*, June 18, 1930. 86.
11. "Bebe Daniels Signs Long-Term Contract." *Baltimore Sun*, October 19, 1930.
12. "The Picture Parade." *Motion Picture*, March, 1930. 59.
13. "The Theatre." *Wall Street Journal*, January 5, 1931.
14. It must be mentioned that contemporary audiences and critics were viewing the complete 91 minute version of the film; surviving copies are missing as much as a third of the original movie.
15. Robert Kimball and Linda Emmet, eds. *The Complete Lyrics of Irving Berlin*. New York: Knopf, 2000. 266.
16. "United Artists Pictures." *Los Angeles Times*, June 1, 1930.
17. "Variety's Bulletin Condensed." *Variety*, June 11, 1930. 15.
18. "Screen Notes." *New York Herald Tribune*, June 16, 1930.
19. "Bebe Tells About Ben." *Los Angeles Times*, March 29, 1931.

## Chapter 18

1. "Bebe Glows as Actress and as Wife." *Los Angeles Times*, December 27, 1931.
2. "What Happens When Stardom Takes a Bath." *New York Herald Tribune*, May 24, 1931.

3. James Ursini and Dominique Mainon. *Femme Fatale: Cinema[apost]s Most Unforgettable Lethal Ladies.* Milwaukee: Hal Leonard Corporation, 2009.
4. Jill Allgood. *Bebe and Ben.* London: Robert Hale, 1975. 112.
5. "Bebe Daniels Waits Stork." *Los Angeles Times,* May 26, 1931.
6. "Bebe Daniels Expects Baby." *Washington Post,* May 27, 1931.
7. Cal York. "Monthly Broadcast of Hollywood Goings-On." *Photoplay,* November, 1931. 84
8. "Bebe Daniels Becomes Mother of Baby Girl." *Washington Post,* September 10, 1931.
9. "Bebe Daniels Presents Lyon with 'Lyoness." *Los Angeles Times,* September 10, 1931.
10. "Suggested by Balzac." *New York Times,* October 17, 1931.
11. Jill Allgood. *Bebe and Ben.* London: Robert Hale, 1975. 112.
12. "Gloria Swanson Is Wed Again to Farmer." *Lincoln Evening Journal,* November 10, 1931.
13. "Notables to Greet Film Star." *Los Angeles Times,* December 21, 1931.
14. "Star Effective in Play." *Los Angeles Times,* December 23, 1931.
15. "Bebe Glows as Actress and as Wife." *Los Angeles Times,* December 27, 1931.
16. *Ibid.*
17. "Lyon Sued by Studio Clerk Over Beating." *Los Angeles Times,* April 14, 1932.
18. "Notables Visit El Capitan to See Colleen Act." *Los Angeles Times,* April 25, 1932.
19. "Comeback for Bebe Daniels." *Hartford Courant,* May 9, 1932.
20. "Ticklish Job on Two Contracts." *Chicago Daily Tribune.* April 1, 1932.
21. "Auction Sale Adds Touch of Actuality." *Washington Post,* August 28, 1932.
22. "Stepping Down from Stardom." *Film Weekly,* November 18, 1932. 3.
23. "New Role for Bebe Daniels." *New York Herald Tribune,* September 3, 1932.
24. "Great Air Show to Aid Charity." *Los Angeles Times,* October 14, 1932.
25. "Putting on a Show." *New York Times,* March 10, 1933.

## Chapter 19

1. "A Report on London's Filmland." *New York Herald Tribune,* July 22, 1934.
2. Bebe Daniels and Ben Lyon. *Life with the Lyons.* London: Odhams Limited, 1953. 183.
3. Irene Thirer. "They Run a Red, White, and Blue Shop." *New Movie Magazine,* February 1934. 47.
4. The shop's actual address was 1151 Glendon Avenue. The building is still standing; today it serves as a restaurant.
5. "2 Views of S.S. American Maid, New Palm Springs Resort Shop." *Women's Wear Daily,* November 23, 1934. 10.
6. "Bebe Daniels Signed for 'Cocktail Hour.'" *Baltimore Sun,* April 9, 1933.
7. "Bebe Sparkles in 'Cocktail Hour.'" *Austin American,* June 18, 1933.
8. Cecelia Ager. "Going Places." *Variety,* June 6, 1933. 12.
9. "Sally and Hoot Are Pals but Sally Travels Alone." *Washington Post,* May 21, 1933.
10. Bebe Daniels and Ben Lyon. *Life with the Lyons.* London: Odhams Limited, 1953. 192.
11. "Our Cinema Chronicle." *Times of India,* May 31, 1933.
12. "Song You Gave Me." *Variety,* August 15, 1933. 14.
13. "Through Britain's Hollywood." *The Globe,* November 4, 1933.
14. "A Southern Maid." *Times of India,* December 23, 1933.
15. "Reel Life in Hollywood." *Daily Boston Globe,* September 18, 1933.
16. Jan Herman. *A Talent for Trouble: The Life of Hollywood[apost]s Most Acclaimed Director.* New York: G.P. Putnam[apost]s Sons 1995. 116–118.
17. "Reel Life in Hollywood." *Daily Boston Globe,* November 28, 1933.
18. Mordaunt Hall. "The Screen." *New York Times,* December 8, 1933.
19. "Daniels' Wb Finale." *Variety,* December 12, 1933. 3.
20. "New Acts." *Variety,* April 10, 1934.50.
21. "Bebe Daniels and Ben Lyon in Stage Debut." *Chicago Daly Tribune,* April 7, 1934.
22. "News from the Dailies." *Variety,* May 8, 1934. 58.
23. "Chinatown Quiet Upset While Bebe Daniels Sups." *New York Herald Tribune,* May 9, 1934.
24. "Met, Boston." *Variety,* October 30, 1934. 12.

## Chapter 20

1. "Veterans of Movies Return to Stage Here." *Baltimore Sun,* February 17, 1935.
2. "Cinema Stars in Stage Play." *Baltimore Sun,* February 19, 1935.
3. "Public Policy." *Billboard,* June 15, 1935. 66.
4. "Bebe Daniels Pulls This One from Film Bag." *Chicago Daily Tribune,* December 30, 1935.
5. "Bebe Will Make Fifth Comeback." *Hartford Courant,* August 4, 1935.
6. "Stanley, Pittsburgh." *Billboard,* January 25, 1936.
7. "Daniels-Lyon Team Heads Oriental Bill." *Chicago Daily Tribune,* January 28, 1936.
8. "Not Wanted on Voyage." *Variety,* February 23, 1938. 14.
9. "London Bills." *Billboard,* February 6, 1937. 20.
10. Bebe Daniels and Ben Lyon. *Life with the Lyons.* London: Odhams Limited, 1953. 200.
11. "Empire: Bebe Daniels and Ben Lyon." *Scotsman,* March 8, 1938.
12. "A Woman[apost]s New York." *Washington Post,* July 5, 1939.
13. Louella O. Parsons. "Close-Ups and Long-Shots of the Motion Picture Scene." *Washington Post,* July 8, 1939.
14. "Ex-Screen Star Adopts Boy." *New York Times,* July 26, 1939.

## Chapter 21

1. "U.S. Acts Staying in Europe." *Billboard,* October 7, 1939. 1.

2. "American Acts in Europe Are Doubling and Tripling." *Billboard*, December 23, 1939.
3. "Bebe Daniels, Ben Lyon in New London Holborn Show 'Haw-Haw'; George Black's 3d Wartime Show." *Billboard*, February 10, 1940. 5.
4. Bebe Daniels and Ben Lyon. *Life with the Lyons*. London: Odhams Limited, 1953. 205.
5. "Vic Oliver Dead." *New York Times*, August 16, 1964.
6. Clarke, Peter. *Mr. Churchill's Profession*, Bloomsbury Publishing, London. 2012. 184.
7. Bebe Daniels and Ben Lyon. *Life with the Lyons*. London: Odhams Limited, 1953. 205.
8. *Ibid.*
9. "U.S. Acts Flee England." *Billboard*, July 20, 1940. 1.
10. "U.S. Acts Hurt by Stiffening of English Alien Law." *Billboard*, June 15, 1940. 1.
11. Bebe Daniels and Ben Lyon. *Life with the Lyons*. London: Odhams Limited, 1953. 204.
12. "Nice People!" *Melody Maker*, August 10, 1940. 5.
13. Grace Turner. "Bebe and Ben—And Breakfast." *Baltimore Sun*, November 23, 1941.
14. *Ibid.*
15. Louella O. Parsons. "Bebe Daniels and Ben Lyon Are Loyal to England." *Atlanta Constitution*, September 28, 1941.

## Chapter 22

1. "Chorines to Stars." *Variety*, January 7, 1942. 54.
2. "Former Favorite Stars Speak Across the Atlantic." *Washington Post*, June 11, 1942.
3. "Radio Highlights." *Washington Post*, May 23, 1943.
4. "Capt. Clark Gable Decides to Emerge from Obscurity." *Austin Statesman*, June 5, 1943.
5. "Stars and Stripes in Britain." *Variety*, May 27, 1942. 32.
6. "Bebe Daniels' Grandmother Passes at 89." *Los Angeles Times*, November 20, 1943.
7. Bebe Daniels and Ben Lyon. *Life with the Lyons*. London: Odhams Limited, 1953. 224.
8. Bebe Daniels and Ben Lyon. *Life with the Lyons*. London: Odhams Limited, 1953. 228.
9. "Follow-Up Comment." *Variety*, June 21, 1944. 36.
10. "Ben Lyon Says Wife 1st Trouper in France." *Variety*, November 8, 1944. 17.
11. "The Adelphi." *The Stage*, February 1, 1945.
12. "Col. Ben Lyon Back Home with Bebe Daniels." *Los Angeles Times*, June 16, 1945.
13. "Louella O. Parsons Reports." *Atlanta Constitution*, June 20, 1945.
14. "Hedda Hopper Looking at Hollywood." *Los Angeles Times*, May 28, 1945.
15. "Denies Divorce." *Atlanta Constitution*, August 23, 1945.
16. "This Town Called Hollywood." *Chicago Daily Tribune*. March 17, 1946.
17. Jill Allgood. *Bebe and Ben*. London: Robert Hale & Co., 1975. 149.
18. "Hal Roach Comedy Carnival." *The Baltimore Sun*, December 27, 1947.
19. "Bebe Daniels Story Time." *Billboard*, November 2, 1946. 96.
20. "Bebe Daniels Cuts Kidisks for Enterprise." *Billboard*, March 8, 1947. 32.

## Chapter 23

1. "Change in Films for Montgomery." *New York Times*. March 15, 1947.
2. "Bebe Daniels Is Signed Up by Eagle-Lion." *Baltimore Sun*, March 17, 1947.
3. "Of Local Origin." *New York Times*. May 6, 1948.
4. Actor Cordell, Jr. "He Named Her Marilyn Monroe." *Atlanta Journal and Constitution*, June 22, 1958.
5. "Played the Innocent, but Discovered Sirens." *The Globe and Mail*, November 26, 1962.
6. "Star Studded Shows for Vets Hospitals." *Boxoffice*, September 25, 1948. 51.
7. "Ben Lyon Promoted." *New York Herald Tribune*, October 23, 1948.
8. "This Is the Life for Me!" *Picturegoer*, February 6, 1954. 24.
9. "Cashing in on the Lyons." *Picturegoer*, June 19, 1954. 25.

## Chapter 24

1. "The Lyons of England." *New York Herald Tribune*, June 24, 1956.
2. "Bebe Daniels, Ben Lyon Making Film Comeback." *Hartford Courant*, May 23, 1954.
3. "Barbara Lyon Makes Vocal Record Debut." *New Musical Express*, April 22, 1955. 7.
4. "From Here & There." *Melody Maker*, May 5, 1956. 2.
5. "Orange Blossom Time for 'Dreamtime' Barbara." *New Musical Express*, April 6, 1956. 6.
6. "Life with the Lyons." *Variety*, October 1, 1958. 30.
7. "Television." *Spectator*, July 22, 1955. 124.
8. "New Lyon Adopted by British Public." *New York Herald Tribune*, May 1, 1958.
9. Jill Allgood. *Bebe and Ben*. London: Robert Hale & Co., 1975. 165–6.

## Chapter 25

1. "Film Star Bebe Daniels Has a Stroke in London." *Atlanta Constitution*, May 21, 1963.
2. "Bebe Daniels Out of Coma After Stroke." *Atlanta Constitution*, May 22, 1963.
3. "Bebe Daniels of Silent Films Ill." *Indiana Gazette*, May 21, 1963.
4. "Bebe Daniels, Former Movie Star, Has Stroke." *Lebanon Daily News*, May 21, 1963.
5. "Bebe Daniels Gains Strength." *Nevada State Journal*, May 24, 1963.
6. "Bebe Daniels Recovering from Stroke." *Atlanta Constitution*, June 24, 1963.
7. "Ben Lyon Stands by Ailing Bebe." *Atlanta Constitution*, August 14, 1963.
8. Robert Musel. "Bebe Daniels and Ben Lyon's Fabled Love Story Goes On." *Los Angeles Times*, March 28, 1967.
9. "Jane's No Bride in France." *Washington Post*, August 31, 1966.

10. "Inside Stuff—Pictures." *Variety*, March 6, 1968. 23.
11. John Kerr. "Memories of Golden 20s of Silver Screen." *Irish Times*, September 23, 1970.
12. Annette D'Agostino Lloyd. *Harold Lloyd: Magic in a Pair of Horn-Rimmed Glasses*. Albany, GA: Bear-Manor Media, 2009. 352.
13. Jill Allgood. *Bebe and Ben*. London: Robert Hale, 1975. 182.
14. *Ibid.*

# Chapter 26

1. "Bebe Daniels, Star of Silents, Early Talkies, Dies at 70." *Los Angeles Times*, March 16, 1971.
2. "Mourn Film Star Bebe Daniels, 70." *Chicago Tribune*, March 17, 1971.
3. "Bebe Daniels, 70, Star of Early Talkie Movies." *Boston Globe*, March 17, 1971.
4. "Bebe Daniels Cremated After Rites in London." *Los Angeles Times*, March 21, 1971.

# Bibliography

## Books

Allgood, Jill. *Bebe and Ben*. London: Robert Hale, 1975.
Daniels, Bebe, and Ben Lyon. *Life with the Lyons*. London: Odhams Press, 1953.
Dardis, Tom. *Harold Lloyd: The Man on the Clock*. New York: Penguin, 1984.
Davies, Marion. *The Times We Had*. New York: Bobbs Merrill, 1975.
DeMille, Cecil B. *Autobiography of Cecil B. DeMille*. New York: Prentice-Hall, 1959.
Lloyd, Annette D'Agostino. *The Harold Lloyd Encyclopedia*. Jefferson, NC: McFarland, 2010.
Lloyd, Harold. *An American Comedy*. 2nd ed. New York: Dover, 1971.
Parsons, Louella O. *The Gay Illiterate*. Garden City, NY: Garden City Publishing Company, 1945.
Schickel, Richard. *Harold Lloyd: The Shape of Laughter*. New York: New York Graphic Society, 1974.
Swanson, Gloria. *Swanson on Swanson*. New York: Random House, 1980.

## Magazines

*The Billboard*
*Motion Picture Magazine*
*Moving Picture World*
*Photoplay*
*Picture-Play Magazine*
*Variety*

## Newspapers

*Chicago Daily Tribune*
*Los Angeles Times*
*New York Herald-Tribune*
*New York Times*
*The Times of London*
*Washington Post*

## Film Archives

Celeste Bartos Film Preservation Center, Museum of Modern Art
Cinematic Arts Library, University of Southern California
Film and Television Archive, University of California, Los Angeles
Margaret Herrick Library, Academy of Motion Picture Arts and Sciences
Motion Picture and Television Reading Room, Library of Congress

# Index

Numbers in ***bold italics*** refer to pages with photographs.

*Advice to Lovers* 107
*The Affairs of Anatol* 56, 67–8
Albuquerque Film Manufacturing Company 27
*Alias French Gertie* 125, 128, 130, 132
*All Fun and Folly* 157
*All Women see The Maltese Falcon*
Allgood, Jill 190
Allison, May 137
*American Eagle in Britain* 168
American Maid 143–4
Andree, Angela 185
*Anne of the Golden Heart* 27
Arbuckle, Roscoe "Fatty" 40, 61
*Argentine Love* 87
Arlen, Michael 95
Arlen, Richard 110–1, ***112***
Arnold, Hap 141–2, ***142***
Arnold, Tom 166–7
*Ask Father* 42, ***42***
Astaire, Adele 87–8
Astaire, Fred 87–8
Astor, Mary 83
Attenborough, Richard 192
*Aunt Matilda Outwitted* 27–8
Austin, William 108, ***108***

Bacon, Lloyd 138
*Bad Women see The Maltese Falcon*
Badger, Clarence G. 92, 96, 98, 101–2, 107–8, 111, 114, 116
*Ball of Fire* 153
Barnes, T. Roy 89
Barrios, Richard 130
Barrymore, John 135, 147–9, ***149***
Barrymore, Lionel 139
Baxter, Warner 141
*Bebe & Ben* 10, 14, 18, 22, 73
Beery, Noah 82
Beery, Wallace 155
Belasco, David 19–20
Belmore, Daisy 125
Bennett, Constance 139
Bennett, Joan 127
Beranger, Clara 77

Berkeley, Busby 132, 141–2
Berlin, Irving 131–2
Binney, Constance 53, 78–9
Birkett, Colin 189
Bison Film Company 24–5, ***25***
Black, George 160
*Bliss* 35
Block, Bob 184
Blondell, Joan 141
Boggs, Francis 21, 23
Boles, John 122–3, 128, ***123***
Borzage, Frank 95
Bosworth, Hobart 21, 23–4
Brady, Alice 53
Brent, George 141
British International Pictures 145–6
Brunet, Paul 43
*Bumping Into Broadway* 43
*By the Sad Sea Waves* 35

Campbell, Maurice 80
*The Campus Flirt* 98–100, 102–3, 105–6, 108–9, 125, ***99***
Caprice, Charles 76–7
*Captain Kidd's Kids* 43
*Carmen* 128
Carroll, Madeleine 158
Castle Records 173
*Catch Me Before I Kill* 179
Chaplin, Charlie 29, 90, 95
Churchill, Sarah 162
*Cocktail Hour* 144–5, ***145***
Colbert, Claudette 132
Columbia Pictures 144
*The Common Enemy* 22, 24
Compson, Betty 137, 139
*Confidential Lady* 157
Conklin, Chester 106
Cornwall, Anne 93
Corrigan, Lloyd 107
Cortez, Ricardo 97, 100, 134–6, 140
*Counsellor-at-Law* 147–9, ***149***
*A Counterfeit Santa Claus* 24
*The Courtship of Miles Standish* 24
Cox, Judge John B. 58, 60–2, 64, 69

*Crazy with the Heat* 28
Crosby, Bing 131
Crosland, Alan 86
*The Crowded Hour* 89–90

*The Dancin' Fool* 48–9
*Dangerous Money* 87
Daniels, Melville *see* MacMeal, Melville Daniel
Daniels, Phyllis 10–21, 24–5, 28–30, 35–6, 76, 109, 124, 143, 146, 158, 163, 170, 185, ***109***
Daniels Neuropathic Institute 17
Daniels School of Acting and Physical Culture 14–6
Dardis, Tom 43
*Daring Youth* 82
Davidson, John ***82***
Davies, Marion 88
Davis, Mildred 43
*The Deemster* 14
Dela Films 156
Del Ruth, Roy 135–6
DeMille, Cecil B. 37–9, 43, 46, 51, 54, 56, 64, 82, 92, 96, 105, 110, 180
DeMille, William C. 77, 79, 92
Dempsey, Jack 58, 72–73, 99, 117, 120, 127, 132
Digges, Dudley 135
Dix, Richard 82–3, 86–7, 100–1, 119
*Dixiana* 128–31, 140
*Dr. Skinnem's Wonderful Invention* 26, ***26***
*A Doll's House* 19
Dove, Billie 137, 139
*Dreamtime with Barbara* 183
*Ducks and Drakes* 55, 60
Dunne, Irene 130

Eagle-Lion Films 176, 179
Eaker, General Ira C. 174
Earhart, Amelia 121
Ederle, Gertrude 108–9, ***108***
Eilers, Sally 137, 139, 146, 158
El Brendel 98

*The Ensign* 18–9
Enterprise Records 172
Ephraim, Lee 166–7
Evans, Constance 160
*Everywoman* 48, 56
*The Exciters* 80–1
Exclusive Films 181
*Ex-Mistress* see *My Past*

*The Fabulous Joe* 172
Fairbanks, Douglas 131–2
Farrell, Charles 156
Fawcett, George 81
*Feel My Pulse* 110, **112**
*The Fifty-Fifty Girl* 111–3, 116
Fitts, Burton 156
Fitzmaurice, George 137, 139
*Fleischmann Yeast Hour* 158
*A Foozle at the Tee Party* 32
Ford, Harrison 92
*42nd Street* 116, 132, 141–2, 145, 148, 150, 153, 171
*The Fourteenth Man* 54–5
Francis, Kay 141

Gable, Clark 165
Gallagher, Pauline 143, 153
Gallagher, "Skeets" 143, 152–3
*A Game Chicken* 73
*Gangway* 166
Gibson, Hoot 24, 139, 146
Gilbert, John 88
Gilmore, Douglas 106
*The Girl I Left Behind Me* 19
*Giving Them Fits* 32
*Glimpses of the Moon* 79–80
*The Good Little Bad Girl* 53
Goulding, Edmund 132
Grahame, Margot 172
Grauman, Sid 121, 139
Gray, Eden 92
Gray, Lawrence 97
*The Green Years* 170
Griffin, Eva de la Plaza 11, 79, **109**
Griffin, George Butler 10–11
Guest, Val 181–2

*Hal Roach Comedy Carnival* 172
Hal Roach Studios 171, 176
Hall, James 98, 100, 108, 111, **108**
Hamilton, Neil 93, 114–6, **93, 114**
Hammett, Dashiell 134–5
Harlan, Kenneth 89
Hassan, Abon 16–7
*Haw Haw* 160–1
Hawley, Wanda 53, 67
Hearst, William Randolph 88
*Heart of the Rockies* 130
Helmore, Tom 156
*Her Own Way* 19
*Heritage of the Desert* 82
*Hi, Gang!* (radio series) 161–5, 175–6, 179–80
*His Children's Children* 81–2, **81**

Hitchcock, Thomas Jr. 117–8
Holland, Albert M. 154–5
*Hollywood Holiday* 152–3
*Hollywood on the Air* 150
Holt, Jack 60, 75, 84
*Honor of the Family* 136–40
Hopper, E. Mason 89
Hopper, Hedda 171
Horton, Edward Everett 131
*Hot News* 113–6, **114**
Hughes, Lloyd 82, 124
Hulbert, Claude 168

Ince, John 125
Ireland, Jill 183

*Jane* 14
*Justinian and Theodora* 24

Kalem Company 26–7
Kane, Bob 84
Keaton, Buster 29, 141
Keeler, Ruby 141–2
Kelso, Mayme **66**
Kenyon, Doris 148
Keystone Studios 28–9
Kibbee, Guy 141
*Kicking the Germ Out of Germany* 39
Kidd, Jim 30–1
King, Joe 83
*A Kiss in a Taxi* 100, 106
*A Kiss in the Dark* 90
Kolker, Henry 106

La Cava, Gregory 111
LaMar, Cedric 139
Lamarr, Hedy 158
La Rocque, Rod 91, 127
Lasky, Jesse 37–9, 43–4, 48, 52, 67, 74, 90, 93–4, 99, 107
*The Last of Mrs. Cheyney* 138–9, 152
Laurel, Stan 86
*Lawful Larceny* 129, 131
Lean, Katheryn 81
LeBaron, William 119, 124, 131, 139
Lee, Dorothy 128
LeRoy, Mervyn 141
*Life with the Lyons* (book) 10, 14, 18, 88, 144
*Life with the Lyons* (film) 181–2
*Life with the Lyons* (radio series) 176, 179–80
*Life with the Lyons* (television series) 184, **180**
Linder, Max 61
Lloyd, Annette D'Agostino 42, 190
Lloyd, Harold 29–37, 39, 42–6, 48–9, 54, 56–7, 61, 72, 87, 92, 96–7, 118, 120, 125, 127, 138–9, 147, 171–2, 180, 182, 189, 190–1, **33, 42, 44**
*Lonesome Luke Loses Patients* 34
*Lonesome Luke's Lively Life* 34

*Lonesome Luke's Wild Women* 34
*Look Out Below* **44**
*Love Comes Along* 124–5, 128–9, 140
*Love in a Cottage* see *Reaching for the Moon*
*Lovers in Quarantine* 92
Lukas, Paul 114
Lyman, Abe 62, **62**
Lyon, Barbara 138–9, 146, 148, 153–4, 163, 170, 175–6, 179, 182–6, 189, **170, 180**
Lyon, Richard 159, 163, 169–70, 175–7, 179, 182–6, 189, 191, **170, 177, 180**
*The Lyons in Paris* 182

MacCloy, June 131–2
Mackaill, Dorothy 81
MacMeal, Melville Daniel 9–17
MacPherson, Jeanie 37
*Mademoiselle Jockey* see *Miss Jockey*
*Magpie* see *The Splendid Crime*
*Male and Female* 46–8, 51, 56, 60, 68, **47**
*The Maltese Falcon* 134–6, 140, **136**
*The Manicure Girl* 90
*The March Hare* 64, 67, **66**
Marsh, Gene 33
Marshall, Everett 128
Matieson, Otto 135
*Maybelline Musical Romance* 150
Meighan, Thomas 46, 48, 51, 91, 139
Miller, Marilyn 102–3, 139, 156
Miller, Max 160–1
Miller, Walter 36
Minter, Mary Miles 53, 73–4
*Miss Bluebeard* 90, 107
*Miss Brewster's Millions* 93, 96
*Miss Jockey* 106–7
Mitchell, Les 175
Mollison, Clifford 147
Monroe, Marilyn 177–8
*Monsieur Beaucaire* 84–5, 107, 129, 148, **86**
*Monsieur Don't Care* 86
Moore, Colleen 139, 141, 190
Moreno, Antonio 80
Morosco, Oliver 19
Mulhall, Jack 54, 64, **65**
Munson, Lyman 178
Murray, Mae 36
*Music Is Magic* 153–4
*My Past* 132–3
Myers, Harry 64

Nagel, Conrad 77, 79
*Nancy from Nowhere* 70
Nargo, Vera 157
*Navy Wife* 153
Neagle, Dame Anna 192
Negri, Pola 95
Neilan, Marshall 116

## Index

*The News Reel Girl* see *Hot News*
*Nice People* 77–9
Nilsson, Anna Q. 78
Nixon, Marion 192
*No Man's a Hero* see *Hollywood Holiday*
Norbig Studios 27, 30
Normand, Mabel 29
*North of the Rio Grande* 75–6
*Not Wanted on Voyage* see *Treachery on the High Seas*

O'Connor, Robert Emmett 125
*Oh, Lady, Lady* 54–6
Olcott, Sidney 85
Oliver, Vic 161–2
*One Wild Week* 67–8, **68**
Ouida 12
*Over the Fence* 34–5
Oxley, David 188

Paddock, Charley 98–99, 102–3, 107, 117, 120, 125
*The Palm Beach Girl* 96–7, 105, 119
Palmer, Gaston 160–1
*Panama Hattie* 166–8
Parnell, Val 166–7
Parsons, Louella O. 123, 136–7, 158, 163–4, 171, 178
Percival, Horace 179, 181
Pickford, Jack 96, 102–3, 117, 120
Pickford, Mary 127, 139, 191
*Pink Gods* 78–9
*Police File* 176
Pollard, Snub 32, 34, 40, **33**
Porter, Cole 166, 168
Powell, Dick 141–2
Powell, William 87, 110–1
*The Prince Chap* 19–20

*Radio Girl* 140
*Rainbow Island* 35
Rambova, Natacha 85
*Reaching for the Moon* 131–2
Realart Pictures 53–7, 60, 63–4, 68–71, 73–5, 78–9, 92, 96
*Red Stallion in the Rockies* 176
Reed, Luther 128
*Registered Nurse* 148, 150
Reid, Wallace 48–9, 67, 70, 77–8, 81
Reinert, Emil-Edwin 156
Renavent, Georges 122
Rennie, James **82**
*The Return of Carol Deane* 156–7
*Richard III* 18
*Rio Rita* 121–5, 128–9, 131–2, 140, 148, 155, **123**

RKO Pictures 119–22, 124, 128–31, 133
Robinson, Edward G. 140
Rogers, Doris 179, 181
Rogers, Ginger 132, 141, 171
Rogers, Will 118
Rolin Pictures 31–41, 43–6, 51, **33, 36**
Roth, Lillian 155
*A Royal Family* 19

*The Savage* 28
Schertzinger, Victor 144
Schickel, Richard 43
Scott, Randolph 144
Selig, William 20–1
Selig Polyscope Company 21–22, 24
Selznick, David O. 139
Sennett, Mack 28–9
*Señorita* 106, 110, 121
Seymour, Syd 160
*She Couldn't Help It* 55, 56, 58
Shearer, Norma 139
Sherman, Lowell 129
*She's a Sheik* 109–10
Shulberg, B.P. 99–100, 107, 116, 118–9
*Sick Abed* 49, 52
*Silver Dollar* 140, 148
*Singed Wings* 54
*Sinners in Heaven* 86–7
*Skippy Hollywood Theater* 175
*The Song You Gave Me* 146
*Southern Maid* 147
*The Speed Girl* 63–4, 69–70
*The Splendid Crime* 93, **93**
*The Squaw Man* 20
Stamford, Jack 168
Stanwyck, Barbara 148
*Stardust* 157
*Stars and Stripes in Britain* 165
Stein, Paul L. 146
Sterling, Ford 100
Stevens, Onslow 148
*The Stolen Jools* 134
Stone, Lewis 133
*Stranded in Paris* 100
Sutherland, Edward A. 70, 90–1, 119, 139
Swanson, Gloria 28, 46–8, 51, 67, 78, 97, 120, 127, 171
*Swim Girl, Swim* 106–9, **108**

*Take Me Home* 116–7
Talbot, Lyle 148
Talmadge, Constance 139
Talmadge, Norma 137
Tashman, Lilyan 116
Tell, Olive 130

Thalberg, Irving 139
*This Is Your Life* 179–80
Thomson, Kenneth 130
Tierney, Harry 128
*The Today Show* 188
Todd, Thelma 148
Torrence, Ernest 82
*Treachery on the High Seas* 156
*A Trip to Paramountown* 78
Truman, Harry S. 174–5
Turner, Otis 21, 23–4
Turner, Russell 183–4
Tuttle, Frank 90, 92
*Two Weeks with Pay* 56, 64, **65**

Ullman, George 85
*Unguarded Women* 82–3, 86
United Artists 131
Universal Pictures 147
*The Unseen* 169

Valentino, Rudolph 71, 84–6, 95, **86**
Vallee, Rudy 158
Varconi, Victor 146
*Volcano!* 96–7, 105
von Eltz, Theodore 69

Wall, Max 168
Wallace, Nellie 157
Ward, Carrie Clark **68**
Warner, Jack 139
Warner Bros. 131, 133, 135, 140–1, 148
Weir, Molly 179, 181
*What a Night!* 118
Wheeler and Woolsey 122–3, 128
*Where the Laugh Comes In* 14
Whiting, Dwight 32, 37–8
*Who Is Guilty* 157
*Why Change Your Wife?* 51
*Wild, Wild Susan* 91–2
William, Warren 138, 140–1
*Woman of the World* See *The Maltese Falcon*
*The Wonderful Wizard of Oz* 22–3
Wood, Sam 81
Woods, Arthur B. 157
*The World's Applause* 79
Wyler, William 147

*You Never Can Tell* 25, 54
Young Deer, James 28

Zanuck, Darryl F. 140–1, 178
*Zaza* 19
Ziegfeld, Florenz 121–3
Zukor, Adolph 85, 99, 107

www.ingramcontent.com/pod-product-compliance
Lightning Source LLC
Chambersburg PA
CBHW081553300426
44116CB00015B/2871